"An excellent variety of great stories, told in superb narrative style."

—John D. Nesbitt,
Spur Award-winning Western writer
and author of Trouble at the Redstone

"Matthew Mayo brings the West alive in this witty and entertaining volume of essays that span from Head-Smashed-In Buffalo Jump to Tom Horn. *Cowboys, Mountain Men, and Grizzly Bears* puts the reader right in the middle of the action, making history not only accessible, but fun, scary, and most importantly, real. Mayo is a writer to keep a lookout for."

—Larry D. Sweazy,
Spur Award-winner and
author of The Rattlesnake Season

COWBOYS, MOUNTAIN MEN, AND GRIZZLY BEARS

Fifty of the Grittiest Moments in
the History of the Wild West

MATTHEW P. MAYO

TWODOT

GUILFORD, CONNECTICUT
HELENA, MONTANA
AN IMPRINT OF GLOBE PEQUOT PRESS

To buy books in quantity for corporate use
or incentives, call **(800) 962–0973**
or e-mail **premiums@GlobePequot.com**.

A · TWODOT® · BOOK

Text design: Diana Nuhn
Project editor: John Burbidge

Art and photo credits appear on page 232.

Library of Congress Cataloging-in-Publication Data

Mayo, Matthew P.
 Cowboys, mountain men, and grizzly bears : fifty of the grittiest moments in the history of the wild West /
    Matthew P. Mayo.
    p. cm.
 Includes bibliographical references and index.
 ISBN 978-0-7627-5431-1
 1. West (U.S.)—History—Anecdotes. 2. West (U.S.)—Folklore. 3. Frontier and pioneer life—West
    (U.S.)—Anecdotes. 4. West (U.S.)—Biography—Anecdotes. I. Title.
 F591.M39 2009
 978—dc22

                                                                                              2009034232

Printed in the United States of America
10 9 8 7 6 5 4 3 2 1

To my dear wife, Jennifer,
for all the reasons, all the time. Slainté!

To my parents, Gayla and Bill Mayo:
my favorite pioneers.

To my brother, Jeffrey,
for being my primo bro.

To Guinness and Nessie—
steadfast and true.

CONTENTS

ACKNOWLEDGMENTS

My thanks to many, including Bozeman Public Library; Colorado State Archives; Library of Congress; the National Archives and Records Administration; National Park Service; Oakland Museum of California; the Pioneer Museum of Bozeman; the Western History Association; Western History Collections, the University of Oklahoma Libraries; and Western Writers of America.

Much thanks to my fine friends Seabring Davis and Carter Walker; to my Black Horse Chums; and to Allen Jones, Erin Turner, and John Burbidge, editors and friends.

And last, but never least, my deepest thanks goes to my dear wife, Jennifer Smith-Mayo, for all of her tremendous help with this book. Hmm . . . how about a burger at Ted's?

—M.P.M.

INTRODUCTION

Igrew up on a dairy farm in northern New England and, just as with people I've come to know who grew up on Western ranches, I wouldn't trade such an idyllic upbringing for anything. Well . . . maybe summers on a Montana ranch. And for that small qualification I blame Mom and Dad. They were raised during the heyday of TV Westerns, and I grew up hearing from them all about Annie Oakley, Marshal Matt Dillon (for whom I'm told I'm named), the Cartwright Clan, Rowdy Yates, Paladin, and so many more. It's almost as if these characters were distant cousins who'd gone West and done well for themselves.

Whenever reruns came on our tiny black-and-white set, I was glued to Little Joe's every move. I just knew that nothing could be finer than life in a log cabin, a pinto horse saddled and waiting outside—just in case—and a saloon a quick gallop down the road. (Riding heifers in a bony Vermont pasture isn't quite the same.) I also read stacks of Louis L'Amour's frontier tales, saw the Duke on the big screen, and vowed I would one day live out West.

With the encouragement of my wife, Jennifer, it eventually happened. I've had the great good fortune to be able to not only live in the West but to study it, delving into its rich history with both arms, and to write about it in fiction and nonfiction forms. And the more people and places and events I learn about, the more fascinated I become. The great era of westward expansion in nineteenth-century America humbles me like no other time period, especially when I read about the hard work, hardships, and heartaches that so many people endured to travel West, often with little more than hearsay and blind faith to guide them. Their talismans a family Bible and the memory of a loved one back East they knew they would never again see. And still they headed West. In droves, singly and by the thousands, on wagon trails through rough, unforgiving country.

As I've researched various projects, I've turned up unexpected gems, tales of bold pioneers, of natives steadfast in their devotion to traditions thousands of years old, and of settlers who built and rebuilt towns and cities in blind devotion to their ideals. For every Custer, Crazy Horse, Hugh Glass, Wyatt Earp, and Sacajawea, there are countless others whom circumstance and time conspired to bury before their tales were told. They carried on in silence, hoping to find that perfect valley for raising crops, that overlooked stream bursting with beaver, that claim veined with gold.

While everyday life in the old West bore little resemblance to the Hollywood back lot sets of the TV shows of my youth, life in the nineteenth-century West was truly gritty—by definition, that which is tough, filled with courage, and uncompromising. In the course of researching these episodes, I didn't need to stray far from that basic definition. A person would be hard-pressed to find a grittier time and place than the old, wild-and-woolly West. Lawlessness, for example, was usually only tolerated for so long before ordinary, hardworking citizens said, "Enough's enough," and did something about the offending individuals. More often than not the practical solution involved a rope and a stout tree branch.

From slaughters, shootouts, and massacres spurred on by all manner of motives, to maulings, lynchings, and natural disasters, these fifty moments have all the gripping elements required of a storyteller: heroes and heroines with impressive potential; villains capable of the foulest of deeds; strength of will to help our characters overcome adversity.

These episodes are set on the plains, mountains, and deserts of the West, locales redolent of the mystique and allure of that special time and place in our nation's history. The book was constructed with three categories in mind: Mountain Men and Indians; Man versus Nature; and Cowboys and Gunfighters. It runs chronologically from the dawn of the nineteenth century to the dawn of the twentieth century. Roughly gathered, these elements helped define my task and gave shape and direction to each chapter. These moments led to others, some to trails that dead-ended, but more often than not to episodes that proved even more fascinating. The result, of course, was that I ended up with far more stories than this book could hold.

The chapters are arranged chronologically so that the reader will gain a sense of how the nineteenth century changed—opening like a promising flower for white European explorers even while becoming a barren, forlorn place for native people. Another segment of the population fell squarely in the middle—the explorers who saw the promise of the land before them and then lost everything in their quest for it. They too are included here, for who among us hasn't fallen flat on his or her face a time or two? The trick, as these admirable people have taught me, is to push ourselves up out of the gravel, wipe our bloodied noses, and head for the horizon.

Though I did use a bit of poetic license by adding dialogue and supporting characters, the fiction writer in me was tempted to let the characters wander a bit more than they actually did. But reining in that impulse and sticking to the facts provided far more grist for the mill. My mother is fond of saying that truth is stranger than fiction, and as much as I hate to admit it . . . she's right. But I'd alter her phrase to say that truth is more fascinating than fiction.

After all, who can conjure a tale more fantastic than the saga of Hugh Glass and his 350-mile crawl across a harsh landscape, his survival reliant more on raw revenge than on the meager foodstuffs he was able to find? Or the seemingly endless travails of Marie Dorian as she crossed an unforgiving winter mountain landscape with her two boys, at the edge of starvation and snow-blind part of the time? Or the vicious treatment of the Cheyenne at the hands of the U.S. Army at Sand Creek? Or the exhilaration and despair felt by John Wesley Powell and his crew as they marveled at the magnificent presence of the Grand Canyon from below and at the same time fought hunger and pounding rapids, day after day, month after month? Or Janette Riker, orphaned in the Northern Rockies in the winter of 1849? She shrugged off despair and hunkered down for the long haul, despite repeated attempts by mountain lions and wolves to dislodge and devour her. She held on until spring, and went on to forge a life as a pioneer woman, wife, and mother.

It is this bold spirit, desire for freedom, and yearning for new, unfettered experience that is at the heart of this book. The history of the Wild West is rich and brimming with gritty characters who find themselves in grittier encounters, resulting in the grittiest of moments. I could go on, but why take the fun out of it for you?

In closing, if this book contains errors, they are mine. If, however, these gritty moments are found to be thrilling, fulfilling, and worthy of further exploration—history is wholly responsible.

Happy trails to you. It's time to saddle my pinto. . . .

—Matthew P. Mayo
Bozeman, Montana
April 2009

1

HEAD-SMASHED-IN BUFFALO JUMP

For more than five thousand years, the Plains Indians hunted buffalo throughout the Rocky Mountains by driving entire herds over high cliffs. The Head-Smashed-In site was in use for many centuries, as evidenced by the thirty-foot-deep deposits of bone at the base. It got its name from the young Blackfoot Indian who wanted to see, up close, the buffalo as they jumped off the cliff.

Stout Tree watched his father and brothers prepare for the great buffalo hunt. His mother readied her tools for butchering the great shaggy beasts. "I want to help," he said finally, standing in front of his father.

The man looked down at him. "Soon you'll be out there with me and your brothers. But not this year. You know that, Stout Tree."

He fought to keep from showing anger, nodded at his father, and left the lodge. He longed for the day when he could be with the warriors all the time. He no longer wanted to merely watch as the warriors drove the buffalo off the cliffs, he wanted to help. He wanted to be the one to wear the sacred buffalo skin with head and horns. He wanted to be the one to lure the herd to the cliffs. He felt certain that he could do that. But that honor had gone to one of his older bothers this year, as it had in years past gone to his father.

One day he would show them all what a fine warrior he was. Perhaps next year. But that did nothing to quell the frustration he felt now. As the tribe moved out from the camps they had set up nearby the cliffs (as they did each year at this time) with each step he studied the cliffs over which the beasts would plunge.

He knew what would happen soon—the panicked beasts would run and push and ram each other in their frenzy. And the decoy warrior, disguised as a buffalo, would run just ahead of the surging herd until at the last moment possible he would jump off the edge to a shelf and crouch there as the animals thundered closer, then flew down past him like great, flawed birds.

Would it not be an amazing sight to see those beasts as no one had ever seen them before? Looking up from underneath would be even better than acting as a decoy warrior. He might not be allowed to participate in the hunt and drive to the cliffs, might not be one of the men who emerged from behind the rocks along the way and frightened the straying buffalo back into the crowd before they reached the cliff's edge, but there was a way he could experience the jump like no one ever had.

Stout Tree's heart quickened as he made up his mind. It would be a matter of slipping away from the women and children and old men—for he was none of these—and finding his way to the base of the cliffs. He had seen the buffalo surge ahead and off the cliff for as long as he could remember, and he knew they flew out into the air before dropping. There was room enough for his entire tribe to stand underneath and see this great wonder. For the briefest moment he wanted to share this news with everyone, but he knew they would prevent him from doing it. He smiled to himself and darted from rock to rock, making his way to the base of the buffalo jump cliffs.

The distant rumbling traveled down from the plain above, and Stout Tree felt the stuttering thuds through the cliff face. The jolting increased in power and he felt it work through him, from his back pressed to the rock wall, into his guts, and out through him. It was like nothing he'd ever experienced. The sound, too, built rumble upon rumble, like a late summer thunderstorm, rolling slow at first, taking all day to reach his village by the river, and then . . . Boom!

Before him a black shape pitched down as if it were a cloud falling. Then another, and another, and he realized he was seeing what he had hoped to see—the falling of the buffalo. Then the noise became enormous. The very rocks under his feet trembled and the sky grew black. Dust plumed into his face and the entire world shook. The rocks on which he stood slid away and he felt himself pulled forward. Stout Tree fell and rolled down the slope, not believing this could happen, astonished even as he became part of the crushing blackness.

It was hours before the warriors had killed all the crippled and maimed buffalo lying in writhing piles at the base of the jump. The women had begun right away butchering the animals at the outer edges. This had been a large herd and the hunters made sure that every member had been driven over the edge and killed. If even one escaped it would join another herd and the knowledge of this place and what it was used for would taint that herd. Such knowledge spread from buffalo to buffalo as a warrior's knowledge passes from father to son.

It was not until He Who Knows the Wind shouted for help, from deep within the middle of the pile of dead buffalo, that anyone knew what happened to Stout Tree. That year's hunt should have been a time of rejoicing for the tribe, but now it was tainted with grief for the young boy who had so wanted to be a warrior.

In his honor, the place was named for him as they found him: Head-Smashed-In Buffalo Jump.

In addition to the Head-Smashed-In site, located near Fort Macleod in Alberta, Canada, Ulm Pishkun Buffalo Jump, the largest in the world, is located just south of Great Falls, Montana. The cliffs there range more than a mile in length, and archaeological digs at their base have turned up evidence of bison bones compacted to a depth of thirteen feet. The site, in use between 900 B.C. and A.D. 1800, was given an extensive mention in Meriwether Lewis's journals of Wednesday, May 29, 1805.

Plains Indians used this method of hunting for thousands of years, with some sites still in use as late as 1800. It was a most effective and relatively safe means of dispatching large numbers of their most valued source of sustenance. They had to make sure that every member of the chosen herd had been driven over and killed. The Plains Indians knew, through experience, that knowledge of the jumps would indeed pass from escaped buffalo to new herds. European hunters did not understand or approve of these methods, though their own methods eventually resulted in the near extinction of the Plains buffalo.

GRISLY EXPEDITION

On May 14, 1805, Lewis and Clark's ambitious expedition was almost left severely short-handed when a hunting party of six men in canoes spied a massive grizzly sleeping three hundred yards from the river. They fired, piercing its lungs . . . and then it bolted after them.

That bear is a brute," whispered Sergeant Ordway to one of the six men in the hunting party. They both watched the massive honey-colored beast as it snored, its back to them, utterly unaware of their presence. They had paused in their slow, low crawl toward the animal. Forty yards away from it, they were still undetected. A low-flying bee lazily circled the bear's head. An ear tip twitched once, twice, and still the bear's massive furred side rose and fell in the steady rhythm of a seemingly deep sleep.

Ordway agreed in silence with the bear's decision to take a nap. It was a cloudless day in mid May and the sun was unusually warm this late afternoon, a warmer day than they'd had in nearly a week.

Ordway raised himself from a crouch in the tall grass of the meadow. He saw movement off to his right. It was the other four men, all sharing glances with him. Following his lead, they stood, raised their rifles to their shoulders, and sighted on the bear. Two of the four stood at the ready, rifles poised, waiting. From their past experiences with the great brown bears, they knew that a following round of shots may well be needed.

The leader felt a pang of regret shortly before he and the other three designated first shooters opened fire on the unsuspecting beast. It was the only thing in the meadow engaged in an innocent pursuit and they were here to kill it. But duty and a hunter's curiosity overcame his moment of weak emotion.

Within seconds the four shots stuttered and boomed across the rolling grass plain. And quicker than any creature of its size had a right to react, the great brown brute rose as if scalded. A blood-chilling roar emanating from the beast froze them all in their tracks—for a brief moment. For that is all they had before the beast's massive claws pawed up great clumps of prairie grass and it lunged, open-mouthed, at the closest of them.

The two men who had held their fire now discharged their shots. Both found their mark. One was but a petty wound but the second broke the bear's shoulder. And for the span of a breath Ordway and his men thought the beast might go down. Each man hurriedly worked at reloading his weapon. But the bear recovered, and broke once again into a full gallop at them.

"Run, men! Run for the river!" Ordway's order was not necessary, as the brute, showing little sign of injury, was already bearing down on them. As it gained ground, the two men at the rear of the small group of hunters broke off toward the beached canoes, lunging at the nearest craft without pushing it into the water. The bear slowed not a whit, bawling and slavering and shaking its head as though a swarm of bees surrounded its face.

Ordway and the other three stumbled to a stop and crouched in a cluster of willow saplings to reload their rifles. After they finished tamping the balls down, they wasted no time in again drawing aim at the beast and shooting. In doing so they managed to keep the bear from a final lunge at the men in the canoe. They also managed to lure the bear's attention to themselves.

But the speed with which the bear recovered and charged astonished them all. Their single shots spent, they threw aside their rifles and pouches and jumped straight off the shaggy rim of a twenty-foot embankment and into the swirling Missouri River below. They thrashed into the water, swimming toward the far shore in an attempt to put even more distance between them and the unstoppable beast they had angered. But it was almost all for naught. The lunging jaws, snarling, shaking head, and great rippling body of the savage creature did not break stride but burst straight after the second shooter, plunging off the same grass knob less than a man's-length behind the shrieking hunter.

A great and rending roar accompanied this impressive action, and the bear pitched forward into the water and lay still, waves pulsing outward from the now-sopping form of the great beast.

For long seconds, no one said anything, so astonished were they that the great bear's roaring and slavering had ceased. The men in the river snorted

Hunting of the Grizzly Bear by Karl (Charles) Bodmer. Lewis and Clark's men thought that eight lead balls would be enough to kill the big grizzly. They were nearly wrong. *Courtesy Library of Congress*

and wiped at their wet faces with their sleeves. They cautiously strode through the shallows to the bear, dark clouds in the water indicating its bloody leaks. A rope was retrieved from a canoe and the bear was dragged ashore. All hands participated in the butchering. It was found that the bear took no less than eight lead balls, two in the lungs alone, before it had expired.

The last shot, fired from on shore by Sergeant Ordway, had blazed straight into the bear's head, stopping its rampage for all time. The men who'd scrambled off the embankment slapped Ordway's great buckskin clad shoulders and thanked him heartily.

"Knowing this country," said the sergeant, "I've no doubt you'll have the opportunity to repay me one of these days." They all laughed, nervous and exhausted, and finished working the carcass. The meat proved not to be worth their time as the bear was past its prime, but the skin was worth taking.

Meriwether Lewis and William Clark's Corps of Discovery, so designated by President Thomas Jefferson, was charged with finding the most direct water route across the country to the Pacific Ocean. Beginning in 1803, this epic expedition lasted two years, four months, and ten days, and covered eight thousand miles. It was a monumental success and provided the world with many first glimpses of the unexplored frontier. The expedition also cleared the trail for the great influx of pioneers who would transform the raw wilderness into a place largely unrecognizable.

3

RUN, MAN! RUN!

In 1809, in what would become Montana, John Colter ran naked and weaponless from the dreaded Blackfeet and into the pages of history. It was not Colter's first skirmish with the violent tribe, nor would it be his last.

Under the jam of logs jutting into the current of the Jefferson Fork of the Missouri River, Colter eased lower into the water until it pooled into his eyes. His lungs and windpipe burned with the need for air, but the gnarled toes and horned, calloused skin of a warrior's bare feet hugged a log inches from his face. He needed to remain still.

He thought back to the events of the past few hours. He and his trapping partner, Joe Potts, should have known better than to drift in their canoes so far into Blackfoot territory. But the beaver were plentiful and so the men had continued on up the Missouri, setting their traps. And then the band of Blackfoot warriors had come upon them with nary a sound, though there were hundreds of them lining the east bank. Colter was sure they would kill them both where they sat, but instead they had demanded the white men come to shore. Colter had done so, reluctant but sure of the outcome should they resist. As soon as he stepped from his canoe, a swarm of squaws attacked him, stripping him of everything but his skin.

"Tell the other white man to come to shore."

Colter relayed the chief's request to Potts. Twice. But it was no good. He knew Potts too well to expect the man to give up without a fight. And he hadn't. Within seconds a warrior had driven a ball into the stubborn trapper's shoulder. Potts returned fire, killing the Indian who shot him. It was the work of a half-minute more before Potts was peppered in a vicious volley from the eastern shore of the river.

Colter gritted his teeth, lest they rattle in the cold water and alert the Blackfeet still searching the shoreline. As he waited for them to leave, unbidden images of Potts's end once again flooded his mind's eye. After the warriors dragged Potts's canoe to shore, shrieking squaws picked clean his companion's body, hacking at the bloodied thing until it was nothing more than hunks of meat and bone. And all the while they flung parts of his friend at him until Colter dripped with his friend's gore.

A great argument ensued among the younger warriors and the chiefs. Colter knew enough of the lingo to tell they were of differing minds as to what to do with him. But from the smirks on the faces of the ring of warriors, he knew this was but the beginning.

A chief stepped forward. "Can you run, white man?"

"I can, though I am out of practice and not that swift."

More smirks and laughter met his remark. The younger warriors began shucking their clothes and extra gear.

The chief led him to the edge of the wide, clear plain. Colter looked over his shoulder at a line of braves, noted the restless shiftings of the younger warriors, then heard the shouts. "Run, white man!" And he did.

Within seconds, the line of warriors broke. He knew the river lay roughly six miles ahead of him over hard ground riddled with prickly pear, sharp rocks, and Lord knew what else. The river's rushing water and brush-lined slopes offered the only chance, however slim, he might have for escape. But the rough terrain already lashed his feet, leaving them bleeding and throbbing. And his chest heaved hard as a smithy's bellows.

He heard the rage in the yelping voices of his followers as they saw him outdistance them. They did not expect that he would be fast on his feet. He had lied to them. Odd, he thought, that a captive's word should be trusted. He quashed a grim smile that licked at his mouth. There would be time enough for gloating later. He hoped.

Bitterness like strong, black tea filled his throat. Without warning blood gushed from his mouth and nose, flowed down his face and chest. He felt no pain. Had he been shot? It had happened before, in a skirmish with the same damnable tribe, but he'd felt that ball slam his leg like the head of a ramming bull. He risked a look at his chest. There was no pain, no visible wound. It must be his heart, nothing more. Never had he breathed so hard in his life.

Colter risked another quick glance behind. The two score or more warriors were still in pursuit but straggling, their strength leaving them. He guessed he must have traveled more than half the six-mile distance to the river. The sound of his breathing, hard and sharp, now held a ragged edge, reminding him of the death rattle of a grizzly he'd killed on the Lewis and Clark expedition. The beast had fought harder than any animal he'd ever encountered.

He drew strength from the memory and surged forward. However slight, such extra effort might mean the difference between life and death. Every tick of the clock's hand counted with an immensity he knew he would only appreciate later, in front of a fire with his fellows, recounting this vicious day.

But his breathing was too ragged, too uneven. And that's when he realized the sound he heard was not merely his own breath but also the exhalations of another joining his. He looked backward. Gaining on him was a young warrior, running full out, the glint of bloodlust in his dark eyes, a lance carried in one hand as if it weighed nothing at all.

They were passing through sparse thickets now and Colter knew that here he may have to make his stand, though it might mean his end. The warrior was gaining on him. As the young mountain man wove his way through the thickets dotting the plains, instinct yanked him to a stop. He whipped low to the ground, kneeling in wait, knowing he could not disguise his heaving breath. Within seconds, the pounding of the warrior's feet filled his ears and a muscled leg flashed in front of him, closer than expected. Colter lashed out with his only weapons—his brawny hands—and gripped that leg with a raw power born of anger. He sprang at the man and slammed the body to the coarse ground.

For the span of a single heartbeat the faces of the two adversaries were inches apart, their eyes blazing at each other. The warrior spun, knocking the white man aside with a sinewy arm and thrusting his lance. But just as the white man's fleet-footedness had shocked them all, so now did the speed with which Colter blocked the lance, slamming an open hand into the shaft and snapping it in two. The blow knocked the warrior off-balance. That brief moment gained was all Colter needed.

Time was his most precious resource and he did not waste a drop. With a knee rammed tight to the warrior's gut he grasped the top half of the lance, stone tip down, and pushed on the ragged haft with his own shoulder. The warrior's defeat was evident in his eyes even before the honed tip pierced his skin. In another heartbeat it was finished. The warrior bucked like an empty dugout in hard rapids, his own blood, hot and red, pulsed from his wide mouth, coloring his teeth with his own death.

Colter stared for but a moment, no sympathy evident on his visage or in his heart. This was no one to be pitied. He yanked the shoulder blanket from beneath the man, the warrior's blood already seeping into one corner of the woven thing.

He tried to ignore the raw, weeping wounds that were the soles of his feet, the lacerated mess of his body, and the fact that his breathing sounded more like something ripped and windblown than that which he relied upon for life. As he peered from behind the thicket, he saw that while the horde of warriors had thinned (indeed, many were doubled over, clutching their sides and heaving into the waving grasses), a few were still advancing with worrying speed. He kept low and, clutching the blanket, thundered on toward the river.

Through the first hours of dark, the numbing cold of the water kept Colter from deep sleep. He briefly dozed, and when he came to, it was a clouded night, perfect for travel across open land. He peered into the dark, listening, then began to swim downstream with the current, hoping he was making the right choice. When he finally pulled himself from the water, he crouched in the undergrowth lining the riverbank.

He did not curse his luck, for he was not a man who believed in such foofaraw, but he knew it would take a heap of hard work on his part to make it out of the land of the Blackfeet alive. These first miles were nothing more than a gift. He faced at least two weeks of hard travel to cover the two hundred or so miles that stood between him and Manuel Lisa's fort. He knew that in the dark, far to his left, stood imposing cliffs. The Blackfeet would not expect him to make such a climb out of their valley. John Colter set off at a lope, the beginnings of a smile pulling at his mouth.

John Colter, who blazed trails with Lewis and Clark and who was the first white man to discover the Yellowstone region's natural wonders, experienced two more run-ins with the Blackfeet before swearing off his wilderness life forever. He married, set to farming in Missouri, and died penniless of jaundice at age thirty-eight in November, 1813, just four years after his series of infamous escapes from the Blackfeet. His wife, Sally, without funds to bury him, left his body in their rough home with a note pinned to his shirt and his old possibles bag around his neck. In it were receipts for plews he'd sold during his six-year tenure as the first mountain man.

4

A BRUTAL END

In 1809, George Drouillard, indispensable half-French and half-Shawnee member of the Lewis and Clark expedition, master of many languages, and expert hunter and guide, was working for the Missouri Fur Company. Deep in Blackfoot country near the headwaters of the Upper Missouri River, he ignored warnings to stay close to camp.

As he guided his horse along the Jefferson River, following the same route he'd taken the two previous days, Thomas James's words of caution rang in George Drouillard's ears. He didn't need the advice, but the kindly remarks, he knew, were prompted as much by the man's fear of losing a valuable resource as from concern for his safety.

He was alert to every slight scuffle and twig snap in the surrounding undergrowth. He shifted his rifle to a looser position in the crook of his arm and noted again that his pistol, tucked in his sash, was at the ready. It was a dangerous game he was playing, and any amount of luck, especially out here in the wild, was about as predicable as a grizzly's temper, but he'd be damned if he was going to sit in that camp in the midst of all those scared men.

Was he not, after all, half Indian himself? And did he not have more experience in these woods than anyone else in the small band? If he wanted to make a mark with this company, then his money was to be made here, in this land crawling with beaver. If it happened to be in Blackfoot and Gros Ventre country, then so be it. If no one made an attempt, no one would ever succeed in trapping here. And there was plenty of beaver to be trapped, his previous two days' efforts proved that.

The trees thinned and opened into a small clearing. He'd noted it yesterday when he returned from checking his traps. He held tight to the river, and though he couldn't see it he knew it was there, but a few dozen yards to his left, gurgling and slapping and constantly flowing. He wished he could quiet it for a moment, for he swore he heard something more than the river and his own horse's footfalls.

There! A faint snapping of twigs. But from which direction? He crouched low, his face to the horse's neck, smelling the musky odor, feeling the beast tense, its ears laid back. From behind, to the right, owing more to sense than sight, he caught a glimpse of movement, dark and low. No mountain lion, but it did stalk him like one. And where there was one Blackfoot or Gros Ventre, there were untold others.

He swung his right leg free and over, clinging to his rifle and to the horse, kneeing it in the belly and urging it on. Two nervous steps forward and then the horse shunted sideways, groaning. They must have shot it with an arrow, as he'd heard no rifle report. The animal remained standing. Drouillard slid to a crouch on the river side of the horse and patted it. If he were lucky they wouldn't have crept behind him yet. He cocked the rifle and laid it over the trembling horse's back, kept his dry mouth clamped tight, and sighted on a dark shape that he swore had appeared just before he focused on it. He held his breath and squeezed the trigger.

The report awakened a clatter of sound. The screams and shouts of what sounded like hundreds of warriors surrounded him. The air whistled with arrows and gunshots. Instant pain coursed up his right leg, and a quick glance showed a short arrow protruding from his calf. He pounded on the heaving barrel of the horse's belly, urging it forward in a wide circle in an effort to keep the poor, doomed beast between himself and the emerging mass of devils.

But it quickly became apparent that he was already surrounded and by too many of them for one man to dispatch. He let go of his cherished rifle, knowing he would never again load it, and pulled his pistol from his belt, keeping his back to the rapidly weakening horse. From its screams he knew it was taking the brunt of the missiles. It could not last much longer.

There, crawling over a log . . . and there! Beside that one, from behind those trees . . . Drouillard let go his pistol shot. As with his rifle shot, he heard a scream and saw a form recoil. He threw the spent weapon at the nearest attacker, watched it strike the man in the head and send him reeling back. Drouillard bounded forward with an oath of anger flying from his lips. He whipped his sizable skinning knife and tomahawk from his belt and crouched to meet the onslaught. The horse slumped to its side, arrows, lances, and bullet wounds puckering its trembling hide.

Drouillard spun on his chosen spot in the midst of the little clearing and growled a long, loud, and deep bellow that did nothing to slow the advance of the attacking horde of warriors. Yes, Blackfeet, he could see them clearly now. All around him, perhaps a dozen, probably closer to twenty.

A lead ball slammed into his gut, pitching him forward for an instant of agony, then an arrow whipped into his chest, drove deep. He felt bone and something more give way inside him. But he did not drop his weapons. He would take as many of these devils with him as God would allow. And despite the arrows that threatened to topple him at any second, he windmilled his arms, bellowing louder than ever.

The next blood to spray in great hot gouts in the clearing was not his but that of the first two Indians who dared advance on him before their fellows, to show they were true warriors and not afraid of close combat. But he surprised them with his knife and tomahawk, and now they were nothing more than wretched lumps at his feet, spewing their last into the forest floor.

He would soon follow them, he knew, but not until his blades tasted more Blackfoot blood. He struck like a madman, like someone who has nothing to lose—the most effective fighter is one who knows he is doomed. He saw an older warrior, thicker in the chest and with more decoration adorning his torso, motion to a throng of younger men, who immediately attacked from the front and sides. As he buried his tomahawk deep into the waist of the nearest, he saw a flash of satisfaction on the face of the older warrior. Drouillard realized too late what they had done and what he, in his weakened state, had not anticipated in time. He looked skyward. Blood flowered from his mouth even as an axe sang down into the top of his head. And he knew no more.

Thomas James was the first to find the little clearing. He reined his horse hard, dismounted and crouched there, seeing but not wanting to see, and all because that damnable Drouillard, the single most capable man in the woods and wild he'd ever met, had refused to listen to reason. Had refused to live like other men—in fear—and now he had met his end.

His men dismounted and stood by him, some of them scanning the woods, others with their gaze locked on the carnage laid out before them. Not a man could believe the scene, for there was the mutilated body of George Drouillard, explorer, trapper, guide, hunter without peer, master of languages, the most skilled interpreter in sign language any of them had ever met. He was the man who some said was the only reason the Lewis and Clark expedition had succeeded. This man could not be dead.

But he was. And as their initial shock wore off, half the men, not bothering to stifle tears, walked among what was left of Drouillard. His head had been removed from his body, mashed and mutilated beyond recognition. His limbs, too, had been hacked away and divided further, as if joints in a meat shop, and his guts had been split wide and dragged like glistening ropes all about the clearing. Some of the men didn't realize that they stood on Drouillard's intestines. The man's horse, pocked and riddled with arrows, fared no better. It too had been hacked open. Several men bent low, hands on knees, and heaved their noon meal into the grass.

Wearing a mask of grimness, Thomas James circled the little clearing. He noted that while Drouillard's weapons were gone, there was blood splashed liberally about the vicinity, most of it too far away from where he fell to be his. Drouillard had given as good as he got, to at least a few of the devils.

The men knew they could not linger in this hellish place, for to do so would mean their own deaths. They dug a hasty grave for Drouillard and placed his mutilated body in the shallow resting place. None of them wanted to admit that what few rocks they managed to lay atop the grave would be insufficient to repel the foragings of the night's beasts. They put the thought from their minds and rode hard for their camp and toward yet another sleepless night.

Although George Drouillard met his end that May day in 1809, the fur trade continued for many decades to come, due in part to the persistence of men such as Manuel Lisa, Andrew Henry, and Thomas James, partners in the Missouri Fur Company. The Blackfeet continued to be a formidable impediment to the fur trappers, but eventually even this fierce tribe was no match for the tide of intrepid explorers heading West.

5

THE TRIALS OF MARIE DORIAN

In 1811 Marie Dorian and her children accompanied her husband on the ill-fated Wilson Hunt trip, a seven-month, 2,073-mile journey to Oregon. After arriving, Marie Dorian, a Sioux, thought her life might offer less hardship. She was wrong.

The second horse was more difficult to kill. It seemed to know that death had come for it. Marie Dorian shot the beast in the temple and stepped back to let it drop. With its death she felt the weight of loss that had become so familiar in her life. First there had been the death of her baby, born on the trail during the Wilson Hunt trip the previous year. Her husband, Pierre Dorian, had been hired to guide the party from Missouri to Fort Astoria in Oregon. It was a bad trip, two men had died, and they all nearly starved.

She watched the horse breathe out its last, the eye staring up at her, already changed like they do, viewing her from death. The snow steamed red as the blood leached outward from the sagged body. And with that killing she had made the choice to stay here at this camp and feed her boys rather than try to ride the horse, already a weakened thing, to find help. The snow was too deep for the horse anyway. They would eat the meat and use their own legs to find help.

She bent over the horse and began the long work of cutting away meat. She knew her boys stood behind her, staring at the dead beast, fascinated with what she was doing. She smiled. They would live. She would not let her husband win this battle. And then she laughed out loud, peeked under her arm at the boys. They giggled at her. She truly must have loved Pierre, she thought, to argue with a dead man.

Days later, the horsemeat nearly gone, she sat in their crude shelter, exhausted and stricken by snow blindness. A twitching movement at her side caused her to flinch. It was Baptiste, her eldest. Her hand felt the tears on his cheek, the smeared dirt and hair matting against his face.

"What is it?" she said to him. She spoke in her native tongue, which she had taught her boys. He just shook his head. She repeated her question, though she knew the cause of his tears, this little boy who had tried so hard through this ordeal to be a man.

"Papa is dead and now you are going to die. We will die, too."

His words squeezed her heart. She swallowed and breathed deep, and said, "No, Baptiste, we will not die. We are only stopped because the snow has made me unable to see. But it will not last. I have seen it before in others. In a few days we will travel again. Now go to sleep."

If her words did not convince the boy, at least they slowed his wretched snuffling. Under her other arm slept Paul, her youngest. She rubbed them both, her bony little starving birds.

The snow was deeper than she expected. Baptiste was tiring quickly, but Marie felt her sight returning. They rested often and she did her best to dig a shelter in the snow. And while they rested, with the cold clear night all about them, her thoughts turned to Pierre.

Only when she looked at little Paul did she grow angry with her dead husband. She could not say she was sorry that Pierre was dead. No, not even for the fact that her two boys would no longer know their father. Only the way he died. No one should be killed like that. And after traveling more than two thousand miles, to be murdered while trapping beaver. . . .

LeClerc lurched into the doorway, grabbing the frame with one hand. He weaved there a moment and looked at Marie, then the two boys playing on the floor. The burly trapper was covered in his own blood. His head was sticky with it and he held one arm tight to his guts, trying to stop a seeping wound.

He slumped to his knees, half in the little cabin.

"Where are Pierre and Rezner?" She knelt by his side, looking at his face, at his wounds.

"Bannocks again. . . ."

"LeClerc! Where is my husband?"

The man looked at her as if finally recognizing her and said, "Marie! You must leave. The others are dead. Yes, Pierre, too. They killed him and Rezner. I, too, am a dead man. You must take the little ones and go."

"Ssshhh. Don't talk, LeClerc. Save your strength."

She looked out the door, then made her boys sit still and quiet. She rounded up two horses and loaded them with what provisions she could find. She helped LeClerc onto the strongest of the two horses. He protested but was too weak to argue. As quickly as she could she led the horses, LeClerc on one and her boys on the other, through the forest and toward the safety of the main trapping camp, four days walk upriver at the mouth of the Boise.

They had not gone far when she heard a loud, heavy thump. LeClerc had fallen from the horse and lay moaning. She tended him quickly and managed to get him back on the horse. But by nightfall he was in poor condition. She couldn't get much more information from him other than that she should never see what the Bannocks did to her husband or Rezner. She knew that what she would imagine would never come close to the horrors the men endured before they died. The Bannocks were ruthless.

LeClerc died in the night. She left him there, too afraid of being caught to give him much of a ceremony. She did her best, assuring the boys all the while that they would be safe once they reached the main camp. Her sons were too young to understand anything other than that they were frightened. But they dared not cry, she had warned them against such things.

Just before dark on the fourth day of her journey, she approached the camp. Before she got there she knew something was wrong. Saw smoke rising from the trees. Still, she had to know. Emerging from the path into the clearing by the river, she registered it all in a sweeping glance. The camp had been burned to the ground and the men slaughtered, their bodies hacked open, limbs severed. One man was missing his head. Nothing of value lay anywhere that she could see.

She did not know how long they had been traveling, but at times the terrain was less difficult, the snow not as deep, and even Paul could walk more often now. Her sight had returned. These all should have been good things, but with each step, she saw in her sons' weak, thin bodies that ever-present specter of death. She tried to always keep her smile, just for them. But she was dying, too.

They trekked for weeks through the Blue Mountains before finding the Wallah Wallah River. They rested, and just before she felt her head nod forward, sleep pulling at her like a heavy weight, she saw something not seen by them in a long time.

"There is smoke in the distance," she said to the boys. They looked at her and Baptiste smiled. She nodded. "I will go for help and come back for you soon. But you must stay here under this blanket where you will be warm." She touched them each on the head and unsteadily walked toward the smoke, hoping that it was not the camp of hostiles.

Long before she reached it she found that she was too weak to continue. She collapsed in the snowy grass of the plain, a whimper of anger forced from her as she dropped, prone, to the ground. The cold snow on her face revived her enough that she pushed herself up, and with thoughts of her children, she crawled, one foot at a time, on her hands and knees, toward that campfire smoke.

When the Wallah Wallah Indians brought her boys to her in the lodge, she wept without shame. That she should experience such good fortune when she needed it most was so welcome.

Marie Dorian and her sons spent fifty-three days in their first camp until lack of food and harsh weather forced them to move on. They traveled through the Blue Mountains for more than a month until, in March, 1814, they made it to the river and were taken care of by the Wallah Wallah tribe. Within a month she and her sons were found by traders from Fort Astoria, her husband's employer.

She married twice more, and spent the rest of her years in Saint Louis, Oregon. She died there on September 5, 1850, revered among her white neighbors as an unassuming woman, but strong, kind, and capable as well. Most of them knew of the hardships she had endured, though none ever heard about them from her.

UNSTOPPABLE MAN

In April of 1823, having been left for dead by his party after a sow grizzly severely mauled him, mountain man Hugh Glass dragged his savaged body 350 miles to Fort Brazeau. Barely recovered, he set out for revenge, not on the bear but on the men who had abandoned him in the wild. Revenge, he felt, was a dish worth serving.

Hugh Glass paused, a scar-knotted, clawed hand resting atop the hilt of his knife, the other hand firmly gripping the stock of his rifle. *His* rifle. Even if he was to be robbed of revenge, he would not be robbed of his closest ally. At least Captain Riley there in Fort Atkinson had retrieved it from Fitzgerald for him. That was consolation of a sort.

Before him, close by the river, sat the fort that contained his quarry, John Fitzgerald. One of the death dealers who abandoned him in his hour of need. He straightened and strained against the tightened ropes of scar tissue that banded his body. It had been more than a year since the mauling. He'd traveled two thousand miles just to be here. No longer did his wounds stink and fester. No longer did he have to fight back beasts real and imagined, though none more vicious than Old Ephraim, the grizzly who had inflicted this hell on him. He'd fought his way through packs of wolves as they trailed him, sniffing at the blood sign he left behind, gritting his broken, jagged teeth, loose in a snapped jaw beneath his flayed cheek as he dragged his festering wounds through leaves and dirt to streambeds where he could rest, soaking in the cooling freshness.

Even his back wound had healed, the worms purged and the flesh closed, with help from the small band of Sioux he stumbled on before reaching Fort Brazeau. But it had been a long year; most of the two thousand miles on foot, another handful of near-death attacks by Elk's Tongue's rogue band of Arikara, bent on revenge for the death of old Grey Eyes. At least that was sentiment he could understand.

He snorted, leaning against the scrub pine in the slow-growing light, watching the fort and not watching it, his scarred visage lost in unbidden mists of harsh memories, of a terrible experience from which he would never escape.

It was spring fruit they were after. And elbow room. He and George Harris had it in mind that they would get away from Major Henry and his little row of ducks. In truth it was his own bullheadedness that prevented him from sticking with the troop that morning. There were among them weak men whose company galled him. He needed to be alone. He often felt a twinge of regret at allying himself with the incompetent leader, Major Andrew Henry, who had lost half the men in a doomed attack on the Arikaras. But Hugh knew he would stay with them. It was not in his nature to give up.

There was a promising berry thicket, then a sudden sound. An awful roaring rose up to meet him, eye to eye, and then rose higher yet. An enormous bear looked down at him. Old Ephraim's on me, he remembered thinking, just before the beast's jaws closed about him. No buckskin in the world could stop those gleaming blades of teeth from popping into his chest and taking with them a mouthful of him. The bear swung him around, and that's when he saw cubs. Two of them. Old Eph was a she-bear. The worst kind.

He had little time to raise his trusted rifle. He was shaking so hard, as if gripped with ague, that he felt sure he wouldn't be able to force back the hammer. But he did, and pulled on the trigger without hesitation. Though he heard the report and knew from years of sure shooting that he had shot true, the beast was on him again, rising to its full height and lashing with curved claws as long as a man's fingers. Glass rolled over and made to crawl away. He remembered tasting dirt and thinking of sure death, of being covered with the stuff. This idea did not appeal to him at all.

Another swipe and his back seemed to peel clean off. He felt his scalp rise, heard the pop as it separated and was pulled away. His arms had been raked to the bone and his right hip, too, a glistening, bare ravine of meat and bone. Hugh saw this and heard the shouts and rifle reports of his fellows as he collapsed back to the ground, undone even as the bear charged away, then returned, slower. It swatted and lunged at him again and the last he recalled was the stink of the thing's final breath as it dropped across him, draped like it was sleeping. So familiar and fitting, he remembered thinking, for they had gone out together. But that was not his end.

For all the close scrapes he'd been through—fleeing the pirate Jean Lafitte, living with the savage Pawnee, the injuries he'd sustained through the long years—they didn't call him Old Hugh for nothing—none could compare with the agonies that coursed through him when he regained the living world. He was fussed over by the men, but they were far from civilization and surrounded by savages. There was little they could do for him. He heard Major Henry's remark about his many mortal wounds, and saw the looks of pity from the men. Waves of pure pain washed through him from head to foot, taking him to unconsciousness.

Two voices, arguing. One shouting, the other shushing, saying, "He can't help but hear us. You must know that."

"No, no, you are wrong," says the other. "Old Hugh is all but gone already." He knew that voice. Yes, it was that John Fitzgerald fellow calming the boy, Jim Bridger. Just a green lad. Hugh could hear Fitzgerald's coarse voice telling the boy it had to be this way or they too would die. What would it matter, he said, for Old Hugh will not know. . . .

The memory brought Hugh back to the present. He sneered in the rising daylight and said out loud, "But he did know." For a long time Hugh stayed leaning against the tree, watching the fort where Fitzgerald was holed up. He was now a soldier and therefore untouchable, they'd told him hours before. Untouchable. Pah. Where there is life there is hope, is there not? This I know well. He grimaced again.

He remembered he had fluttered in and out of wakefulness for a time, gleaning that Fitzgerald and Bridger had been promised money to watch over him until he passed on. So they were convinced that he was all but dead. Would that they had not spoken—but then he might not have lived. They revealed their cowards' plan in low whispers over him, thinking him beyond knowing, beyond caring.

They divvied his goods like buzzards picking a corpse—his possibles sack with flint and steel for fire making, tomahawk, knife, powder, shot, and percussion caps. And most unforgivable of all, Fitzgerald hefted his rifle. A wilderness man's only trusted ally and that scoundrel took it. Rage burst in him and still he could not call out, could not make them hear him. He felt this theft to his marrow, yet was unable to act. He knew then, at the moment of hearing their cowardly footfalls vanish in the crackling undergrowth, that he would live. And he would make them pay for what they did.

He pulled from his reverie in the woods beyond the fort, the day's new light warming the far side of the clearing. Thoughts again came flooding to him, filling his head, the memories of more pain as he wobbled in semi-consciousness for four or five days. He remembered a wolf dragging away the blanket with which he had been covered. He grudgingly recalled the fact that the two men had left him within arm's length of a stream. The water proved as restorative as any bought tincture. And oddest of all, a rattlesnake, resting within reach, provided nourishment after he dispatched it with a rock to the head.

When his strength had sufficiently returned, still unable to walk, he had crawled toward the Missouri River, dragging his broken, raw body more than 350 miles to Fort Brazeau where he was treated with awe and reverence. Too late for that, he thought. For he wanted nothing but to see the look of horror and shame on the faces of those two men, the looks he had earned every right to see. For they hadn't left a dying man to die. They had left a living man to starve to death.

He shifted and scanned the fort's ramparts for signs of morning life. It had been right to let the boy go. Bridger had promise. And the deep and real fear in his eyes on seeing Hugh had been enough to satisfy the scarred man. But Fitzgerald should be another matter.

One of two men who left mountain man Hugh Glass for dead, Jim Bridger, later forgiven, went on to become one of the West's most famous frontiersmen.

Courtesy Pioneer Museum of Bozeman

Hugh stretched again and ran a hand over his hairy face, rubbed his eyes deeply. He had been so sure for so long and he wasn't used to being unsure. Especially not now. This was the most galling of all moments in the ordeal. Turned away with the task only half complete—at least he had retrieved his rifle. Wagh! Too much thinking, not enough action. He hefted the beloved weapon, cradling it and staring at the fort. Fitzgerald would pay. Someday.

And with that, Hugh Glass turned back to the forest and disappeared.

The saga of Hugh Glass has been recorded in many forms including films, books, songs, stories, and poems. And it endures because his unbelievable trek is a prime example of the power of human endurance and blind will to live. That Glass's motivation was revenge speaks highly of the man, for he went on to forgive those who wronged him—though it's doubtful he ever forgot.

Young Jim Bridger, one of the forgiven, went on to establish his own great fame as a legendary mountain man, guide, explorer, hunter, and businessman. It's probable that his early dose of humility and forgiveness at the hands of the mighty Hugh Glass helped shape the respected man he became.

7

THE TOUGHEST OF MEN

In 1824, on Captain Jedediah Smith's second westward expedition, a massive, bawling grizzly bear emerged from a thicket, bypassed the entire line of men and horses, and made straight for the young leader.

It had been a long day of walking and riding, following the Cheyenne's South Fork, carefully skirting the low and painful prickly pear cactus. The small band of explorers and free trappers, led by Captain Jedediah Smith, a man known for early rising and light fare, had slipped into the reverie so familiar in life on the trail. The men trudged along, leading their horses through the low, sparse growth, their mounts slowing occasionally to sniff at something that might prove toothsome.

Daylight would leave them within a few hours. The group pushed through a thicket of scrub growth saplings on their way to the river, still a mile or more away, where they intended to camp for the night.

With no warning a massive brown streak burst from the midst of the thicket. It was a huge grizzly and the bawling roar it emitted was matched only by the snapping of its jaws. Horses jerked free and reared high, slashing the air with their hooves, neighing as if they were on fire, eyes rolling white in their frenzy to find escape.

The bruin burst upon the line of men at their middle, menacing the lot of them with its rage before bolting straight for the head of the line. It leapt at Captain Jedediah Smith, grabbed the startled young man by the head, and dragged him down. As their leader thrashed on the ground, shouting and twisting under the bawling beast, the men were immobilized for less than the time it took to draw breath again. Four of them had their long guns poised for a shot at the savage creature, but with Smith rolling about with the beast on top of him, then he on top of it, a clear shot at the rippling brown hide seemed impossible. Something had to be done.

Jim Clyman, second in command because of his age and experience, shouted, "Don't shoot the Captain!" and charged at the bawling mass of bear and man, yelling and waving his arms. By that time the bear had turned its attention to Smith's unguarded belly, where its biting jaws snapped ribs and even the steel of Smith's long knife. The other men followed Clyman and, moving closer, let fly volley after volley of lead ball until the brute succumbed to the assault, leaving a grisly mess in its wake.

Several of the men quickly reloaded their rifles, lest any more of the beasts be lurking in the surrounding undergrowth. The two youngest men were sent out after the three horses that bolted, and the rest of the men huddled about their leader sprawled on the scrubby growth of the little clearing. Smith's head was a glistening knob of blood and bone—the scalp had been peeled back as if it were the lid on a vessel. It swung from the right side of his head, attached now only by a hinge of skin and hair. His face was sagged and his left one eyebrow was torn away. His left ear dangled by the merest flap of skin. With bleeding hands Smith lightly touched his glistening scalp, his skull, the ear.

His midsection fared better, though his belly and chest were slashed and torn. His snapped ribs made breathing excruciating.

The men gathered around, staring down at him, not knowing what to do. If it were a snakebite, they would have known how to make a poultice to draw out the poison, likewise a snapped leg could be splinted. But a man freshly mauled by a grizzly—and one as fearsome as the expired brute at their feet—was a problem outside their experience. They were at a loss.

But their captain not only still breathed, he stared back up at them. It almost seemed he was about to speak. They bent closer. Smith held his head in his hands and through clenched teeth, said, "Two men, get to the river, bring water. Help me sit up now. And someone get my spare shirt to stop the blood flow."

These were men of action. Now charged with tasks, they were relieved to be useful. When they had Smith leaning upright against the nearest solid object at hand—the dead bear's broad back—Smith beckoned with a curved finger for Jim Clyman to bend closer. "Jim, I need you to take needle and thread and sew my scalp back in place. Cut the hair away so you can see what you're doing."

Clyman stood up, his mouth wide as if he were about to shout to a friend in the distance. "Captain, I'm no doctor." As if to prove it, he held up his two thick, scarred and trembling hands.

Smith moved his head slightly side to side and said, "You're the one for it, Jim."

The slim, older man swallowed, nodded once, and headed to his parfleche for scissors, needle, and thread.

"Wouldn't you like a taste of the whiskey, Captain? Might help the pain."

Jed Smith looked up at one of his crew, a well-meaning trapper named Evans, and said, "Thank you, no. You know I don't drink liquor, Eli. But you go ahead if it'll make you feel better."

The younger man nodded, feeling chastened, then his eyes widened. "Your Bible, then, Captain?"

Smith mustered a weak smile and said, "Thank you, Eli. That would be most welcome."

Clyman returned with the scissors and cut away the captain's hair as best he could, asking another man to support the scalp as he did so.

Light footsteps and snapping sounds from the direction they'd been traveling turned every head toward the thicket, rifles raised—and out emerged two men carrying canvas buckets sloshing with river water.

"Some of you men go on ahead to the river and set up camp. I'm afraid we may be there a few days yet. I suspect I'll feel poorly tomorrow." And with that, half the group broke off, rearranged gear on their horses and headed for the river. Both clusters of men were somber and quiet, for while they knew the captain was an oddly powerful presence, especially for so young a man, they knew, too, that he had taken a mighty knock.

Clyman gingerly picked bits of twig and grass from the matted scalp and glistening head and used some of the river water to wash the wound.

"Get on with it, Jim."

"Now don't rush me, Cap'n." But Jim ran the thread tight through a folded hand, smoothing the unruly, coarse fiber. "Boys," he said, "get prepared to hold him down. This is going to hurt like the devil himself was doing it."

"Can't be any worse than what has already befallen me, Jim. Now get on."

Poking the thread through the skin still attached to Smith's head proved a more difficult task than Clyman expected. He winced with each push, biting the tip of his tongue and making hissing noises.

Jed Smith sat stock still and as upright as he could, grunting now and again when Clyman pulled the thread too hard or when the needle failed to pierce the skin easily. It took the better part of an hour to reattach the captain's ragged scalp to his skull, during which time he barely moved, barely groaned.

"Captain," said Clyman, wiping his sweating brow with his forearm. "That ear's too far gone—"

"Sew it on, Jim. Do the best you can and sew it on."

Clyman nibbled his moustache and murmured, "I'll do my best." But in truth, he was correct. There was little to be gained by sewing on the mauled ear. When he was through it was not a pretty thing. He stood a few feet back from Smith and scrutinized the job.

"Thanks, Jim. Now boys, I'll need help getting on that horse. Someone walk alongside so I don't topple." The captain looked rough. His pallor had grown chalky. Sweat stippled his forehead and he was hot to the touch.

"He's getting a fever, boys," Clyman barked. "Time to move." The three men who remained, in addition to Smith and Clyman, wasted no time in hoisting the ailing man onto the horse. He groaned and looked close to fainting, but as had been the case throughout the ordeal, he uttered no curses or complaints.

In expectation of their arrival, the advance party had erected the outfit's one tent, now solely for the captain's use. When he arrived they eased him from the saddle and set him up in the tent with as much care as the rough men were capable of.

In ten days he'd healed enough, by his estimation, to continue his westward trek toward fresh trapping territory and, of greater importance to Smith, unexplored wilderness.

"Old Jed" Smith took to wearing his hair long in an attempt to conceal the welted braids of scarring that encircled his head, dipped above his left eye, and ringed his drooping and misshapen ear.

Despite a string of such close calls in his eight years of roaming the West, Captain Jedediah Smith was not the average hard-living, devil-may-care man of the mountains. He was quiet, not boastful, and preferred his Bible to liquor, tobacco, and swearing. His thirst for exploration was unquenchable and unmatched. Among many notable experiences in his short life—he died alone, overwhelmed by Comanches in 1831 at age thirty-two—he was the first white man to blaze a land route to California.

8

WHO WANTS
TO BE CHIEF?

Between 1830 and 1836, painter George Catlin visited numerous North American Indian tribes. During a visit to the Mandans, he chronicled the Okipa medicine lodge ceremony: Whoever best withstood the pain was a candidate for tribal leadership.

He recalled the popping sound the skinning knife made as it poked through the young men's pinched skin, reaming a hole for the wooden skewer. And he recalled how the young men, each in turn, fought to maintain smiles for the benefit of him, the artist, even while their eyes showed their obvious agony.

George Catlin stared at the blank canvas before him, then lowered his gaze to his field book. From his raised seat as guest of honor, he opened to the first sketches he made earlier on this, the fourth and final day of the ceremony. He was told that he and his two fur-trading companions were the first whites to ever witness the ceremonies from within the Mandan's sacred space. And what they witnessed began innocently enough.

The first day's events started with the village's young men assembling for their coming-of-age ceremony. They sprawled around the medicine man, laughing and in general good humor, even though for the next four days they would not be permitted to eat, drink, or sleep.

None of the early dances and ceremonies prepared the painter for the brutal scenes that unfolded before him on the fourth day. One by one the young warriors advanced to the center of the lodge on all fours, all the while clutching a medicine bag in their left hands. Harshly they were set upon by two men with scalping knives and sharpened splints. Great pinches of skin were pulled upward and the two-edged knives were used to ream channels through the flesh for the splint. Such wounds were inflicted at each shoulder, below the elbows, through the thighs, and below the knees.

The full operation took no longer than five minutes for each young warrior. Throughout the ordeal, the brave struggled to evince no sign of discomfort on his stoic face, taking great care to show Catlin that he was smiling, for he was aware of the strange powers of the foreign medicine man, the *Te-ho-pee-nee-wash-ee-waska-pooska*, the white medicine painter.

Cords were secured to the various splints skewering the young man's flesh. He was raised off the packed-earth floor of the sacred space by men outside, hauling on the rope ends. Attendants, their faces painted in brilliant colors, draped the skewers with the young man's own shield, bow, and quiver. As the straining youth was raised higher off the floor, heavy-horned buffalo skulls were also hung from the skewers. The youth, sufficiently weighted, was hoisted high above the crowd. Still he didn't cry out from his obvious pain.

During the proceedings, the young men each beckoned to Catlin. "See me," they seemed to say in their peculiar leer. "I am no coward. I am as manful as any in this place." And indeed, for some minutes after most were hoisted high, they were able to retain a cavalier attitude toward their searing pain.

Catlin felt tears roll down his own cheeks and he did not care who saw them. He took pains only to wipe them away lest they spatter on his sketch pad and obscure the scene he so feverishly rendered. And yet, with each passing moment the bizarre scene grew stranger, so much so that Catlin felt himself tensing, even forgetting to sketch.

He wished for the mad ritual to end but, at the same time, felt shame that he could not bear to look away. At the moment when he thought the scene would draw to a merciful close, men rushed in with poles and spun the hanging youths in slow circles. At first the braves endured the twisting and pulling at their thongs and skewers, but the older warriors with poles turned them faster and faster. Soon cries of anguish filled the domed lodge. And still they spun, their voices weakening.

Within fifteen minutes, the youths passed out from pain and exhaustion, their heads lolling loose on their necks, their tongues sagged and flopping, their tethered limbs the only things moving, although not of their own volition. They were lowered to the floor and allowed to regain consciousness. The cords attached to their shoulders were removed, but the objects on their legs were left attached.

As the youths became aware, they crawled, dragging their hideous weights, to one side of the lodge, where a medicine man with a hatchet awaited. The participants held aloft the little fingers on their left hands, praying out loud to the Great Spirit, and then each laid the digit down on a buffalo skull, wherein it was severed with a single blow. The more stout-hearted youths offered the pointing finger of the same hand. No soothing medicines were offered, nor were attempts made to bandage the stumps.

Catlin had swallowed hard and, as queasy as he felt, he continued sketching, hoping to capture some little sliver of the horror and revulsion he felt, but also something of the obvious importance of the proceedings to the Mandan.

There seemed a lull and the artist, breathing a sigh of relief, looked at his white companions, but they shook their heads and nodded toward the lodge's one door. The agonized youths were dragging themselves and their weights outside to the village center. Catlin noted the puckered, bloody flesh of the young men as they made slow progress toward daylight.

The youths dragged their freakish prizes before a cheering crowd of hundreds. Once outside, they were hauled to their feet and their wrists were strapped in leather. They were forced to run around the perimeter of the crowd until the weights tore from the flesh, at which time they were allowed to stagger home to their own lodges to be nursed by their families.

Several youths were unfortunate enough to still be plagued by dragging skulls and other objects. Even after several turns around the village, they had to continue circling, dragged by assistants. And when, as was the case with one last unfortunate, the splints did not tear from the flesh, he was forced to crawl through the crowd and out onto the prairie. He would have to wait for three days with no assistance, fasting further and praying until the flesh on his wounds rotted enough that the splints separated of their own accord. The youth, for the sake of his honor, would not slide the splints from his wounds.

All that Catlin learned in the preceding days threatened to overwhelm him, and yet he knew that if he did not quickly capture the vivid scenes played out before him, he would lose the essence of them forever. And the heart of the artist beating deep within him would not let that happen.

George Catlin inhaled deeply, glanced up toward the smoke hole in the roof of his guest lodge, noting the perfect, early-day light shafting down and illumining the chamber. He looked down at his palette, relaxed his grip on the brush, and began to paint.

Setting out in 1830 with the intention of painting every native tribe in North America, George Catlin ultimately managed to visit and document an impressive forty-eight tribes before many of them disappeared through disease and warfare. His traveling Indian Gallery, comprised of six hundred paintings and thousands of artifacts, toured the eastern United States and Europe for years before Catlin accrued too much debt to continue. His attempts to interest Congress in buying the collection failed—the members disliked his public opposition to their Indian policies. A creditor assumed the collection and it sat in a warehouse for twenty-seven years before his heirs gifted it to the Smithsonian Institution in 1879. Catlin died seven years before, certain that this dream would never come to fruition.

RABID AT THE RENDEZVOUS

At the mountain man rendezvous of 1833, near what is now Pinedale, Wyoming, a rabid wolf rampaged through the encampment, biting horses, cattle, and men. Within weeks, those bitten began showing telltale signs of hydrophobia.

His head throbbed with the baying of a thousand hellhounds circling in his skull and kicking up cinders. Before he opened his eyes, Rafe knew two things: He shouldn't have had so much Who-Hit-John, and it truly couldn't be morning yet. He opened his right eye. Nope, still dark. Then what was all that damnable noise? Something poked him in the ribs. Gustin, his trapping partner.

"Hey, Rafe, you awake?"

"Yep, what's the commotion?"

Before Gustin could answer, a man's scream sounded from across the field. Growling and barking rose up at the same time, then sounded as if it were moving away, leaving behind the eerie notes of a moaning man. Rafe sat up. He heard Gustin cocking his rifle.

"No shooting in camp."

"I don't care. I ain't gettin' no hydrophoby."

"Good Lord, is that what that was?" Rafe reached for his pistol and kept one hand on Sweet Belle, his rifle. All around them men were running in the grass, shouting, lighting brands. It was still hours before daybreak.

He heard Gustin grunt, then say, "Afore you woke up, there was commotion amongst the horses. I figure some got bit."

"From the sound of it, a man got bit, too."

"Wonder who?"

"Dunno, but the last thing I want to do is wander around out there, still half drunk, and get bit by a crazed dog or wolf or whatever that thing is."

They said nothing for a few moments, and just sat listening to the commotion. Finally Gustin said, "I can't stand it. Ain't nobody out there any drunker'n you or me." He stood up, shrugging out of his blankets. Rafe did the same. Truth be told, he didn't feel that drunk any more. The thought of hydrophoby laying him low seemed to pull him to his senses.

As they walked toward the commotion, their weapons held at the ready, Rafe said, "I've seen what it does to a man. Fella on a riverboat clawin' at his own face, barkin' like a mad dog, and chasin' people. Even bit himself on the arm. A few of us tried to corner him and he just pitched himself overboard, drowned eventually, still slappin' at the water and snarling."

Gustin shook his head. "I don't aim to go out like that."

They walked to the edge of the gathered crowd, peered over shoulders. Rafe spoke to a small Frenchman he knew by the name of LaBoeuf. "Bit? Who is he?"

"Ah, Rafe, yes, he is a young man, first timer here, George Holmes. A good boy." He shook his head and turned away. "So sad."

Gustin and Rafe pushed in closer. In the flickering glow of torches, they saw the young man half sitting, the side of his head and face a mess of blood and hair. His eye seemed unharmed but the ear was mangled, and the cheek and lips were torn and laid open. A disheveled man who Rafe knew as Larpenteur, one of Fontanelle's men, leaned close, dipping a cloth in a tin of water and swabbing the young man's head. "Someone bring whiskey. He'll need it." A corked bottle was offered and the man splashed the rag, then handed the bottle to the trembling young victim.

The group of men was surprisingly quiet, though some of them were splitting off as more torches and lanterns arrived. Shouts of anger could soon be heard in various directions. Savaged horses and cattle had been discovered and more men from other campsites were trailing over. Word had spread. Soon the entire rendezvous would know of the threat of the dreaded, madness-making disease.

Three days later the rendezvous was a more somber affair than Gustin had ever seen. "It's over, Rafe."

"What is?" said his partner, clamping the lid on his stew and squinting through the fire's smoke.

"We got the wolf. One with the hydrophoby. Only right since Fontanelle's our new employer and his party's the one that got the most damage."

"Hardly over, Gustin."

"What do you mean? We got 'im."

"Twelve men bit, and I don't know how many cattle and horses. I've heard tell a bit man can be fine for a year or more, then of a sudden take a fit."

Gustin grunted, said nothing.

"Guess we'll know tonight."

"Yep."

On their third day out following the annual gathering, Rafe thought that this had been the strangest rendezvous he'd been to in some time, maybe ever, and not one that he'd care to repeat. At least not until next year. He swore he was still foggy headed from the last night's celebration, which had been marred by the disappearance of the second of the bitten men.

The first had raged and screamed and ventured off on his own in the night. He was not found the next day. And the second did the same, though he'd been much quieter about it. Rafe didn't think they found him, either. Figured the poor man wanted it that way. And now George Holmes was holding them up, acting strange, not wanting to cross any streams let alone rivers. He had to be calmed down. Tossing a blanket over his head hadn't worked since the first day.

During the rendezvous, he and Gustin had joined up with Fontanelle and the American Fur Company. So far they seemed a solid band of men. Fontanelle himself was a decent sort. As Rafe thought this, he caught Gustin's eye, and looked over his shoulder.

Speak of the devil, thought Rafe. Up rode the boss man himself. Rafe sat up straight, looking beyond Fontanelle. There were the two men who'd been charged with keeping watch on Holmes at the last stream, a mile or so back, until Holmes's fit had passed.

"What is this?" said Fontanelle, incensed, looking at the two men.

"He went crazy on us, Mr. Fontanelle. We couldn't stop him. He was foaming at the mouth and coming at us. We didn't want to shoot him. Finally he commenced to ripping off his clothes, then he just run off over yonder. Screaming and barking like he was a dog or something. I don't want no hydrophoby, no sir." The bearded man shook his head, the long feather in his hat band wagging.

Fontanelle sighed and said loudly to the group of men, "We'll stop here. I need two men to help us with young Holmes. They tell me he has refused to move any further. If we can get him to the fort, we'll arrange to have him sent back east to his family."

Gustin wheeled his horse around and Rafe followed suit. Be good to show a willingness to help, being the newest members of the party. He knew that's what Gustin was thinking, too.

When they arrived back at the stream, the young man could not be found. But there was a trail of clothing that left off, in the distance, with a ragged shirt swaying from a low branch. Fontanelle looked at the two men who had let Holmes escape, and shook his head. Rafe saw the boss man's jaw muscles working, then Fontanelle nudged the horse into a run. The four men followed.

"Spread out!" shouted Fontanelle.

Though they spent hours looking, they never found George Holmes. But for the rest of their days, they all knew that the poor young man had died in the wilderness, crazed and alone.

While it is easy to forget that Louis Pasteur's 1885 vaccine removed the threat of rabies (or "hydrophoby," as it was more commonly called on the frontier), the disease was a source of constant anxiety should one be bitten by any animal acting out of the ordinary. Mountain men were especially susceptible, dealing as intimately as they did with all manner of wild creatures on a daily basis. Cases of rabid animals running rampant throughout camps and settlements, biting people and other animals seemingly at random, abound in the pages of history. Even today there are flare-ups of the disease in pockets throughout North America.

10

ENORMOUS JAWS

In his famous journals, trapper Osborne Russell tells of wounding a grizzly while working in the Northern Rockies. As he and his friend circled a copse, a bear stood full height and roared at Russell, its mouth wide and its teeth grinding. "His enormous jaws extended and his eyes flashing fire. Oh Heavens! Was ever anything so hideous?"

There," whispered the Mullattoe, trusted friend and fellow mountain man of Osborne Russell. The burly man pointed at a copse of willows 150 yards ahead. Since leaving the fort and the river, Russell had been watching the purple of the ridges ahead as they tapered up into layers of white cloud. As he swung his gaze around, he chided himself for not paying attention. But the Mullattoe, it seemed, was always on the alert. Sure enough, dead ahead was a large, humped form, pawing and snuffling at the moist roots of some boggy plant. The men turned their horses quickly lest they catch sight or scent of the bear—horses were not fond of such beasts.

The grizzly didn't see the two men as they dismounted and approached, crouching low. Russell knew what his friend had in mind and gritted his teeth as they stepped cautiously toward the oblivious, digging beast.

Now within one hundred yards, the Mullattoe knelt, aimed his rifle, and touched off a shot that caught the brute in the left shoulder. The bear rose and spun in the air, gnashing its teeth and whipping its head side to side. It dove for the nearest cover, the willow thicket just behind.

"Let him go, let him go! He's a dangerous varmint," said the shooter, already reloading his rifle. But Russell knew they had dealt the beast a life-threatening blow, and it would surely meet a hard end if they didn't finish the gruesome task. Russell was also fairly new to encounters with the great, brawling beasts about whom he had heard so much.

Together the two men walked the outer edges of the willow copse, rifles cocked and at the ready. With each step they heard a heavy snuffling rising in intensity, as if the breather had run a great distance. Then the noise stopped. The men traded glances quickly. The Mullattoe nodded, and Russell poked his rifle barrel into the willows, rapping it lightly against a stout shoot.

A low, rumbling growl rose just in front of them, less than a man's-length into the shadowed thicket. They had taken barely a step backward when a massive, earth-colored blur exploded from the trees and launched at them. The bear's flashing jaws were wide and set for grappling, and its large eyes seemed to glow from within.

The men were overwhelmed and ran as fast as their moccasin-shod feet would carry them, each in opposite directions and each secretly hoping the bear would choose the other to follow. Russell chanced a quick glance over his shoulder and saw the bear break off its pursuit of him and instead turn back after his friend.

The Mullattoe heard the brush crashing behind him. Stopping, he spun where he stood, steadied himself, and released another shot. But he was hurried and the ball whistled too high. The bawling beast, startled by the sound, and still showing no sign of injury from the shot it took in the shoulder earlier, spun back around and resumed its attack on Russell. The lean young mountain man, who still hadn't fired a shot at the beast, found himself hemmed in on all sides, trees on three and a kill-crazy bear on the last. He stood, petrified, facing the rampaging beast.

Beyond the bear, Russell glimpsed his friend frantically reloading his long gun. Hurry your task, man! Was all Russell could think. He raised his rifle, more out of reflex than intention.

The bear, within ten paces of Russell, rose on its hind legs, taller than a man, and pawed the air, its mouth thrown wide as it bellowed loud and raw oaths. From that short distance Russell could smell the beast's foul breath as it roared out its hate. And just before it once again dropped to all fours and charged at the man, Russell pulled the trigger. His rifle barked flame. Out of pure accident the ball found its true mark, coring the grizzly's heart where it stood.

But still the bear surged forward, howling its pain and rage and confusion, covering half the distance between it and Russell before it dropped to the ground as if sledged, but a few paces from the shaking trapper.

The Mullattoe ran up beside the bear, rifle aimed at its chest, his own lungs working like a bellows. Rising smoke and the smell of burnt hair from the close-fired shot filled the little clearing.

"You alright?"

Russell said nothing. Just stared at the dead brute at his feet. His head, arms, and legs all shook as if he were in the grip of a deep fit. The Mullattoe tugged on the younger man's sleeve. Russell shook his head and looked at his bearded friend, blinked hard, and nodded.

The Mullattoe patted his shoulder. "Let's get this thing butchered before it decides to come at us again." He knelt by the bear, slipped out his skinning knife, and set to work.

An hour later, the bear skinned, the fat and meat bundled on their horses, they headed back to the fort. The Mullattoe's spirits were high as they rode, the tall golden grass rustling with their horse's steps. Russell kept a smile, lest his friend think he was less of a man than he ought to be, but inside he decided that he would never again molest another wounded grizzly bear.

Just because they were mountain men doesn't mean they weren't deathly afraid of grizzlies and other denizens of the dense woods and open plains. Perhaps that's why Osborne Russell outlived so many of his contemporaries. He spent nine years traveling the Rockies and the Missouri River as an employee of the fur trade. In 1843 he left it behind and headed to Oregon where he played an important role in establishing the Oregon Territory's first form of government. While there he studied law and later was appointed as a civil judge.

But we would know none of this if Russell hadn't also been one of the few of many men of the mountains to also have a penchant for recording his deeds. His plain-spoken humility and genuine wonder at the natural world around him make his Journal of a Trapper *still highly readable.*

11

CARGO OF DEATH

In 1837, at Fort Clark, Dakota Territory, on the Missouri River, a Mandan chief stole an old blanket from a crewman aboard the riverboat St. Peters. *His camp had 1,700 members, but within weeks only thirty of them were left alive.*

What the hell's the matter with that one?" the captain gestured with his chin at the Negro deckhand who had been in the same spot for days, on the deck with his back snugged up to the cabin.

"He's got the ague. Happens to someone every trip upriver." The first mate stared at the slender shivering man and wondered where his filthy wool blanket had got to. The poor fool had been wrapped in it, moaning, earlier in the day.

"If he doesn't snap around by the time we're ready to cast off for Fort Union, leave him here."

"But sir, he's—"

The captain looked at his first mate. "I don't care what he is or isn't. You heard me. Make it so."

"Yes sir." As soon as the captain turned back to the wheelhouse, the first mate walked over to the huddled form on the deck and nudged him with the toe of his boot. The man was, if anything, more active than he had been earlier. His arms and neck were covered with some type of rash and his long, thin fingers raked at the raw lesions.

"Hey, deckhand. Time to get up."

The face that turned to stare up at him was hardly the same one he had seen hours before. That one had still been recognizable as the deckhand's. This was gray as cigar ash and dark as shadow in the valleys—the sunken eyes, the concave cheeks, the puckered mouth. The man's eyes were shot through with blood veining away from milky centers.

It took the first mate a few seconds to overcome his surprise. "Where's your blanket?"

The man's mouth worked like a slow fish, then he said something. The first mate bent low. "What?"

"Mandan took it . . . from me." His head dropped back to the deck and he closed his eyes. His chest worked harder than ever, though still he dug with surprising vigor at the rashes that covered his arms.

The first mate straightened and looked toward shore, where the Mandans were milling about the dock, yammering and showing each other their cheap manufactured goods they'd traded for, knives that wouldn't last a month of use, hatchets that would chip. Still, they seemed satisfied. Didn't see any old dirty wool blankets, though. Indians, he thought. If it wasn't nailed down, you could be sure it'd be gone.

Alexander Culbertson, bourgeois of Fort McKenzie on the Marias River, had tried to reason with them, but the Blackfoot chiefs would not budge. "I tell you, Harvey's keelboat cannot come upriver just now because it is carrying a deadly disease. Two men have already died on that boat."

The interpreter, a gimpy old voyageur turned squaw man, rambled on, while Culbertson watched the stone faces of the Blackfoot chiefs. Nothing about their perpetual scowls changed to let him know they understood. Maybe the mouths grew a little tighter, the eyes a little harder. He knew they didn't want to leave—they needed the manufactured goods Harvey's keelboat carried. But he also knew they could not wait for a week, let alone a month. The buffalo hunt was almost upon them and they needed the meat and robes for the long winter ahead.

One chief spoke in that halting, clacking way they had, never once taking his eyes from the bourgeois. Then the interpreter told Culbertson that if he did not wish to see Fort McKenzie burned to the ground he would get the keelboat there right away.

Culbertson sighed. "Look, I know it's time for your big buffalo hunt. If you don't get to it, it'll be a long winter. For all of us. But if I let that boat up here and it's carrying the pox. Well," he raised his hands and let them drop to his sides. "I can't be held responsible for the deaths it will cause. And it will." He shifted his gaze from the chief to the interpreter. "You tell him that."

The old trapper said, "She really carryin' the pox?"

"No way of knowing. But why should we risk it just so he and his tribe can have new knives and beads and tobacco? Now tell him. And tell him I don't like to be threatened when I'm trying to do right by everybody." The bourgeois folded his arms across his chest in a final show of defiance.

The chiefs just stared at him as the interpreter chose his words, if the merchant could guess, with more care than before. He was in the middle of this, after all. There was a long pause while the talking chief and the head of Fort McKenzie stared at each other, then the chief said something to the interpreter and walked away. Culbertson watched him go, then said to his interpreter, "That man's not happy."

"Nope."

"But at least he's alive."

"For now."

"What do you mean by that? I stopped the keelboat from Fort Union, didn't I?"

"Mr. Culbertson, the pox don't just travel by boat. I know a number of folks who lived through it fifty years back. It came on fast, laid many a Mandan and Assiniboine low. And with nary a boat in sight."

For the first time in a long time, Culbertson wasn't quite sure what to do.

"Besides," said the interpreter. "Last thing he said was that if you didn't get that keelboat up here lickety-split, they're going to burn the fort."

Any thoughts the merchant had of not bringing the pox upriver disappeared like smoke in a windstorm.

It must be a punishment. But for what? Mandan Chief Four Bears, *Mah-to-toh-pa*, did not want to believe what others of his tribe said, that the disease had come from the whites. Why would the whites do such a thing when he, Four Bears himself, had always welcomed the whites and dealt with them as he had all friends? He sat on the dirt floor of his lodge and touched his face. The oozing boils were there. And he knew that he now looked like his wives and children had before they blackened and died.

He had not even had the strength to wrap his own family in buffalo robes.

He had failed in his duties to them as father and husband. And he had failed in his duties to his people as chief of the Mandan.

And because he had witnessed the drawn-out agonies of his family's final moments, he knew what would soon befall him. While it did not frighten him, his rage consumed him—it was the most complete anger he had felt in all his days.

He would fast and die with honor. All about him his people were doing the same. He was told of a stricken woman who smothered her children and then hung herself. Her warrior husband had already turned black and died of the disease. Others of his people hurled themselves off cliffs, drowned themselves in the river, and shot themselves and their families. Anything to escape the unstoppable foe that rotted and blackened their skin. Now he understood what drove them to do such things. It was not weakness, it was pride.

And so shall I face the Great Spirit, he thought. And with great slowness and pain, Four Bears donned his finest war regalia, necklaces of bear claws, a headdress for only the most sacred occasions, his weapons, the war bow and lance, and presented himself before his people for the last time. And at last he, the Mandan's greatest defender of the whites, agreed with his people. He spoke to them of this, of the anger he now felt for the whites. "Black hearted dogs, they have deceived me, them that I always considered as brothers have turned out to be my worst enemies."

Speaking was painful for him. He trembled and his breath came in rapid gasps, but he continued. "I do not fear death, my friends. You know it. But to die with my face rotten so that even the wolves would shrink with horror at seeing me, and say to themselves, that is Four Bears, the friend of the whites, that I cannot abide."

His people stood before him, sad and beaten, but as he struggled to grasp the ragged edge of life that was left to him, he continued with his message. "Listen well what I have to say, as it will be the last time you will hear me. Think of your wives, children, brothers, sisters, friends, all who are dead or dying with the sickness caused by those dogs the whites, think of all that my friends, and rise together and not leave one of them alive. The Four Bears will act his part."

And later that day, July 30, 1837, having tried to incite his people to make war with the whites, Mandan Chief Four Bears, *Mah-to-toh-pa*, died of smallpox.

The St. Peters' trip from St. Louis to Fort Union touched off an epidemic of smallpox that affected nearly every Indian tribe from the Platte to the Rockies. The plague traveled overland to the Arikaras, Pawnees, and Minnatarees, while the St. Peters itself carried the smallpox upriver to the Assiniboine, the Crow, and the Blackfeet. Within a year the disease had killed at least fifteen thousand Northern Plains Indians—more than the Army would kill in combat in the next turbulent sixty years.

12

WAGON TRAIN WOES

In the summer of 1844, while traveling west on the Oregon Trail, the Sager family endured a seemingly endless string of unfortunate events.

The real trouble began when nine-year-old Catherine leapt from the wagon onto the wagon tongue, intending to jump free of the moving vehicle. It was a maneuver the children had performed for weeks as the family rolled along with the rest of the wagons on the Oregon Trail. Henry and Naomi Sager and their seven children had joined the train in April, 1844, heading for Oregon and leaving their Missouri homestead far behind. But on this June day, the eldest of the five Sager girls caught her dress on the handle of an ax and slipped.

Given that the oxen were such slow, methodical creatures, it amazed her that it all seemed to happen so quickly. She heard her own screams, heard her father's shouts, and felt the wide iron rim of the wagon wheel roll over her left leg. The bones snapped and her body flooded with hot pain. Her right leg barely escaped the same treatment, being canted at an angle from the fall. Several of the other children saw it and began to cry.

"Get back, the lot of you!" Henry shouted at them as he dragged his screaming daughter out from under the wagon. Another few seconds and the rear wheel would have rolled over her torso, almost surely killing her. His hands trembled as he picked at the flowered fabric of her dress, now matted into her wounds. He bellowed to his wife, knowing she would be of no use, weak as she was in the wagon, cradling the baby Rosanna, barely two months old. A wagon rollover the month before had knocked his wife unconscious and nearly killed her.

Henry Sager, not known for his ambition and focus in life, now seemed to come into his own, as he had in previous crises along the trail. He turned to his second oldest, Francis. "Help your mother. We need a fire and bandages. And stop them others from cryin'. They're upsetting Catherine." At the sound of her name, the injured girl focused on her father's face. "Papa, oh Papa. . . ." Then she lost consciousness.

He was relieved, for he had seen the full extent of the heavy wheel's damage: The skin of her thigh had been mashed and split as if it were a piece of overripe fruit. He saw the wet gleam of bone poking through skin in at least two spots. Lest she wake beforehand, he worked to realign as best he could the unnatural angles of the ragged and mangled leg.

By this time other members of the train had gathered and offered help. He dared not look up. Already he knew some of them thought him a fool for all the accidents that had plagued his family. In addition to the wagon rollover in which they had all ended up scraped, bruised, and battered, the girls were shot at by a sentry one night, then twice they had troubles with children catching fire. Even as he tended his daughter he prayed silently that Catherine's accident was the last of their misfortunes.

"She don't need a doctor. I can make it right." Henry Sager stared up at the faces surrounding him, his traveling companions, neighbors on the trail these past months. Now that they were almost to Fort Laramie he felt he knew them as well as he ever knew anyone, except perhaps his Naomi. But right now he didn't seem to recognize them. They all stared at him as if accusing, as if he had caused this to happen to poor Catherine, his eldest girl. She whimpered.

"She's coming around, Henry. She needs a doctor!" This time the man who said it grabbed the eldest Sager boy. "John, run back down the line and yell for the doctor. There's one traveling somewhere in the train back behind us. German, I think. Hurry!"

Henry finished tending the girl, shoving away the helping hands of the women. When the doctor arrived he inspected Sager's work and said he could do no better. All that fuss, thought Henry. Told them she didn't need a doctor.

The following weeks and months were a series of agonizing days for Catherine Sager as she endured the jolting, jarring journey in the wagon with her weakened mother and crying baby sister. Then on August 28, less than a month after Catherine's accident, Henry succumbed to the camp fever, typhoid, that had been creeping up on him for weeks since his frantic participation in a buffalo hunt.

They buried him by the banks of the Green River and moved on. A year later the family was informed that his grave had been violated, his body disinterred by Shoshone hoping to scare up valuables. His scattered bones bore evidence of having been feasted upon by coyotes.

Not to be outdone by her husband, within a month after his death, Naomi Sager was also laid low by typhoid . . . and scarlet fever. She spent her last days flopping about in the unforgiving wagon, too ill to rise. On September 11, with her pulse nearly undetectable, she fluttered her eyes wide open and said, "Oh Henry, if only you knew how we have suffered!" Then she too died. She was buried beside the trail and the train moved on.

Fellow travelers, Mr. and Mrs. William Shaw, had promised the Sagers that they would make sure the children were placed in the care of the well-known Whitman Mission in Waiilatpu (now Walla Walla, Washington). Until the train drew close enough to the mission, the Shaws cared for the seven newly orphaned youngsters as if they were their own offspring, sharing their dwindling rations in a stretch of barren, forbidding landscape between Salmon Falls and the Snake River.

The tough terrain was matched only by frigid nighttime temperatures, so cold that one of the distraught orphans, little Hannah Louise, wandered alone from the train one night and was found nearly dead of hypothermia. In time she recovered, only to be captured by the Indians three years later and succumb to measles.

Had the Shaws known what horrors awaited the Sager orphans at the Whitman Mission, they surely would have figured out a way to keep the children with them. In 1847, barely three years after they were left in the care of the Whitmans, the seven Sager orphans became unintentional participants in the Whitman Massacre. The orphans watched as their adoptive parents were shot and hacked to death. The two Sager boys, John and Francis, were among the dozen whites killed by angry members of the Cayuse tribe. Hannah Sager, then six, was taken captive and died from lack of medical attention due to the effects of measles.

Catherine, Elizabeth, Matilda, and little Roseanna (renamed Henrietta Naomi in her parents' honor) all survived, though they were taken captive

Like the one pictured here, most families traveling west in a wagon made the journey with few mishaps. The Sager family's Oregon Trail trek in the summer of 1844 was filled with unusual misfortune and woe. *Courtesy National Archives*

and became victims of malnourishment and sexual abuse. Their freedom was secured a short time later through a trade for hard goods, including blankets, clothing, guns, and tobacco. The surviving sisters went on to marry and raise families, and each wrote about her experiences along the Oregon Trail.

For every tale of a wagon train disaster, there are hundreds more that tell of families who enjoyed their treks to new lives on the frontier. Scores of journals kept while on the trail provide valuable and unique insights into the lives of these emigrants.

13

CANNIBALISM IN THE MOUNTAINS

In May of 1846, eighty-seven men, women, and children set out across the Plains on a new, unproven route for California. They struggled across the desert and, in October, climbed into the High Sierra in the teeth of sudden, savage snowstorms. Trapped in impenetrable passes, many members of the Donner Party perished that winter. Others survived by any means necessary.

In his feverish slumber, the starving man, William Eddy, was visited by nightmares. He had known they couldn't stay in their miserable camp any longer, had known that someone had to leave. He'd always been a man of action, God curse him for it. That's why they had risked their lives and those of their children and made the trip across the Plains in the first place. Now he realized that fate had played them hard. Still, no matter the end, there could be no other way. Not when they'd had nothing to eat for weeks but a sticky, sopping mess made by boiling down the animal hides they'd used as roofing.

When his small group departed the camp at Truckee Lake, he knew that the people they left behind were doomed. There could be no way any of them would survive the winter by staying there. He nevertheless prayed to God with every painful, faltering step that his beloved wife and children would live until he could return. If luck existed, then they surely deserved their dose of it. He joined a group that numbered seventeen in all—ten men, five women, and two boys. They set out to cross Truckee Pass and make it down the western slopes of the Sierras for help. And they had made it down. But after that, the torturous trek was little more than a wash of pain and snow and freezing cold temperatures.

And when he awakened in what seemed a bed in a cabin, he knew he was surely dead. Then a second, terrible thought struck him. If he had died, which parts of him had been eaten? Surely they began with the legs. Despite his atrophied state, they were the thickest part of him.

"Are you better?"

The words did not make sense. He tried to speak, opened his eyes at the same time, and saw a young woman's face staring down at him. She looked worried.

"What?" he finally managed to say.

"How do you . . . feel?"

"Where am I?" He tried to rise, suddenly remembering where he was, who he was, and what had brought him to this place. "Where are the others? They lived?"

She pressed him back down flat and said, "You're in the Sacramento valley, in a settlement, safe and sound now. You made it over the mountains, though from the state of you I don't see how. The others were brought back earlier today. You were too weak, otherwise I would have told you."

"Are they . . . ?"

"Yes, they are alive."

"How . . . many?"

"Five women and a man. Foster, I believe is his name."

He made to rise again. "I should see them."

"You can't leave. You're not in any fit state to walk. Your feet were in terrible shape when you staggered in here."

"But they found them?"

"Yes, yes, I told you. . . ." Then her voice grew quiet, but he heard her. "They followed your bloody footprints back to them."

They were to be the rescue party for all those starving people back at Truckee, back at Alder Creek. His wife, Eleanor, his babies. All the others. Were they still alive? How could they be, boiling hunks of old hides for food? How long before . . . No, it wouldn't come to that. Not for them. Not for Eleanor or his children.

Then he slept again. And dreamed of the people who had left Truckee Lake with them a month before. They had made it to the top of the pass only to get lost in the snow. The damnable snow. Storm after storm, never ending. Ten of them died. Stanton had been the first. Too weak to go on. And then it was Christmas Eve, and two more had died, Uncle Billy Graves had begged them to eat his body, told his two daughters who were on the expedition to eat him, that it was their only hope of survival. The words had stung them all like slaps to the face. It was unthinkable. But it was the truth.

Christmas Day dawned bright, cold, and snowing. And they lost Pat Dolan then. It was another day before they could partake of his gift to them. All but Eddy and the two Indian guides. They couldn't do it. Not yet. Then Lem Murphy and Jay Fosdick. They were eaten. That's when Foster had gone off the beam, suggested to him they eat one of the women. Then he threatened to kill the two Indians, but Eddy warned them and they left. Didn't matter, though, because they found them near death and frozen, and Foster shot them. Then they all ate them, too.

Slashing and peeling back the clothes had been the hardest part, because then it was still human. That and making that first slice, knowing it was the leg or arm or back of a man you'd talked with and worked with and walked beside for all those months on the damnable trail. How do you go on after that? But you do, God help you, you do go on. And in his dream the faces rose up from the snow, hauling with them their flayed, skinned torsos, the half-eaten limbs stripped to the white bone. And the eyes snapped open and, though no words came from the mouths, his ears rang with their voices and his head filled with sounds that he knew would never stop.

The woman huddled close by the tiny guttering flames of the damp-wood fire, staring through sunken eyes at the gaunt, lifeless husk that had been her neighbor and friend. Her face was a drawn thing of frostbitten skin stretched drumlike over bone. She swallowed once and closed her eyes. None of the others of this group, camped beneath the snows at Alder Creek, held out hope for help from the seventeen who had left before Christmas. Since their departure from this hell camp weeks before, the numbers in the camp had dwindled with each passing day.

Those with constitutions already weakened by exposure to frigid temperatures and malnutrition were the first to go. Mostly men, it seemed. Funny that they'd turn out to be so weak after all. And since they had run out of hooves to boil and furs to cook, and the last family dog had been devoured weeks back, there was nothing for it but to start in on the dead.

She liked to think of herself as practical, and this situation was no exception. There was meat on legs, on arms, that came away in strips, peeled off

On the Way to the Summit (the Donner Party), by William Gilbert Gaul. Despite repeated attempts in the winter of 1846–1847 to cross the High Sierra, savage snowstorms stymied the Donner Party. *Collection of the Oakland Museum of California, Kahn Collection*

the bone as if it were a poultry carcass. She tried to convince herself that this was no different than dressing out game, a deer perhaps. She did her best to make sure the children didn't see what she was doing, hiding her grisly task behind the drifted berm where the bodies of the dead had been laid out. She draped a grimy remnant of tattered sacking over the face of the man whose thigh she was slicing into. It would not do to have him stare her down at this task. Despite the cloth, she looked repeatedly at the motionless head, the body rocking with each dig and slice of the knife.

She didn't hear her daughter come upon her. "Oh mama."

The tired disappointment in the child's voice was something she could not stand. She paused, her hand still on the big handled knife, and said, "Get back inside, damn you. Get in now or so help me. . . ."

Her voice was thin as the dinging of a far-off brass bell on this clear, cold morning. She tried to keep it steady but it shook and cracked. Soon she heard the child turn and the snow squeaked on the path under her rag-wrapped feet. The mother wiped at her nose with the back of a grimy coat cuff and set to work with renewed vigor on the upper thigh, peeling away strips and laying them neatly on a cloth at her side.

She would see the children through this. Where there is life there is hope, however hopeless the situation might seem. And though she had no way of knowing if they would survive, she trusted that God would see them right. He had to. Or she would go crazy, like her neighbors at Alder Creek.

It is doubtful that most people, in a similar situation, would act any differently than did those of the Donner Party. But that does not make the tragic tale any easier to swallow. On October 31, 1846, after two unsuccessful attempts to summit Truckee Pass, the Donner Party, by now a dragging mass of exhausted, starving people, reduced through attrition from eighty-seven to eighty-one (forty-one of them children), decided to stay put for the winter. They split into two camps, one along Truckee Lake, the other six miles back at Alder Creek. The doomed groups hastily lashed together lean-tos, tepees, and all manner of crude shelters in an effort to beat the snows.

It was mid-April of 1847 before the last of four bands of rescuers from settlements on the western slopes of the Sierras was able to reach the ill-fated pioneers in the Truckee Lake encampment. Of the eighty-one souls who hunkered down beneath Truckee Pass the previous autumn, forty-seven survived. The last to be rescued was a well-educated German named Lewis Keseberg. When his rescuers turned up, they found him preparing his next meal—the liver, brains, and lungs of a young boy.

14.

MISSIONARY MASSACRE

Within a few short weeks in the fall of 1847, more than half of the 350 members of the Cayuse tribe of Wallah Wallah (Oregon region) died of the white-man's measles. On November 29, 1847, angry survivors blamed missionaries Marcus and Narcissa Whitman for bringing this disease to them.

Marcus Whitman spun around in his chair by the fire. "Narcissa, what was that? Is someone here?"

His wife stared at him. She couldn't remember ever seeing him look so poorly. It's no small wonder, she thought. With the measles running rampant through the mission and even more so the Cayuse tribe at the mission grounds. "Yes, it's Tiloukaikt. He and Tomahas would like to see you. Oh, why can't they just leave you be for the afternoon, at least. You just returned from there."

Marcus pushed heavily up out of the chair. "He is the chief, Narcissa. And he lost a third child himself to this dread disease just this morning." He stood, his back to the fireplace, and rubbed his large calloused hands roughly over his face. But the others in the room, his wife and the children, adopted orphans all, already knew this. Narcissa saw that the strain on her husband would soon be too much for him to bear. He was a strong man, but the lack of sleep and constant care he lavished on the Cayuse were taking a mighty toll on him.

They had traveled the entire length of the Oregon Trail in 1836, eleven years earlier, to set up a mission. Indeed, she had been one of the first two women to cross the Rocky Mountains. And though the intervening years brought with them various hardships—taking in scores of weary travelers and adopting many children orphaned along the wagon train trails—this latest challenge, the measles epidemic, was the test of tests.

"Rest, Marcus. I'll tell them to come back later."

Whitman, despite his fatigue, shook his head. "These people need more than we can give, but at least we can offer solace, Narcissa."

Then they heard raised voices in the outer room. Marcus looked at the alarmed faces around him and smiled weakly. "They are just upset. All will be well." He crossed to the door and pulled his wool coat tighter about him, his King James Bible clutched in one hand. It was a brisk day, as expected in this territory in late autumn. "Narcissa, bolt this behind me. I won't be long."

As he unlatched the door a groping brown arm forced through the crack, feeling for anything it might grip. It was Tiloukaikt. Whitman could now see his face, the face of an angry, grieving father. The face of a man who could not understand why whites rarely died of the disease but the Indians seemed to have no immunity at all to it.

Whitman forced the man back into the outer room. There before him stood Tomahas, tribesman of the chief. Whitman firmly closed the door behind himself, and saw MaryAnn Bridger, one of his adopted flock and the half-breed daughter of Jim Bridger, pressed in fright to the far wall near the stove. He smiled and nodded to assure her that all would be well. He maintained his smile as the two Cayuse men approached him.

Never had they seemed so stirred up, so bold as to stand within inches of him. He could smell wood smoke and sweat rolling in waves from the chief, the man in whose home he had been mere hours before. Now, in the chief's eyes burned a hard anger. For the flicker of a moment no one spoke. So penetrating was the Indian's stare that Marcus felt the lifelong underpinnings of his faith sway beneath him.

Then it was gone and it was again as if his old friend Tiloukaikt had come to him with his woes, the worst a man can endure, and he knew once more he was the helper, the confessor, the healer to these savage people that he set out to be all those years ago. He sat down at the table and gestured for the two men to do likewise, though only the chief sat. Tomahas paced the floor. Marcus faced Tiloukaikt, hoping to coax him from his agitated state. He rested his work-worn hand on the closed Bible. Perhaps passages of scripture would help assuage the man's grief. As he reached to open the Good Book, from behind him the scream of a young woman split the very air of the room. And then sudden agony, quick as a rifle shot, wracked his body.

Tomahas had angled around behind Whitman while Tiloukaikt engaged the doctor in conversation at the table. What good was talk now that three of his friend's children were dead? Dead of the white man's measles. Barely half of his people were left alive who were but a month ago a proud band of Cayuse warriors and families, 350 strong. This never happened before Whitman brought more and more whites to take away the Cayuse hunting grounds. This Whitman was an evil that must be stopped, and according to Cayuse custom, if a healer failed at his task, that healer's life was to be taken in retribution for the deaths he failed to prevent.

Tomahas looked down on the head of the man seated in front of him, nodding and speaking. More words. Words that would do no good now. People were dead and more would soon die. He saw Whitman's hand reach for the Bible. The cause of it all. At first there were only a few bringing their beliefs, their "faith," with them. Some said it was a good faith, one his people could understand. But then others came. And soon more. And with them, disease. And now his people were treated like camp dogs while the new arrivals, settlers they called themselves, spoiled the land, taking all the meat and leaving none for the Cayuse.

The white doctor's hand spread wide on the black book, his thumb reaching to open it to all those words. And Tomahas felt nothing but anger for the words that would do no good. The hate boiled in him, rising from his guts to his head, and in one swift motion his hand slipped the tomahawk from his belt, raised it high, and drove it downward, straight into the cursed white man's head. Jim Bridger's half-white daughter screamed behind him. Then Tiloukaikt stood, slashing at Whitman's face with his long knife. The blood slapped Tomahas like rain. The chief rounded the table and jammed his rifle in Whitman's neck. Then there was the shot, straight into the neck, and Whitman flipped from the chair.

MaryAnn Bridger ran for the door to the other room, shouting, "They're killing Papa!" But Tomahas didn't care. Tiloukaikt finally saw the truth.

Narcissa unbolted the door to the kitchen and told the children to stay away. MaryAnn would not scream without cause. And now she was banging on the door, saying they were killing Marcus! She flung the door wide and Tiloukaikt and Tomahas were stumbling outside, shouting as if drunk.

Marcus lay sprawled on his back on the floor, his face a mask of blood. His jaw moved and red bubbles rose and popped through holes in his neck. Narcissa dropped to her knees, the screams of the children surrounding her as they saw their adoptive father's condition. She put a hand to his chest and whispered close to him. "My love, don't leave me. I will make you better. I will nurse you to health and we can leave here. My love. . . ."

Screams and shouts from outside snapped her from her reverie. The children! She ordered them upstairs to barricade themselves in. Through the window, she saw men, women, and children (some her own adopted young) running across the yard. They were chased by Cayuse men, shouting and with axes held high. A second later she felt a tremendous pain in her chest. She dropped to her knees beside her husband's prone form. Though she knew she'd been shot, Narcissa rose and struggled up the stairs after the children. Prayer was the only thing she could think to do.

Soon they heard wood tearing, glassware smashing, and an Indian shouting. "The house will be burned around you. Come downstairs!"

This was the voice of an old friend among the Cayuse. He would not lie to them. Narcissa was brought outside, carried on a settee, and then she screamed. The last thing she saw was a ragged ring of Cayuse men staring at her with narrowed eyes, rifles pointed at her. And then they opened fire.

Her body pitched, jerked, and flopped to the ground. One young Cayuse, who had attended her husband's sermons in the past, lashed Narcissa's lifeless face over and over again with a riding crop.

Such gruesome scenes occurred throughout the mission. By day's end, on November 29, 1847, eleven men, one woman, and two children lay dead. Three more children, stricken with measles, died soon from lack of care. Among the murdered were two of the Sager children, orphaned several years before along the Oregon Trail. In all, forty-seven survivors were taken captive and endured a month of hardship that included malnutrition and sexual

assault before being ransomed by officials at the Hudson's Bay Company on the Columbia River, twenty miles downstream.

Within weeks, mountain man Joe Meek, whose half-breed daughter had been among the murdered, trekked to Washington, D.C., and demanded to see his cousin by marriage, President Polk. As a result, and after much legislative wrangling, Oregon was established as a territory on August 14, 1847, with Joe Meek as a U.S. Marshal. Eventually, after being relentlessly pursued for two years, the five perpetrators of the Whitman Massacre, Tomahas and Tiloukaikt among them, gave themselves over to white authorities. They were tried and hanged.

15

DON'T MAKE HIM ANGRY

In 1847 Crow warriors murdered the pregnant Flathead Indian wife of mountain man John Johnston. He vowed revenge, and for the next two decades he was dogged by the Crow nation's finest warriors.

It had been a damn long time since he'd come West to scratch around in the dirt looking for riches in Alder Gulch, Montana Territory. It'd been even longer since he'd been in the navy. He hadn't minded that either. There was regular food, even if you had to eat without looking too close at what you were putting in your mouth. Weevils tended to work their way into the flour and sometimes made it from the pan to your plate. No matter, they sure as hell didn't kill him. He snorted and murmured, "Rather have weevils about now than the blasted Absarokas dogging me these six years."

Johnston preferred mornings like this, though he could do without the sting of the wind that had kicked up in the last few miles. He kept up his steady pace, Hawken in his right hand, gripped in a thick fur mitten. He felt a spot of cold at the base of his trigger finger where he'd slitted the mitten for quick shooting.

He had found over the ten years he'd been traveling the Rockies that afoot was the only way of getting about, especially in winter. It tired him sooner than if he'd been ahorseback, but he'd always relished the feeling of clean air icing in through his nose, the frosty buildup on his beard around his mouth as he put one snowshoe in front of the other, over and over again, knowing (without knowing just how he knew) the direction he wanted.

His side ached up high, more than the older wounds. This one had been healing nearly three weeks now. The Crow warrior had been a crafty devil, launching himself out of a tree. If he hadn't yelled on his way down, that big knife looking like it was going to split John's head like a gourd, he would have been done for and no mistake. He'd left the trail, looking for a spot to do his business when he heard that screech coming down at him from the pine like a mountain lion and a coyote tussling.

"Man had kept his pie hole shut he'd have had Liver Eater's scalp on his lodge pole. Only thing he has now is one less liver and a whole lot of happy varmints chewin' him down to bone and not much else." Even so, the warrior had managed to nick him pretty good. Felt the blade dig in between his ribs before he forced it back out of himself and right into that devil's own body.

That warrior had died right there, flopped on him like they was a married couple. Johnston had rolled the Crow off him, noticed he was no more than a boy and almost felt a twinge of pity. Then he remembered Swan's wide forehead, perfect black hair, that regal nose with a little bend in it, her smile just for him. It had been a long time since anyone had smiled at him just because they liked him. And then they'd killed her. For no good reason. Hell, they didn't even have a bad reason. Just killed her. And their baby.

He'd looked back down at the dead boy-warrior and, with the Crow's own knife, slit the Indian open like he was gutting a fat trout. The innards flopped out, steaming on the snow. He reached in up to his wrist and seized the boy's liver, held it up and squeezed it tight in his fist, the blood streaming down his own arm, then threw it at the dead man's face. Close enough for what those fools expected of him.

It was only when he walked away that he remembered he'd been stabbed in the side. Johnston stripped down and washed it with snow, let it bleed a bit, then smeared bear grease into it and wrapped it. It would be sore the next day, he thought. And he was right. But every day since then it had mended more.

And this morning he'd set out early from his meager camp backed up against a granite outcropping. It had been a good spot to spend the night. Made him feel as though his sleep would sustain him, especially with Crow still dogging him like water slapping a river rock. They would not catch him with his pants around his ankles. But he would catch them.

He'd vowed it six years before when he'd returned to his cabin to find that those greasy, stinking heathens had killed, scalped, and mutilated Swan, his Flathead wife. Nearby he'd found the half-chewed remains of their unborn child, prob'ly a boy by God, tossed in the dirt like stove ash.

As he'd buried a kettle he'd filled with their gathered bones, he'd vowed that the Crow would pay dearly for their butchery. That woman was no harm

John "Liver Eater" Johnston spent twenty years feuding with the Crow Nation in revenge for the murder of his pregnant Flathead wife, and although he denied actually dining on the livers of his foes, eyewitness accounts say otherwise.

Courtesy National Archives

to them, nor was the baby. But John Johnston, by God, was. And he'd proved it too these past six years.

The Crow didn't call him *Dapiek Absaroka*—Crow Killer—for nothing, and the whites took to calling him "Liver Eater" Johnston. And why not? For every Crow liver they thought he ate, the heathens believed that the warrior wouldn't get his ultimate rewards in the happy hunting grounds. Fine with him.

He halted in his snow trek, pushed the back of one furred mitten to the side of his nose and snotted hard like a bull, then spat and wiped at his beard with the mitten.

He switched his rifle to his other hand and worked his free hand's fingers open and closed to get the feeling back in them. He jogged forward, kicking up soft mountain snow with each shuffling stride. His breath pushed out ahead of him, the wind at his back. He'd altered his direction to accommodate it.

He did not like being unable to hear what was happening behind him, and every few dozen yards he snatched a quick glance backward, alternating shoulders. It was Blackfoot territory and he wanted to get through this pass before dark. He figured he still had forty miles to cover. With every stride he looked forward more and more to the warm welcome he would receive at his Flathead kin's winter camp. He cherished making these visits in his midwinter downtime from trapping, and was grateful that they still considered him kin, though his wife was dead.

He shifted his rifle back to his left hand and peeked over his shoulder. And what felt like a length of frozen log slammed into his head. He fell face down in the snow—no time to raise his arms—and laid still. And even in that sliver of an instant, before pain seeped in, he knew as sure as the sun would rise tomorrow that another Crow warrior had caught up with him. He lay quiet, his eyes not wanting to open, and watched the snow.

The man would not shoot him or lance or tomahawk him in the back. He would flip him over first. It was their way. Admirable, he had to admit. And as the warrior jammed his lance hard in his side, just about in that new wound, Johnston lashed out like a striking snake and grabbed hold of the lance, using it to push the Crow off balance.

It worked, and though his head still rang like a bell and his vision flickered with shards of daylight, he could see well enough to attack without stopping, driving the Crow backward until the man was on the ground and Johnston straddled him, pummeling the Indian with fists like river rocks.

The pain in his head, the pain in his side, they would heal. Would the pain in his heart ever heal? He didn't think so. He landed another mad stroke against the warrior's dark face until he felt something snap.

Much has been said and written about John "Liver Eater" Johnston, with the result that today the myth of the man is more well known than the fact. He did indeed conduct a twenty-year war with the Crows, though eventually, through mutual consent, he became a tribal brother to them. They had grown tired of losing fine warriors to him and he had long since grown weary of fighting off their attacks. Johnston lived for many years more, employed variously as a woodhawk, marshal, soldier, peddler, and guide. In the last month of the nineteenth century, he grew ill and moved to a veterans' hospital near Los Angeles. He died on January 21, 1900. He was seventy-five.

18

ABANDONED IN THE WILDERNESS

In the autumn of 1849, in what would become Montana, Janette Riker, her father, and two brothers, stopped their wagon for a few days to hunt buffalo before continuing over the mountains to Oregon. The men left camp early on the second day and never returned.

Janette Riker held her hand above her eyes, the late September morning sun providing enough light for a last glimpse of her father and two brothers as they waved from a ridge before disappearing down its far side on a daylong quest for buffalo.

She smiled, relishing the solitude, and turned back to camp. It would be a rare day alone, something that hadn't happened in the three months they'd been traveling westward toward Oregon. Now that they had reached Montana Territory and the mountains, her father decided they'd rest here in this small grassed valley to make minor repairs to the wagon, let the two oxen fatten on the lush green grass, and hunt for buffalo in preparation for their trek through treacherous mountain passes.

"We'll do our best to be back before dark. And remember the rifle—keep it close to hand at all times."

Janette smiled at her father.

"Now girl," he said, trying to look stern. "You know that I don't want to leave you here alone while we hunt, but I need both boys with me if we are to haul back as much meat as we can."

"Yes, Papa." She smiled at him, her head tilted to one side.

For a moment he stared at her, his daughter, his oldest child, now seventeen. How could it be? The vision of her mother, save for the dark hair, but alike in so many ways. And now here she was, already older than his Martha when they had met and married.

He kissed her forehead and strode past the boys, speaking over his shoulder, "I'm on my way to find buffalo. What are you two going to do all day?" The lads, like spring colts, stumbled and pushed at each other to catch up with him. "'Bye Janette!" said the boys almost together.

"Good bye, good bye! Bring me back a buffalo robe!"

She sat up all night at the fire, keeping it blazing, jerking upright when a knot snapped or a coyote pack passed, yapping like arguing children. And when dawn began its slow melt into daylight, it found Janette still sitting upright, staring bleary eyed at the smoldering coals. Off to the side of the fire, her stew pot had grown cold. When there was light enough to reveal the edges of the far hills, the young woman set out, bundled against the frigid morning. She knew the direction they took the morning before and fully expected to meet them as they returned. She brought along a small satchel of biscuits she had made the previous day. They would surely be hungry.

By midday, she was lost. She ran for nearly an hour, her sides feeling as though they might split, her heart pounding in her neck, her breath coming in gasps. If she could find the stream, perhaps she could follow it back down southeast to their camp. It was another hour before she found a stream, and she prayed that it was the right one. Within twenty minutes she emerged from behind a thicket below their camp. The fire was long cold. The oxen still grazed not far from the wagon and barely lifted their heads when she shouted.

"Hello the wagon! Helloooo! Papa?"

The cold and wind increased with each passing day, and as her father used to say back in Missouri, she could smell snow on the air. All it would take would be one mighty storm to freeze her solid. She finished fastening down the heavy canvas wagon covering, stepping back to regard her shelter, half of it made from logs she had cut from the trees growing close by the stream, the rest made from bent saplings lashed together. She'd chinked the gaps as best as she could with moss and sod, and had piled a berm of earth tight to it all around for insulation. It wasn't the most handsome structure she'd ever seen.

"As long as it keeps the weather out," she said, picking up her father's axe and sinking it into the chopping block. She spent the rest of the afternoon transferring goods from the wagon to her new home.

The next day, with an ache in her heart and tears on her face, she pulled the trigger of her rifle and dropped the remaining ox dead. The first had been eaten by wolves two nights before, and this one had received injuries such that she doubted it would remain well much longer. She recalled what she could of the grisly task of butchering and set to work cutting up the beast for her winter food supply. She salted it to preserve it and carried it all down to her shelter.

The next morning the sky darkened and felt heavy, as if it were pressing down on her. She knew what this meant, could smell it, and within an hour small, slow flakes of snow began to fall. She spent the rest of the day dragging more wood close by the shelter. When she fell asleep that night she was, if not happy, at least content that she had done what she could for herself.

By the morning, the snow was up to her knees and was still falling so thick that she couldn't see twenty feet. It snowed for the better part of the next three weeks and completely covered her crude little shelter. She had to climb outside several times to unblock the smoke hole for the little wagon stove.

A sharp sound like a man coughing or sneezing awoke her. It was dark in the shelter, as it always was, even during the day. Her fire had gone out and she knew it was night, for she could see nothing but black through the smoke hole. She lay still, listening. Her first thought was of her father and brothers. They had finally made their way back to her. But they must be cold and sickly, that's why she heard a cough. She sat upright, listening. Close behind her, just outside the chinked wall of logs and bent saplings, through the snow, she heard the familiar scratching and whining, like a dog wanting to be let in.

Only she knew it was no dog. It was a coyote or wolf. It must be the ox meat, she thought, because every night they circled for hours. Last night the mountain lion stalked her shelter again, circling and growling, a low, guttural sound that rippled through her and made her want to scream. She had quieted herself with a mouthful of quilt, trembling as if stricken with a fit. The lion paced and growled and sometimes swatted at the top of the shelter. The canvas and branch roof sagged under its weight, but the smoke seemed to repel it and she was pleased that, if she needed to, she had enough wood inside to keep the fire alive for another two days.

But she longed for sunlight and she longed for sleep. Night after night being stalked by lions and wolves and coyotes was no way to live. She sat back in the chair and rested her forehead in her hands. Despite the occasional whines of the stalking dogs circling her buried little home, she slept.

She'd lost count of the days, but as near as she could figure it had been more than five months since she built the shelter, and as she hauled the canvas top up over the hoops of the wagon, covering it once again, she saw the last of her house give way and churn downstream, logs and chunks of sod mixing with slabs of gray ice.

The entire valley began flooding the day before. She woke to water rising halfway up her boots. Her blankets had soaked up enough weight that she had to drag them out one at a time and up the bank to the wagon.

It seemed the rain would never end. For two weeks, it kept coming down. The water rose to just under the hubs of the wagon's wheels and there was no way to make a fire. She hadn't thought to drag enough firewood into the wagon to last even more than two days.

Three days later the water receded enough for her to step down out of the wagon for the first time in nearly two weeks. The ground was spongy and she sank in up to her ankles, but she didn't care. It felt good to walk, though she was weak. Without fire she had been reduced to eating raw corn meal mixed with water into a paste. And the last of her meat, though she'd salted it last fall to preserve it, was raw and difficult to keep down.

There were six of them. When they rode up to the wagon they just stared at her. She did the same. She had the rifle across her lap but didn't feel frightened. These were the first Indians she'd seen up close and though she knew better than to judge them by their first appearance, she had to admit they seemed friendly. She was so weak from rationing the last of her rancid food that she had no strength to do more than stare back at them.

Finally one rode forward and spoke to her in enough English that she understood him. But she couldn't reply right away. It had been so long since she'd heard another person's voice that suddenly she was overwhelmed with emotions. Her eyes filled with tears. She wiped them away hard with the back of her hand. He asked her the same question again.

"Who you?"

She swallowed and said, "I am Janette Riker."

And for an hour they conversed in a halting manner. He stopped often and spoke to the other five in their language. She studied them and decided that, come what may, life with them had to be better than starving to death here, alone, in this miserable little valley in the mountains.

The party of Indians were so impressed with this young woman and all that she'd been through that they fed her, loaded some of her possessions on a horse, and brought her to the fort at Walla Walla, after which little is known of her. It is said she married and settled down to homestead and raise a family. Of her father and two brothers, no trace was ever found. It is assumed they fell in a ravine or just became lost in the vastness of the Northern Rockies.

17

FISTICUFFS WITH A UTE CHIEF!

In the summer of 1852, Richens "Uncle Dick" Wootton, fur trapper, scout, and Indian fighter, drove a large herd of sheep northwest from New Mexico to the gold fields near Sacramento, California. A Ute raiding party stopped him in the San Juan Mountains of Colorado. Within minutes, the hot-headed mountain man had attacked the Ute chief, his skinning knife laid tight to the startled chief's throat.

Dick, you think it's wise to give them Mexicans rifles, pistols, and knives, same as us Americans? You figger you can trust 'em? We got nine thousand head of sheep, after all, not to mention our pack mules and them goats for leading the herd." The speaker was a tall man with a week-old beard and half of his left eyebrow missing.

Richens Wootton, Uncle Dick to his friends, looked up from tying off the last of the rations to the back of a mule. "You worry about your own affairs and I'll worry about this outfit, all of it my own and no one else's. And when I want your advice I'll ask for it."

Wootton watched the broad-backed man walk away, knowing then and there he was going to have trouble with Mack Shipley. And from the way the fourteen Mexican herders and eight Americans he'd hired as guards were arranging themselves in little groups, only three days into the journey, he knew there would be trouble from other quarters as well. Mack was one of those fellows that weaker men bowed to, and he wasn't afraid to bully others into getting what he wanted. Wootton, not for the last time, regretted hiring the man and his friends, but there had been few other options. Not many men were willing to risk their hides herding sheep through Indian territory.

Weeks had passed since they left Taos on June 24, 1852, driving sheep along the emigrant trail. The going was slow, made even more so by having to drive the herd from the established trail every few miles for forage. Before long they had made it well into Colorado's San Juan Mountains—Ute Indian country—and Wootton had told his men to keep extra vigilant. That night he rearranged the trade goods he planned to offer the Indians as payment for using their land.

Gun shots pulled him from a light sleep. He scrambled to his feet, hefting his rifle.

"Uncle Dick!" It was Mort, one of the few men he could trust. "It's Utes. They're on us!"

"Drive 'em off, men! Fire over their heads if you can." Off to his left, in the dark, he saw one of his Mexican herders shouting at a couple of men on horseback. He rushed to his side in time to drive off the riders, thwarting their attempts to abscond with three pack mules.

For the rest of the night, the men stayed awake, and though they were allowed to rest in shifts, most patrolled the perimeter of the herd, their weapons cocked and ready for the slightest untoward movement.

Daylight brought with it welcome relief, for with each passing minute they could see further afield. When a large Ute party thundered up to camp just after sunup, the men, with barely a cup of coffee and a hard biscuit each, were tired, grim, and in no mood for games.

The band of warriors galloped directly into camp, scattering the men and making a great stamping show of themselves. They had little regard for the guns trained on them.

Having dealt with Utes many times before, Uncle Dick was able to converse with this Chief Uncotash.

"You will pay tribute. This is sacred land and you are trespassing here!" The man was fairly shouting at him and Wootton worked hard to remain calm. He knew that losing his temper would not help them get on up the trail.

"Let us reach the Uncompahgre River by tonight and we can bed down the sheep. Then we will powwow and you will be paid."

The chief was not convinced, and his unchanging stare pinned Wootton to his spot. Wootton offered further assurance by offering to send two of his men with the chief's band to ride ahead and help select that evening's campsite. The chief seemed satisfied with this and, though the two men Wootton selected were unimpressed, they rode off, surrounded by Ute warriors.

Soon after the herd set forth again, shouts from one of the forward herders brought Dick riding up. The two men he'd sent with the Utes thundered in.

"What are you doing back here?" he shouted.

"We know what you're going to say, Uncle Dick, but them Injuns was fixing to do us in."

Before Dick could respond, thunder from the distance ahead rolled at them—one hundred Ute warriors, with Chief Uncotash in the lead. He galloped to within two feet of Dick Wootton and immediately began shouting. The surrounding warriors also bellowed and shook their rifles and bows, though none quite matched their chief's exhortations.

"You have offended Uncotash, Chief of Utes!" The chief raged. Without warning he barked orders to his band. The Indians peeled away in small groups and surrounded each of Wootton's men.

Wootton swallowed and said, "Now Chief, these men were just scared, that's all. You are the greatest warrior here, of that there is no doubt. And your power cannot be—"

But the chief had stepped down from his horse and bellowed in Uncle Dick's face, interrupting the drover's explanations with shouts and pushing Wootton with his chest.

If I don't make my move now, thought Wootton, I will forever regret it. And considering how these men are acting, forever might be a short time. Uncle Dick rammed his powerful body forward into the chief and knocked the thin man to the ground. He struggled to grasp the wiry chief's arms, then pin them. He managed to land a solid punch to the chief's chest, which slowed the old dog for a moment. Wootton was thankful that the warriors kept their distance. He knew it would be unthinkable for them to interrupt another man's fisticuffs.

Finally Wootton had the squirming chief pinned and in a swift move he whipped out his long skinning knife, the flat of the blade pressed tight to the chief's throat. Wootton, his face inches from the chief's, growled in the Ute tongue that he'd better surrender. There was no movement, and as Wootton stared into the dark eyes of Uncotash, he saw a mix of raw hate and respect warring on the man's tensed countenance.

Then something seemed to give way and the chief barked to his warriors to back away and allow the herd to be moved to the river, as originally agreed.

Later that evening, after they bedded down the herd, the chief and Uncle Dick passed the peace pipe and struck terms. Wootton proffered generous amounts of such items as flour, ammunition, tobacco, and trinkets, and Uncotash, who had lost face in front of his warriors, seemed pleased with the deal. As an extra assurance against chicanery in the dark hours, Wootton demanded that a Ute warrior remain in his camp overnight, to be released in the morning when the herd moved on.

Later on the trip, when he discovered that six of his men had struck a deal with a following wagon train to sell them sheep from his herd, Wootton forced the six out of camp at gunpoint, making them swear, under penalty of death, to never return. It worked, and while the remainder of the trip offered its share of woes, rustling from within was not one of them.

In all, Richens "Uncle Dick" Wootton, traveled 1,600 miles with nine thousand sheep, twenty-two armed hired hands, a string of pack mules, eight goats to lead the way, and one trained sheep dog—all in less than six months. They lost less than one hundred head on the journey. He sold the herd the following spring for fifty thousand dollars, ten times what he had paid for them.

Word of Uncle Dick Wootton's successful sheep trek to California spread like prairie fire, and others soon followed his lead. The next to launch a successful sheep drive was legendary scout and mountain man Kit Carson, who drove a herd of three thousand sheep through much the same terrain, and made thirty thousand dollars—enough for him to purchase his own ranch in New Mexico.

In addition to his lifelong pursuit of new experiences and daring exploits, Uncle Dick Wootton was also renowned for his quick temper and harsh treatment of anyone he felt had wronged him. When on the trail he would sleep with a loaded and cocked gun by his side. If awakened in the night, he would literally shoot first in the direction of the offending noise and question his actions later. This often resulted in the loss of a horse, but on at least one occasion did prevent a deadly raid.

18

MASSACRE AT MOUNTAIN MEADOWS

On September 11, 1857, 140 men, women, and children of the Fancher party emigrant train stopped at Mountain Meadows, in southern Utah, to regroup their eight hundred head of cattle. They were attacked and pinned down for five days by Mormons and Paiute Indians, then tricked out of their enclosure by the same Mormons—who sought free cattle and goods.

Why should we surrender our arms to them?" The man who spoke was a burly giant, taller than his fellows by at least a head, and he commanded attention.

"Hoyt's got a point," said a wiry man who no one had seen without a cob pipe bobbing between his lips. "But I'll tell you what," he pulled the pipe from his mouth and poked it in the air, keeping time with his words. "We don't get some water soon we're in trouble." Most of the men nodded, dug at the dirt with their tired boots. "Besides, what choice we got? Not like they ain't going to run off our cattle anyway."

Again, the men nodded. The big man spoke again: "I don't trust 'em, dammit."

"What's not to trust? They're Mormons, God-fearing folk, same as you and me."

"Why do they need our guns? Why can't they just leave us be? We'll move on quick enough."

"Said they'd protect us from the Paiutes."

The big man threw up his arms. "Hell, they been shooting at us with the Paiutes for three days!"

"You don't know that was them."

"You know as well as I do some of them Indians are just whites with their faces blackened. I don't know what they're playing at but I don't like it."

"You don't have to like it, Hoyt. Just go along with it and we can get out of here. The families are going to need water soon."

For a long minute no one said anything, then the big man folded his arms and said, "Alright. Let's go."

John Doyle Lee knew it was wrong from the start, but he was in too far to turn back. How do you reject a lifetime of hard work and devotion to a cause, to your God? Still, it felt wrong. But that didn't mean they wouldn't get away with it. And when they did, the cattle, the money, the loot would make their meager lives immeasurably better.

The Mormons in his area of southern Utah were not prosperous by any means, and most of them had many mouths to feed. It was a hard life. When word reached them that one of the biggest and most promising wagon trains they might ever see would be passing their way, Lee and his neighbors knew that this was an opportunity to enhance their own situations and at the same time eliminate Arkansans, people from the same place as those who had murdered one of the brethren for taking that Arkansas farmer's wife. This form of blood atonement would sit well with Brigham Young and put them in a favorable position in the eyes of the Church.

"Tempt them with safe passage, brethren," Higbee had said. "Get the emigrants to surrender their arms. Then we will tell them that they may leave our lands in peace."

And as soon as Major John Higbee signaled to them, waving his arms like a windmill and shouting, "Do your duty!" the slaughter began. Each man was shot while the women and children watched, screaming and shouting and trying to run. Then they, too, were quieted, mostly with blows to the head.

The Paiutes were there as a convenience, Lee knew. Again, it was Higbee who thought of bringing the Indians in on the plan. He said that if they played it well the Paiutes would receive any potential blame.

It was all for "blood atonement," or so Higbee had said. That's why they opened the throats of so many of the emigrants—children, women, boys, girls, babies, men, it didn't matter who. The blood must flow. That there were upwards of one thousand head of prime Texas Longhorn cattle, all manner of other stock, plus wagons, and untold loot the pioneers had packed in, was incidental to the righteous killing that must be done. It was all sanctioned, said Higbee. Have no fear.

But even as Lee shot the huge bearded man beside him, the man who had glared at him these past few minutes as they had marched side by side, walking away from the wagons, and even as the man fell groaning and clutching his chest, his neck spasming and his hateful eyes fixed on Lee, even then John Doyle Lee knew they just might get away with this. As the next hour wore on and he found two young teenage girls hiding in the brush not far from the growing piles of bodies, even as they were beaten and raped and cut, even as he saw his neighbors, men he broke bread with, men he attended services with, even as he saw them hack off fingers and ears for the jewelry attached to them, yes even then he thought they might just get away with it.

And with each passing moment his bloodlust grew and with it the familiar feeling of superiority that came from his church, from more than within himself, that feeling of victor over vanquished. When it was all over, the ground squelched with blood under their boots as if it were mud after a hard rain, and the bodies of the women and children and men lay naked and bloody in piles. The Mormons drove off the stock and the wagons.

In late September of 1857, a group of men passed through Mountain Meadows on their way west, coming upon two piles of hacked-apart, naked human remains. One pile was composed of women and children ranging in age from but a few months to twelve or so. The other pile was built of men, also naked, slashed, and cut apart.

The travelers guessed that the bodies, which by now had been savaged by wolves and crows, had been there for more than two weeks. They hurried on and alerted authorities. Investigations began within weeks, but it wouldn't be until the following spring that the bodies were gathered and buried, and nearly twenty years before anyone was brought to justice for what has come to be known as the bloodiest episode to occur on an emigrant trail. After two decades the Mormon Church offered up John Doyle Lee for execution as a scapegoat. To date he's the only person to have been officially punished for the slaughter at Mountain Meadows.

Seventeen young children, all seven years of age and younger (the age at which Mormons still believe children are untainted and innocent), were left alive and absorbed into the Mormon community of Southern Utah. But two years later, when investigations proceeded, the Mormons told investigators that these children had been kidnapped by the Paiutes and had lived with the Indians since the killings. The children knew better, and said so. And yet the Mormons continued to contradict themselves for years to come. In 1999 when the church attempted to prettify the area, bulldozers unearthed a mass grave of bones from the massacre.

19

REAP WHAT YOU SOW

In 1858, lawman Jack Slade tracked horse thief Jules Beni to Julesburg in northeastern Colorado, only to be shot five times by the outlaw. Slade lived and Beni, outraged, vowed to kill the lawman. But Slade got wind of the plan.

Beni! I'm calling you out! You're a cowardly horse thief and on behalf of my employer, the Central Overland California and Pikes Peak Express Company, I aim to hang you for it." Joseph Albert "Jack" Slade let his words carry down the deserted street of the thief's namesake town. He'd tracked him here to Julesburg after his latest thefts. Slade listened for a response, leaning against the rough boards of the sign painter's shop, the scent of gum spirits strong in his nose.

"You talk too much, Slade."

Jack spun to his left, pistol raised, as Beni stepped out from behind a sprawling stack of burlap sacking. He raised his gun but Beni was already in position, and emptied five shots into Slade, who lurched, convulsing with each stinging punch, into the dirt street. He dropped to the ground, dust rising in little clouds where he landed.

For a few seconds there was no sound, just the echoing memory of Beni's last shot. Angered locals drifted out from behind their locked doors. Some of the braver souls ventured over to Beni, who toed Slade's boot. "Hey, hey . . ." Beni shook his head and turned to the approaching cluster of townsmen on horseback. They were armed.

"We want you out of here and now," one of them shouted as they bore down on him. "You've killed a lawman and we don't want you around here." The tall man who'd been talking racked in a fresh cartridge as the horses reined up a half-dozen yards away.

Jules Beni regarded the man for a moment, looked at the others knotted close by, grim-faced and all armed with shotguns and handguns. He mounted his horse as three more armed and mounted men rounded a corner and joined the group.

They chased Beni for a few miles past city limits, then turned back. When they returned they were amazed to find Jack Slade struggling to his feet, several people rushing to support him. The man had taken five shots and still he lived.

Jack Slade spent most of the months since the Julesburg shooting at his ranch in Cold Springs, but had not kept secret the fact that he would make Jules Beni pay for his thieving, murderous ways. And he did not have long to wait.

His foreman rushed in one morning while Slade was still at breakfast.

"What on earth . . . ?" said Slade, looking up from a ledger book beside his breakfast plate.

"Sorry, Jack, but I thought you'd want to know we just got word that Beni's planning on ambushing you here, on your own ranch."

Slade set down the pencil and said, "What makes you think that, Cal?"

"Little Slim knows a few fellows, one of them swears it's going to happen before the end of this week."

Slade stood, wiped his mouth, and said, "Then we'll be ready for him."

Three days later Slade and his men captured Beni a mile from the house and barns. "Get down, by that fence line there, and keep your mouth shut."

"What are you going to do, Slade?"

"Well, I ain't going to hang you, Beni. You're past that offense." Slade nodded to the four men behind Beni. They stripped him of knife and gun and lashed him to a fencepost. All the while Jules Beni screamed his rage and fear at him. Slade drew his gun.

"Boss, ain't you going to. . . ."

"Shut up, Cal." Slade stepped in close and one by one shot off each of Beni's fingers. The man's screaming turned Slade's cowboys white, and some looked away. Slade leaned in toward the writhing man. Spittle and tears slicked Beni's red face, his features contorting.

Slade said, "Steal another horse, will you?"

Beni shook his head. "No, no, no, I won't, I won't!"

Slade stuck the pistol barrel in Beni's mouth, waited long enough for the horse thief's eyes to bulge, then said, "I know you won't," and pulled the trigger.

While his somber, shaken crew rode away, Slade hacked off Beni's ears, thinking that one of them might make a decent watch fob.

Six years later and six-hundred miles north, in Virginia City, Montana, a man cried, "Sheriff, Jack Slade's on a binge again. You got to come quick!"

J. M. Fox sighed, folded his newspaper neatly, and stood up. He strapped on his gun belt and checked his badge. Can't that man keep himself sober for more than a week at a stretch? Fox hadn't been in the job long, but he knew by God when a man was a nuisance. He'd arrest him, drag him to jail, fine him for the damage caused, and send him on his way tomorrow. Same thing every time with every drunk. But Slade was different, dangerous, even when he was staggering.

It didn't take long to find Slade. Random shots rang from the Nugget Bar and a cluster of men stared in the open door. "I'd appreciate help from a few of you boys," Fox said as he stepped up on the boardwalk, drawing his pistol. A few of them nodded and two fell in line behind him.

He walked into the bar to find Slade stood weaving in the middle of the room. The owner, bartender Billy O'Connor, ducked behind the bar, the tip of his shotgun's barrel just visible over the shining surface, now pitted and pocked with bullet holes. Fox hadn't seen this much damage in a long time. As if in response to his thought, one of the men behind him whispered, "You should see what he done to half the shop fronts on Main Street."

The low voice caught Slade's attention and he looked at the sheriff. "Why, hello Foxy. Come to arrest me again?"

"Yes, Jack, I have. You've had too much fun for one night."

Slade staggered to the bar and splashed whiskey into a broken glass. His pistol clunked to the floor. Fox stepped in and, with the help of the two men behind him, subdued Slade.

They wrestled him to the jail and were met there by Alexander Davis, the head judge of the town's newly formed people's court. He had an arrest warrant for Slade.

Fox began to read it but Slade snatched it from him and ripped it into little pieces.

"You'd better watch your step, Jack Slade," said O'Connor from the doorway, still toting his shotgun. "This won't sit well with the Committee!"

Slade laughed and said, "Well, Billy, a fellow Vigilance Committee member. Don't lecture me—I'm on your side, pal." He whipped out a pistol he had concealed in his coat, pressing it to the judge's temple. "So help me, Judge Davis, I will kill you and all your smug people's court."

Fox and his men disarmed Slade and within a half-hour riders were sent out to nearby mining communities with the request to bring back public approval of punishment for the bullying drunk. The six hundred gathered miners, most of whom had been affected at one time by Slade's bullying and drunken sprees, to a man agreed to hang Slade. They were sick of him.

A tearful and shaking Slade begged for forgiveness, for someone to fetch his wife at their ranch. But the twelve-mile trip proved too long. By the time she rode in on her lathered horse, wild-haired and screaming for the proceedings to stop, Molly Slade's husband was still swinging, having strangled to death several minutes before.

Fresh off a run of righteous justice, the citizens of Virginia City, Montana, fed up with rampant thievery, formed a Committee of Vigilance and, within three months, hanged twenty-two suspected road agents, including their own Sheriff Henry Plummer. Not deserving death for being a public nuisance, Slade nonetheless ran afoul of the very vigilante group he had helped form, and was hanged on March 10, 1864.

Following her husband's untimely demise, Molly Slade had a zinc-lined coffin specially built that she filled with whiskey to preserve the body. She kept it under her bed until the roads opened later in the spring and she could transport him to his birthplace in Illinois. She never made it beyond Salt Lake City, where Slade was buried and remains to this day. His wife was accompanied on the 475-mile trip by one of Slade's close friends, whom she later married.

It is rumored that Slade, as a reminder of his time working to help clean up the Sweetwater Division (a rogue's wasteland and stretch of line operated by the Overland Stage Line), kept as his watch fob the dried ear of one of his victims.

20

LEAVE WELL
ENOUGH ALONE

Captured by raiding Comanches in the Fort Parker Massacre of 1836, nine-
year-old Cynthia Ann Parker was eventually made one of the chief's wives
and bore him two sons and a daughter. At thirty-four she was recaptured by
Texas Rangers and, along with her infant daughter, was reunited with her
white family . . . but not for long.

Why won't she eat, Mama?" the little girl stared at the strange woman
who had come to live with them a few days before. The girl had a
fistful of her mother's dress and peeked through the kitchen door to where the
stranger sat on the edge of the bed, staring at nothing. "I thought you said she
had a baby, Mama?" Her mother's hand slapped down on her mouth, covering
it so fast the little girl had no time to react.

"Hush now!" her mother's face burned red at her like when she scolded
her two older brothers. Then her mother did a strange thing. She let go the
girl's face and picked her up, hugging her close and whispering in her ear, "Aunt
Cynthia's baby died, honey. And we cannot talk about it, do you hear? Ever."
Orlena hugged the child again and shifted her eyes to the half-open door of
the little room beyond.

Cynthia stared back at her sister with those blue eyes that were truly
more Indian than white. Even in her grief, Cynthia Ann's stare chilled the
spine of the woman in the kitchen, who knew then that her long-estranged
sister would soon die.

From the little bedroom, Cynthia Ann Parker, Naduah to the Comanche, her
adopted people, heard the little girl and something inside her tightened and

felt as though it might snap. Her own little girl, Topsannah, Prairie Flower, would have been this girl's age, but she would never see the sun rising over the Staked Plains, would never know her mother or father, never know the love of a warrior husband such as her own devoted Peta Nacona.

He had been rough when they first met, and treated her as the child she was. But within a few short years, long enough for her to become one of the People, Nacona had chosen her as his wife. She was pleased, for she knew that in time he would become a great chief and mighty warrior, and so he did.

It was at just this time of the year, when the world grew again and birds nested along the riverbanks, that Peta Nacona's people raided the place in which she had lived with her white family. Parker's Fort, they called it. She remembered much more than she would ever tell anyone of that day, of her life before the time of the Comanche. Of the smell of smoke and dirt and grease of the warrior with whom she was forced to ride, of her brother, John Parker, and his five-year-old's cries as he was pulled from their mother's arms.

She remembered the screams and how she could not turn her face away from seeing her grandfather die. While he still lived, the Comanche had ripped off his genitals. Her grandmother was stripped of her clothes, raped, and pinned alive to the ground with a lance. She was later told that the old woman lived through it. Over time, while she could not forget these things, she did come to understand the Comanche way. After that raid so many years ago, a Tenowesh couple took her in and treated her as their own daughter. In time, Naduah even forgave Peta Nacona for leading that raid.

The unrest with the whites ripped the threads of her adopted Comanche people apart, but still she remained for twenty-four years and was a devoted wife and mother to the only family she really knew. They had been good times, raising her sons, Quanah and Pecos, and tending to her husband, who was happy with her. Unlike the other warriors, he never took another wife.

And then came the raid, the killing raid of the cowardly whites that was timed so her people's warriors were away. Two young warriors and sixteen women were shot, clubbed, and trampled to death by the whites. She, too, was almost killed that day, and would have willingly fought and died had it not been for Topsannah. She had held up her baby to show the white men, the ones who called themselves Texas Rangers, so they might see that she was

The only surviving child of Comanche captive Cynthia Ann Parker, Quanah Parker went on to become a celebrated chief of the Quahadie Comanche and counted Theodore Roosevelt among his hunting companions. *Courtesy Library of Congress*

carrying a child and would not kill her. It had worked. And the young man Goodnight stayed the hand of the soldier who would club her in the head.

But now she knew it was a mistake to have trusted the whites. She should have died there that day. They not only took her from her people, they would not let her return, ever, to her family, though she pleaded with them and her heart was sick for her sons and her husband. The man, Isaac Parker, who said he was her uncle, took her and Topsannah to live with his family. But she tried escape again and again, stealing horses and riding off with her child.

But each time they rode faster and with more men. Each time she was recaptured and forced back to her brother's house. She knew she was an irritant to them, and that was her only enjoyment during her time as a captive of the whites.

"I don't know what to do anymore with that sister of yours, Orlena. We give her everything a body could wish for. Home, bed, food. Hell, the government even gave her a parcel of land and one hundred dollars a year. What more does she want?"

"Keep your voice down. She'll hear you. She's not well."

"I know she's not well. I'm the one whose house she's living in. How do you think it will look to the Parker clan if your sister decides to starve herself to death right here in my own house?"

"The Comanches took her when she was nine, then we take her back from them when she's a grown woman with a family. And now she's lost her baby. Oh, it's heartbreaking."

"I know it, and I'm sorry about that, but damnitall, I ain't to blame. Comes a time when you have to toughen up and accept the Lord's plan. Carryin' on that way, cuttin' her hair off and wailin' like she was an Injun. Hell, she ain't a Comanche any more than I am."

In 1863, Naduah learned that Pecos, her youngest son, had died of smallpox. Shortly after, her baby daughter, Topsannah, became ill with influenza,

then died of pneumonia. Naduah mourned as a Comanche, with wailing, prayer, and self-mutilation before starving herself to death. After his wife's abduction and subsequent death, Peta Nacona never remarried, dying eventually of a wound he neglected through his grief.

Of the family of five, only the eldest child, Quanah Parker, lived. He became celebrated as the last chief of the Quahadie Comanche Indians, and though through the years he made compromises to protect his people's interests, he was shrewd in his negotiations with whites, never fully trusting them. In keeping with Comanche tradition he had eight wives, five at one time, and fathered twenty-five children. He eventually became the wealthiest Indian in the United States, visited Washington on behalf of his people, and hunted with Teddy Roosevelt. Chief Quanah Parker lived to be sixty years old, dying of pneumonia on February 23, 1911. He was buried beside his mother.

BACK FROM THE DEAD

In the early 1860s, at a quartz mine near Pony, Montana, M. D. Hatheway ambled into the bush after a grouse he'd shot. A cinnamon bear reached it first. Hatheway slipped and fell before he could retreat, and the bear was on him.

M. D. Hatheway cracked open the shotgun and thumbed in a shell as he walked into the woods uphill east of the cabin. "Tired of my beans and biscuits? Youngsters today are spoilt." As oldest—and orneriest—partner in the little quartz mine, he spent more time by the cabin than did the Kid and Rusty, scaring up game for the stewpot and making sure the jug was safe. "Might be I'll find a plump grouse or two, show them boys who's the meat maker."

Minutes later, he left his usual trail and worked toward a thicket he hoped might be home to a game bird or three. Within seconds he was rewarded with an explosion of sound only a few feet to his right. He spun, sighted, and squeezed the trigger. And the bird kept flying. "Godamighty, if that ain't wrong, I don't know what is." He kept watching the fluttering form in case it decided to fly back and die at his feet. Nope.

He sighed and stuffed in another shell. That made two left. And don't think Rusty wouldn't count 'em. "What makes a man that young so blamed cheap?" A squirrel scolded him from a nearby aspen. He squinted at it and had just decided to let the little rascal have it when, to his left, another bird exploded upward. He spun on it, covered it, and let loose the shot. The old fowling piece hammered his shoulder, but seeing that bird fold up and drop made the bruise worthwhile . . . almost. It slipped into the scrubby thicket down the slope below him. He plunged in after it, racking in his last shell as he wove between saplings and knobs of brush. Without warning he nearly collided with a cinnamon-colored grizzly that had come into possession of the unexpected sky-dropped grouse.

"Godamighty!" Hatheway was torn between wanting that bird and wanting to run. Even as he dithered the bear turned on him, clicking its jaws and pawing at the earth, the plump grouse, *his* grouse, between those front legs on the ground. Hatheway noticed how the bear's curved claws bounced and flexed with each stamp of its forelegs, how its lips shook as it chuffed at him.

He stepped backward, paused, the gun held across his chest. The bear bellowed and charged. He had just enough time to pepper the brute in the face with his last shell of bird shot. The beast howled in rage and pain and pawed at its face, swinging its shaggy head in great arcs. Hatheway wasted no time in groping his way up the gravel slope, but he slipped and slid backward a few feet trying to gain purchase, still half-turned toward the bear. And then it was on him.

The light brown beast swatted him hard on his ribcage. As Hatheway rolled he felt something inside let go. He ended up on his back, and before he could flip over the bear straddled him, its hot breath blasting into his face. He pushed himself upslope with his feet. As the bear lunged at him, Hatheway raised his legs and kicked it square in the bawling, bleeding face, driving his hobnail boots into that maw as hard as he could. It set the bear back a step, but only served to make it angrier. He'd barely gained a foothold on the slope before it came straight at him, open-mouthed this time.

He still held the shotgun in his right hand and he pushed it up at the grunting, bleeding face. The snout drove at him and the bear fastened its jaw down on his arm. The gun dropped from his grasp and the bear shook Hatheway like a near-empty flour sack. The bones in his arm popped and snapped like dry twigs.

He drove his left fist into the bear's nose, then its eye. The bear let go of the old man's right arm only to snatch up the left, tearing at it with its yellowed teeth and whipping it side to side. All the while the powerful front paws raked him, head to belly, as if the bear were burrowing through him. Through his ringing ears and the beast's gruff roar he heard another sound, higher pitched but no less urgent. He realized it was his own voice, screaming, frightened, and angry. It didn't help.

The last thing he thought of before the daylight filtering through the trees faded to black was that the bear's breath smelled worse than Rusty's ripe, wet socks draped over the stovepipe.

He came to in his bunk, in the cabin, the boys looking down at him. Then he remembered what had happened. The squirrel, the grouse . . . the bear. Memories of the great bawling head, inches from his own, the dark eyes staring straight into his, forced a shudder that wracked him from head to toe.

The kid bent low near his face and said, "How you feelin', M. D.?" The young man looked about to cry, so Hatheway decided to lie to him. It took him two attempts before his sore throat could offer words. "I been worse, kid."

A man coughed. Hatheway widened his eyes. Rusty was bent near, staring at him. "We got it, M. D."

Got what? He thought, and his question must have shown on his face, because Rusty said, "The bear. We got the bear that done this to you." He nodded at the old man.

"How bad . . . ?"

"The bear? Not much trouble, really. We went out first light and found it right enough, close by where you tangled."

"But . . . how bad . . . am I hurt?"

"Oh." Rusty straightened, leaning a hand against the wall. "Hell, M. D., you ain't ready for the cold ground just yet. I'm still waiting on a decent meal, you know."

On the boardwalk just in front of the sign maker's shop, a fat man in a grey suit walked by an old, hunched man. He stopped, turned, and hurried back. He stepped right in front of the codger and leaned in, scrutinizing him closely. "Nah," he said. "Can't be. Must be losing my sight."

"Milt," said the old man, a smile cracking the raised pink grooves running up and down his face.

The fat man stepped backward. "M. D.? Nah, nah, can't be!"

"It is me, Milt, sure as the sun rose today."

The fat man leaned in again and said, "But we printed your death notice in my paper a few months back. Heard you were killed by a grizzly up to the mines at Pony."

As he wiped the tears of laughter from his eyes, Hatheway said, "I'd appreciate a copy of that death notice, Milt." He looked his chunky friend in the eye and said, "For future reference." Then they headed to the bar.

M. D. Hatheway may well be one of the few people to survive a severe grizzly mauling only to find that he actually didn't survive it. When they returned from a day of hard labor at the quartz diggings to find their elder partner missing and no food on the stove, M. D. Hatheway's partners set off in search of him. They found him near dark, a bloody mess from head to foot, with both arms chewed and broken. Early the next day one of the miners tracked and killed the offending grizzly. Four months later in Butte, the scarred Hatheway was regarded with shock by old acquaintances, for they had read of his death in the paper some months prior. He was greatly amused by this and kept the clippings "for future reference." Rumor has it that he managed free drinks from shocked old friends for quite some time.

22

THE LONG WALK

*In 1863, Colonel Kit Carson was charged with subduing the Navajo upris-
ing in New Mexico by any means necessary. He destroyed water sources and
crops, slaughtered livestock, and burned villages. For the Navajo, that was
just the beginning of their ordeal.*

Deshna sat on the bunk in the dark little room and thought that if his
family had lived, they never would have been happy here. After Carson burned their homes and forced them to this place, they were told that
there would be plenty to eat here at Bosque Redondo. That crops would be
abundant and he would be able to raise sheep once again. Very little of this
came true. And now he was the only one left of his family. He could not help
remembering what it had been like years ago.

They were never wealthy but they had been happy with their small flock of
sheep and crop of corn. It had been enough. At least before the cavalry came.
He tried to tell them that not all Navajo were raiders, not all had guns. Most
were too poor to bother with such things. Most were concerned with making
sure their children were fed. But the men in blue did not want to hear it.

And then came the terrible winter of 1863 when Kit Carson and his army
burned down his home and crops, slaughtered his sheep. He heard later that
any man, woman, or child who raised a fist or tried to flee was shot in the head
on the spot. He did not believe this for a time, despite the burned homes and
crops, the slaughtered animals. He knew such things could happen, but the
shootings? Then he had seen the bodies of people he had known his entire life.

Yes, Carson was smart, thought Deshna. By ruining his people's food and
water he could do whatever he wanted with them. Without sustenance they
could not fight back.

The food given to them on the march was rotted and useless. And there
was not enough of it. They were all so hungry. And then his wife had the baby
by the roadside. The soldier closest to them said there would be no resting, no

stopping. He was fat and had lip hair like a badger. The fat man kicked his wife with his boot. When Deshna jumped to his feet the man drove his gun into the side of Deshna's head. When he awoke his wife and baby were gone. It took him most of the day to find them again.

The people shuffled along in line—the food they were given was little better than what a rat would eat. The meat was rancid and Deshna's father grew weaker after retching from it.

For a week they traveled, and then one night while they slept the air grew much colder. The wind was worse than the snow that came with it, and by morning they were all shivering and huddling under the one blanket they had between them. When they awoke, his father was no longer among them. His body was there but no life was left in it.

His mother insisted on staying with his father's body but more soldiers came along and forced her to walk on. They were not allowed to give his father a proper death ceremony. They didn't even have a spare blanket in which to wrap him. Deshna laid his father there at the roadside along with so many of his people.

Days later Deshna awoke to find his wife and newborn son dead beside him. It happened in the night as a blizzard piled more snow on them than he had ever seen at once. He found his daughter and mother close by, huddling with other people he did not know, but that did not matter. As cold and tired and hungry as he was, he somehow found the strength to stand before one of the soldiers and shout at him, cursing him for the raw injustice of it all. People he knew waved to him to stop, that he would make it worse for them all, but he no longer cared.

All about him people leaned against each other, many half-naked and all hobbling as if they had walked on jagged shards of pottery for days. Why were they forced to do this? What right did the whites have to burn their homes and take their lands? The soldiers, staring from beneath their heavy clothes, could not answer him. Surely they could see how wrong this was, even if they could not understand him.

It was only when he saw his mother and daughter, crying over the bodies of his wife and week-old son, that he relented. He fell to his knees and hugged his wife a last time. The soldiers prodded others to move on but they passed him by. And only when those at the end of the line limped by did the last of the soldiers prod him to get up. He had to leave his wife there, hugging her baby tight to her chest, even in death.

Deshna watched his mother rub his daughter's back as the girl retched. He saw the little bumps of his daughter's spine, like knuckles, through the thin dress. Shame gnawed at him worse than hunger ever could. His child was so thin and his old mother so stooped and gnarled—he knew it was his fault. He should have been a better provider.

He recalled all this from the long distance of five years. His daughter had died within months of arriving, too weakened from the journey to survive in the prison that was Bosque Redondo. His mother too had died, though only last year—too soon to hear the news that Barboncito had helped negotiate a treaty that would allow them all to return home. He knew he should be excited like the rest, but he did not care. There was no home any more for him in Dinetah. There was no home here at Bosque Redondo. There was no one for him to share this news with, no one to care for any more. He was alone and all because of the United States government. There had been no reason to any of it that he could recall. No reason at all.

Not for the first or the last time did Colonel Kit Carson wonder what sort of disaster had he gotten himself involved in. Brigadier General James Carleton had given him full command to stop the Navajo uprisings, then had given him orders to drive the Navajo off their ancestral land. He had burned them out, poisoned their water supplies, slaughtered their livestock, trampled and burned their crops, and shot those who resisted. And then they were forced on Carleton's fool march along three hundred miles of soulless terrain in which they were treated little better than a pack of diseased curs.

And as he stood before Carleton's desk listening to the man rave, he wondered if what he did to the Navajos had really been necessary.

"It is the best way. Hell man, it is the only way," said Carleton, stroking his ample moustaches. "Once they all finally dragged themselves here—and they are too slow for their own good, I tell you—the Navajo began to learn modern agricultural practices. Soon Fort Sumner will be a model on which all future Indian reservations will be based." Carleton drew in a vast breath and seemed to pose for a portrait, though Kit Carson was the only other person in the office. The more Kit knew of the man, the less he liked him.

In 1863 Kit Carson, acting on Army orders, destroyed Navajo food sources and razed villages. The Navajo were then forced to walk three hundred miles to an ill-equipped reservation. Five hundred died on the journey. *Courtesy Library of Congress*

But Carleton had been given a free hand in setting up this so-called model society. Carson had to admit that in conversation and on paper the plans held promise. But he knew Indians, and Carleton didn't.

"Sir, placing the Navajo and the Mescalero Apache together is asking for trouble."

"Nonsense, Carson. Do they not both speak the same language? They are alike in every way. Whatever disagreements they may have with each other can be settled through diplomacy. We'll teach the savages a thing or two about social order. They are but children, Carson, and we are here to mold them into useful citizens."

Of the nine thousand Navajo who surrendered and submitted to the long, torturous walk from their homeland in Arizona to Fort Sumner, three hundred miles away in Southeast New Mexico, five hundred died on the trail, many of frostbite and exposure, some of exhaustion, some were shot for displaying frustration and anger. Navajo women and children were stolen in the night as raids from enemy tribes grew so frequent that soldiers charged with guarding their captives' welfare simply turned a blind eye to the kidnappings.

Once they arrived at Bosque Redondo, the Navajo were treated as forced laborers to bring to fruition Carleton's grand schemes of an agricultural paradise in which his tamed savages might thrive. In reality they labored for long, back-breaking hours each day, were poorly rewarded for their services, were poorly fed, poorly clothed, and suffered in a myriad of other ways. Finally, in 1866, with the grand scheme little more than a failed, limping shadow of its architect's vision, Carleton was relieved of his command. Two years later the Navajo and the U.S. Government came to an agreement that, although salted with numerous contingencies in favor of the government, allowed the Navajo to return to their homeland, Dinetah.

Kit Carson, mountain man, scout, and soldier, and by all accounts a most honorable man, regretted the tactics he was forced to use to subdue the Navajo. He died at age fifty-eight, on May 23, 1868, a few weeks before the Navajo went home.

23

AGAINST ALL ODDS

On July 18, 1864, at 5:00 p.m., 150 Sioux warriors attacked a teamster's train headed to Fort Union, New Mexico. Robert McGee, a wagon-train orphan and still a young boy, was the only survivor.

In the time it took ten-year-old Robert McGee to turn and shout for his boss, Mr. O'Linn, the Indians were upon them. The train of teamster wagons numbered a dozen and each wagon had at least one driver. Some wagons had two men, one riding shotgun. But they seemed no match for this many Indians. They'd held them off three times on this trip, but everything was different this time. The oxen bellowed in agony as they were slaughtered where they stood, arrows slamming into their solid flesh with audible thumps.

Running toward him with his great hands outstretched, Mr. O'Linn's eyes bulged wide with fear. As Robert watched, unable to move from the side of the wagon, the burly man was sent sprawling face first on the ground with a blow to the back of the head. He twitched and shook his head, tried to rise, but an Indian warrior, shirtless and clad in dirty cloth trousers and with a partially shaved head, sprang from his horse's back. As he landed he drew a blade from his belt, drove a knee between the big man's shoulders, and batted off the teamster's old felt topper. The warrior snatched a fistful of hair and, slicing with his knife, yanked back hard on the man's head.

Robert saw a line of blood appear high on Mr. O'Linn's forehead, then he saw the Indian's arm muscles bulge. The savage growled and shouted, a smile stretching his mouth wide, as he yanked backward hard on the man's hair. The teamster's scalp rose. For a brief moment Robert saw bone, bare skull, before gore oozed over it. Mr. O'Linn screamed and screamed as if he would do so forever. The Indian leaped to his feet, holding aloft the pathetic thatch of wiry gray-brown hair, howling and hooting like an animal.

From behind, a powerful hand gripped Robert's shirt at the neck as he struggled to climb the side of the wagon. He was pulled down, his arms forced upward, cries of surprise lodged in his throat as his shirt wedged against his windpipe. Next to his head the powerful rear legs of a horse drummed at the earth. As he tried to regain his legs, the Indian who had dragged him shouted something Robert couldn't understand. It sounded like he was saying, "Keeyo! Keeyo!"

The dragging stopped as abruptly as it began and he rolled backward, flipping over and coming to rest on his belly. Before he could raise his head someone kicked him hard in the side of his chest. He felt instant sharp pain deep within himself. His vision blurred and tears welled in his eyes. Rough, powerful hands grabbed him, flipped him onto his back, and ripped off his shirt.

The boy struggled to regain his wind, finding he could only draw shallow breaths so sharp was the pain within his chest. And he knew something had broken. He looked up to see a tall man staring down at him. He was adorned with feathers flopping loose in his hair and his long face regarded the boy as if Robert smelled like an overfilled latrine.

Without warning the tall man lashed out and struck Robert hard on both sides of his head with a massive lance adorned with feathers and dirty hide wrappings. Despite his dire state Robert couldn't help but stare at his attackers. Never had he seen so many Indians so close up. As he stared, the chief pulled a pistol from a woven sash about his waist. He never once took his eyes from the boy's, nor did the gritted teeth and angled mouth shift. He raised the pistol up beside his own head as if he were listening to it, then he cocked it.

With the speed of a bullet Robert realized what was about to happen. He scrambled backward, his breath still stuttering in and out of him, his head pounding like a war drum. He clawed at clots of sandy dirt and wispy grass. He tried to flip around and gain his legs so he might run, but powerful feet lashed out once again and slammed him back to the ground, belly up. Then the chief shot him. He only remembered the first shot, the pain flowering in his gut and up into his chest. There were other shots, at least two others, but he wasn't sure. He did hear fast talking but it was more musical now, like laughter. And though he tried, he couldn't keep his head from wobbling.

Dozens of warriors surrounded him, looked down at him, and yes indeedy, as his father used to say, they were laughing at him. He tasted dirt and something else, something like liquid metal in his mouth, and pushed at it with

ROBERT McGEE,

Scalped by Sioux Chief Little Turtle in 1864.

Robert McGee in 1890—alive and well twenty-five years after he was scalped, shot, stabbed, and left for dead. *Courtesy Library of Congress*

his tongue to get rid of it. Nothing made sense just now. He wondered if Mr. O'Linn would come help him with the oxen soon.

Robert watched the chief through his shimmering veil of pain. It was like seeing the flat prairie stretching far out before you on a hot day, and knowing there was no way you were ever going to reach the end of it, never going to see those things in the distance that everyone kept saying were mountains. The chief had a bow now, and had drawn the string back hard. This was not happening, Robert knew. Because these things did not happen to people. And especially not to him. He had suffered enough, had he not? That's what the nice woman on the wagon train had said. What was her name?

He saw the arrow flying at him, then pain worse than anything hit him like a team of oxen slamming directly into his right shoulder. The blow lurched his entire body upward and he heard howls of laughter, felt more kicks.

Then another blow, much like the first, drove his other shoulder backward into the earth beneath him. He tried, but couldn't sit up, couldn't move. It was as if someone were standing on his chest. Yes, that was it. He struggled to open his eyes. He must have looked funny because rounds of laughter spurted out again, even as he finally got his eyes open.

And he saw the one who had stood over him, who had shot him and driven arrows into him. That man was now leaning over him again, the expression on his face finally changed. And Robert saw with clarity now a face that he wished he didn't have to see. It was the face of someone who was not quite done. The man held up a curved blade in front of Robert's face. The blade itself was dark but the edge had been honed keen and glinted in the late day sun. He tried to scream, because he knew what was coming next, but the sound he made was more like the burbling growl that had come from that black bear cub he'd seen tied outside the store back in Leavenworth.

Kids had poked at it with sticks just to watch it snap and growl at them. He felt like that bear now. And as the knife met his scalp, he could feel it and he tried to pull away. The roaring howls of the Indians surrounding him rose in pitch, and then it felt like someone drizzled water across the top of his head. It wasn't as bad as he expected it would be. And then he felt a tremendous pulling that wrenched his body against the arrows that held firm to the earth beneath him.

The pain in his head could have filled Mr. O'Linn's freight wagon. And still he didn't lose consciousness. He next remembered kicks raining into his body like head-size rocks pummeling him from all sides. And other pains followed, flashing colors and motions, like silver birds just above him, tearing at him with their beaks. The sticky sweat parted enough from one eye that he could see more clearly. And he saw that the silver birds were knives. He was being slashed at and stabbed—he felt the blades sink into his chest, arms, legs, and he knew this would kill him.

The beating and slicing and stabbing stopped and he heard the laughter again, as if from a distance.

Two hours later soldiers from nearby Fort Larned, hearing that Sioux had been spotted in the area, came upon the massacre site. They found but the one survivor, young Robert McGee. Only much later did he learn of the extent to which fortune had shined on him that July day in 1864. The band of Sioux warriors who attacked the teamster train was 150 strong and led by the notorious Chief Little Turtle. Robert McGee was photographed twenty-five years later. He preferred to wear a hat most of the time, though he often obliged the curious with a recounting of his harrowing ordeal.

24

CHIVINGTON'S LEGACY

On November 29, 1864, after months of Indian unrest and attacks on whites, Colonel John Chivington of the U.S. Army, ignoring the white flag of peace, ordered an attack on the camp of Black Kettle, a peaceful Cheyenne chief. Of those in the camp, two-thirds were children and women. When the smoke cleared, soldiers rampaged and atrocity became the word of the day.

And to think it all started with a cow. A damned crippled, stolen cow. At least that's what that loudmouth, Plunkett, told him. He said that a Cheyenne warrior named High Forehead had killed a Mormon's cow. And now this. Corporal Quimby stared about him, his heart telling him to look away from this field of horror or he would never be free of these sights. But the eager mind of the young soldier goaded him into lingering on each slaughtered body, the stiffening corpse of every man, woman, and child.

Though he served in the First Colorado Cavalry under Silas Soule, and glad of it, Colonel Chivington was in charge on this particular day. And Chivington had said that this was just and right. Soule seemed to feel that parley should have been the order of the day, and the two men had argued viciously in front of the troops.

But he had seen the hatred in the eyes of Chivington's Third Colorado Cavalry and its blood-thirsty Hundred Day Volunteers. Plunkett told him they were men who had lost wives, daughters, sons, neighbors to bands of roving Dog Soldiers—the renegade Indians who wanted nothing to do with peace. They only wanted revenge for raids that just bred more raids, an eye for an eye. It was more than Quimby could keep up with. All he knew was that it led to him riding in with his regiment from Fort Lyon under Captain Soule's command.

It almost didn't seem to matter now as he watched the men, some of whom he had shared cups of coffee with just the day before, riding slow back over the battleground that had been this peaceful Cheyenne village. The men stopped often, firing a shot now and again into what looked like a pile of the dead. "Them are mercy shots," Plunkett told him. "Them soldiers are doing the savages a kindness by ending their misery."

But then Quimby saw one of those same soldiers lean in with a pigsticker and hack at lifeless fingers, separating them at the joint to get at the dead Indian's rings. Some of the men scooped fingers, ring and all, into bloodied sacks swinging from their waists, the gore pooling and dripping, staining their own trousers.

To his right he saw three soldiers hack at a dead woman, one sawing at her head, another slicing off her breasts, a third busy cutting between her legs. A Cheyenne child stood nearby, watching them. One of the men shouted at the child, but he just stood frozen. The soldier's words carried on the wind to Quimby: "I'll hit the little son of a bitch." The soldier stood, aimed his pistol, fired, and missed. The second man joined him, fired, and missed. The third man laughed, said something about how women can't shoot straight, and pulled his pistol. As Quimby heard the report, the child spun in place, dropped, and writhed, clawing at the ground. The three men laughed as they resumed working on the dead woman.

Quimby leaned low out of his saddle and retched. He wanted to ride away from here as fast as his horse could take him. But it wasn't even his horse. He had heard that if he disobeyed orders he would be shot. But Captain Soule had ordered his own men not to fire. It was all so confusing. When they first rode up, the men all noticed that Black Kettle's tent was hung with the stars and stripes, snapping counterpoint to the white flag just below. Audible sighs of relief rose from the ranks. A full surrender would make an attack unnecessary and wrong. But Chivington had ignored Chief Black Kettle's flags of peace.

The colonel's men had surrounded the little village and opened fire with heavy artillery. And within hours of their arrival at dawn, the river bed was glutted with the dead, mostly women and children. There were very few men among the villagers, and those that were there seemed old and crippled with rheumatism. Weak return fire had come from the riverbanks where the few remaining warriors had holed up, digging into the dirt for cover. Word came down the ranks that Chivington's men found fresh white scalps in some of the tents. This fueled the anger Quimby saw pulling at the faces of the men, and they attacked the remaining Indians with renewed vigor.

He saw his friend Ralston sawing away at a dead child's head, trying to separate the scalp from the skull. He hoped it wasn't a girl. That would be even worse somehow. He had seen men holding breasts and genitalia from women. One soldier had stretched something of the sort over his saddle horn while others wore them on their hats, smiling and riding around the site like proud cocks.

Quimby forced himself to look away, out at the patches of brittle-brown prairie and tufts of snow, the wind now lifting great clouds of black smoke from the village and swirling them far away, miles and miles away from this hell. For a moment his face relaxed and he thought of home, of the little farm in Vermont and the warm, spiced smells of his mother's kitchen on a cold autumn day, and of the equally pleasing smells of his father's stable at night, the cows slowly munching hay.

"You look like you been bawlin."

Quimby snapped his head up, looked straight at one of Chivington's lieutenants. Dewey was his name.

"All weepy like you lost something dear to you." He smiled then. The chaw in his mouth had stained his teeth a phlegm yellow. "You an Injun lover, boy?"

He managed to shake his head no.

"Best not be." He leaned toward the young man, his saddle creaking. Quimby noticed the matted, bloodied scalps hanging loose in a loop of rawhide from Dewey's pommel, silver ornaments dangling from some. The horse twitched its withers where the scalps rubbed. Its shoulder, normally the color of fine-baked bread crust, was black with blood.

The lieutenant narrowed his eyes and stared at Quimby, then rasped a hand across his big jaw, working his tobacco. Quimby saw dried blood on the man's hands. "You get down there now, and if anything that looks like a savage moves, you pop 'em one in the head, you hear me? And get yourself a scalp. Prove yourself."

"Corporal!"

The shout startled them both and they turned. Captain Soule walked up to them, leading his horse. "Corporal, I thought I told you to head due south with Tinker after that last small band of stray horses. If I recall there were five or six of them. Do your best to retrieve them."

"Yes sir."

The entire time Soule spoke he stared at Chivington's man. There was a glint of shined steel in the captain's eyes and Quimby knew that Chivington's

Protecting the Herd, by Frederic Remington, circa 1907. The Sand Creek Massacre resulted in the slaughter and mutilation of hundreds of Cheyenne, most of whom were women and children. *Courtesy Library of Congress*

man saw it, too. The man was outranked but his blood was up. Soule was daring the rogue to try something. Instead the man fixed Quimby with a cold stare and yanked hard on his reins. Within seconds he was at full gallop back down the long slope toward the riverbank and the scene that was marked by the random wailing of a ragged handful of children and women.

Smoke built in a gathering cloud over the torn remnants of the village. A gunshot sounded. A cornered dog barked without letup. Another gunshot rang out, then Quimby no longer heard the barking.

"Corporal." Soule's voice, softer now, cracked the silence.

Quimby looked at his captain, whose own eyes were rimmed red and whose mouth hung partly open, as if he were about to speak. But he said nothing. A full minute passed. Then, without turning his head, the captain said, "Corporal Quimby, go. Go now."

Quimby rubbed his thumb and fingers hard into his eyes and whispered, "Yessir." Then reined his horse south.

Though known as the Sand Creek Massacre and Battle at Sand Creek, the incident is also widely regarded as the Chivington Massacre. Ample evidence suggests this name is well earned. Initial boasting included a public display of one hundred Cheyenne scalps taken by Chivington's men, and the claim that five to six hundred warriors were killed in the attack. A vocal minority disputed Chivington's claims before Congress and succeeded in painting him and his men as looting, mutilating murderers who massacred two hundred Cheyenne, two-thirds of whom were women and children. During the massacre, Chief Black Kettle's wife was shot nine times. He carried her that night to Fort Lyon, where she was operated on and survived.

Colonel Chivington was never held accountable for the atrocities he encouraged to be committed that day. The following April, Chivington's most outspoken critic, the young Captain Silas Soule, was murdered while strolling one night shortly after his wedding.

25

FETTERMAN'S LAST MISTAKE

Captain William Fetterman was famous for his hatred of Indians. And later, when dead, he would be more famous for underestimating them. He long maintained a boast that if given eighty men, he could cripple the entire Sioux Nation. On December 21, 1866, at Fort Phil Kearny in Dakota Territory, he had eighty men under his command when he was lured into an ambush by Crazy Horse.

While the Sioux warrior slapped his face as one would an insolent child, Adolph Metzler saw the veil of amusement stretched over the native's wide, harsh features. What he saw underneath was the same anger so evident on the faces of all the Indians around him. They were everywhere! And still more came. And at that moment he knew with perfect clarity that he would die very soon. The revelation stayed his swinging fists and battered bugle and rocked him hard. Or maybe it was the bullet that slammed into his gut. Something burned in his side and he looked down at his right hand as it clutched at his tunic. But it was not his hand, could not be. It was so covered in dark blood that it looked like a glove. And it dripped like syrup.

A well-thewed arm slipped around his neck from behind, squeezing tight. It forced his jaw hard to one side. His nose mashed against the muscled forearm. He smelled sweat, felt grease, and saw slashes of blood on the arm. Or maybe it was war paint.

Instinct drove his free left arm upward hard. "Gaaah!" The sound came from his own mouth. At the same time he bit at the sinewy arm that was crushing his throat. The limb loosened its grip and he knew before he looked that the mouthpiece of his bugle had landed well.

He spun on the warrior. The brawny brute had dropped to his knees, his hands clawing at his face, thick blood spouting between his fingers. As Metzler suspected, the mouthpiece of his bugle, his only weapon, had driven straight into the man's eye. The warrior flopped to his side and the gory mask of his face sagged.

But Metzler was given no time to consider what he'd done, for a long stick appeared as if conjured, protruding from his lower chest. He stared at it, unable to understand what it was. At the same instant as it occurred to him that it was an arrow, the full roar of the battlefield—the shouts of the Sioux warriors, mad and giddy at the same time, the never-ending screams from the cavalry men, his fellows—filled the air, and he knew this was nothing but a slaughter.

And even then the hot anger that welled in him was not felt for the Indians so much as for the foolish officers who had caused this to happen. Captain Fetterman had made Colonel Carrington look the fool. Carrington was no commander, but he was a decent enough man. And intelligent. And his last words to Fetterman and Lieutenant Grummond, before they left the stockade, were an order: "Under no circumstances pursue the enemy beyond Lodge Trail Ridge!"

Metzler remembered Carrington had said it several times. And then as soon as Fetterman caught sight of the handful of Sioux warriors on the ridge, the Sioux began taunting them, going so far as to stand on horseback and bare their backsides at the men. It enraged Fetterman. Metzler and other men around him actually laughed. If Fetterman heard them he didn't let on.

Then someone pointed at the Indians and said, "That's Crazy Horse!" Of course, there was no way he could know that, but Fetterman howled an oath and spurred his mount and men on directly toward Lodge Trail Ridge. Some of the men said it was a trick, that they were being led into a trap by the warriors. But Fetterman and Grummond, if they suspected as much, also thought the Sioux were inferior in every way to the U.S. Cavalry.

Even Metzler, just the bugler, had heard Fetterman, more than once in the month the captain had been at the Fort, say how if given eighty men he could cripple the entire Sioux Nation. This was the sort of talk that stirred the men, especially given the fact that Carrington had done so little to retaliate—really, he'd done nothing—for the lives lost while the men were on daily wood patrol in the surrounding hills. Carrington would send out troops to lend support once the men had gathered what wood they could and were headed back to the stockade. Even to Metzler it seemed a poor way to run the stockade.

From *Frank Leslie's Illustrated Newspaper,* January 19, 1867. Surrounded by thousands of Sioux, within forty minutes all eighty men of the Eighteenth Infantry Regiment from Fort Phil Kearny were killed. *Courtesy Library of Congress*

All this occurred to the young man in a pang of regret for the life he would never get to live, for the girl he would never marry, for the children and home he would never have. But it was too late. Even as he thought all this, the sounds of the battlefield came rushing back to him with sudden force. He saw, from his swaying position, the savages stripping the bodies of men still convulsing in their death throes, their bodies run through with the shafts of spears wagging with each twitch and scream.

Not ten feet away a warrior jammed his long knife straight into the bottoms of one man's feet. The poor soldier was still alive, though one arm had been severed and his face hacked, his nose and chin mere oozing smears. The face tried to scream, but only a blood bubble rose from the mouth, then burst. Metzler did not know who it was, and of that he was glad. He could not bear to know. What if it was Charlie Timms? They had shared rations just that morning for breakfast.

Metzler struggled to keep his balance. It felt like the most important thing to him at the moment. He felt sure that if he dropped to the ground the savages would be on him, stripping him and hacking him to pieces. And he could not bear the thought of knives in his feet, of greasy fingers gouging his eyes out of their sockets while he screamed. He prayed to God, he prayed to his mother, he gritted his teeth together so hard they felt as if they would grind to powder.

The day had been cold but now he felt quite warm, almost as though he should take off his tunic. So warm now. And then he felt his left leg give way. He looked down at it—still there but it was folding of its own will, though not in any way God intended. As the pain washed up from his broken limb, he toppled and screamed, his own howls blending in with eighty others, shifting on the wind like a strange choir. The excited yelps of the Sioux were the dominant voice, the soloist who knows whose show it really is.

Captain Fetterman was not far from him. Metzler had seen him but a few moments before, but now there were few other boys in blue still standing. At least, by his count, he had taken two of the red devils with him, for he knew where he was going.

And he knew he would never again see his dear mother, his sister. He hoped she would wed well and not make her future in Indian country, for it could never be settled by whites. There were just too many Indians. And what's more, the Indians were right. Despite the horrific mutilations and screams still sounding all around him (though now with less frequency than mere minutes before), a grim smile worked at his mouth. They were right after all. It was their land, not the whites', and the Indians knew they would never be bested.

Metzler's head slipped to the side, his left cheek resting against his shoulder. He couldn't lift it now, but he saw that a squat Indian, shorter than the others that were moving in a bunch behind him, stood watching him. He and the Indian studied each other. The Indian spoke now, in an impatient tone and without taking his eyes from Adolph Metzler, and gestured with an outstretched arm. A buffalo robe was handed to him and he approached Metzler. The young bugler tried to turn his head but it would not agree with him. Still, he saw the man bend over him, stare at his face, and say something in a tone that could have been a father talking to a son, wishing him well before a long journey. Adolph almost understood him. Then the man covered him with the blanket.

The Sioux called it the Battle of the Hundred Slain. Within forty minutes all eighty men of the Eighteenth Infantry Regiment of Fort Phil Kearny were surrounded, with no possibilities of escape, by two to three thousand Sioux warriors. In another half hour, the soldiers all were mutilated beyond compare. All but one.

It is believed that Adolph Metzler fought and killed several Lakota Sioux at the Fetterman Massacre with no weapon but his bugle. Though the Sioux eventually killed him, they did not mutilate his body as they did all the others on the battlefield. Instead they placed a buffalo robe over him in honor of his bravery.

26

FRIENDS TO THE END

On September 24 and 25, 1867, Scot Moore rode 260 miles in less than thirty hours to fetch a doctor for his dying friend, Oliver Loving. His path between Fort Sumner and Las Vegas, New Mexico, took him through rough country infested with Navajo warriors. Moore made the trek on behalf of rancher Charles Goodnight, who refused to leave his best friend's side.

Billy, let's keep 'er going, eh?" Oliver Loving squinted at Billy Wilson, his traveling companion and scout.

The young man looked up from stuffing their jerked meat back in his saddle bags. "But we're in Comanche country, Mr. Loving. Best to travel at night. And besides, you promised Mr. Goodnight we'd not travel in the daytime."

The older man scowled and said, "Darn it, Billy. I'm here and he ain't and I say we gain ground when and where we can. We haven't seen hide nor hair of those damnable Comanches anyway, and even if we did, I swear you and me could keep 'em at bay with a few well-placed rounds."

The men rode in silence for the next four hours. When midday drew close they stopped near a rocky outcrop. Loving circled it in hopes of scaring up a bit of shade. As Wilson watered his horse from his hat, Loving, still mounted, bounded around the rocky knob, shouting, "Billy, they're on us! Comanches!" As he raced by, Wilson mounted and stabbed heels at his horse's belly.

As they kicked up hard dust, Wilson risked a look over his shoulder. A party of a dozen mounted Comanche were close enough now that he could hear their hooting, angry cries. Three arrows sailed by, one close enough that he felt it slice the air beside his head. He bent low and drew his pistol, snapping off shots, and galloped after Loving, not far in the lead. It was then he noticed the two arrows wagging from Loving's leg.

Wilson saw that the older man was headed for a riverbank, a decent spot from which to launch a defense against the attacks. When he got there he and the horse nearly flew over the edge of the dry wash. Loving had hastily lashed his reins to a stub of mesquite. He was on his back, his rifle and pistol in hand. Wilson noticed Loving's horse quivering, a bloodied rear haunch drawn up. Loving's face shone waxy-white and he looked up at Wilson from staring at the arrows in his leg. A blood trail led from the horse to Loving.

Throughout the afternoon they repelled three attacks, but by then it was apparent to them both that they would not last the night.

"You have to go back to the herd, tell Goodnight I'll meet up with him in Fort Sumner. And I'll have the contract bids, too." He winked, his face now ashen and pasted with sweat.

"No sir, Mr. Loving. I'll not leave you here with the Comanche circling like buzzards."

The older man ignored him and said, "Once it's full dark, you'll ride back to the herd. But ride like the devil himself is on your tail!"

Wilson opened his mouth to protest but Loving said, "It's the only way, Billy boy. I'll make it yet. I'm a tough old bird and it'll take a sight more than a couple of unruly Comanche to stop me from selling off that herd."

"He never should have traveled by day. I told him that much. He's as stubborn as a three-legged mule."

Scot Moore nodded at the big man standing before him, his unkempt beard streaked with grey. He guessed this was as close as he or anyone would ever get to seeing Charles Goodnight shed a tear. There was never any doubt in Moore's eyes that the cattleman felt a deep bond with the man who lay dying in the next room—Oliver Loving, Goodnight's business partner and best friend. "But how did he get here to Fort Sumner, Mr. Goodnight?"

The big cattleman looked up as if seeing the young man for the first time and sighed. "Billy Wilson rode back to the herd. By the time I got to where he'd been, Oliver was gone. Come to find out he'd been found by Mexican traders. They're the ones who brought him here." He looked back through the doorway, his face wrinkling in concern at what he saw. "He'll die without a doctor, for certain. And even with one . . . I can't get anyone to ride to Las Vegas for the one sawbones within range." He looked up at Moore again and said, "I'd go but I'll not leave his side." Goodnight nearly spat the words, so strong was his conviction that if he did, his friend would die. "I'll pay any sum."

Scot Moore, long a friend of both Loving and Goodnight, shook his head, not believing what he was hearing. "I'll go, Mr. Goodnight. And I don't want any pay."

"No, Scot. That's not what I meant. You just arrived in town and you're all done in."

"No matter. He's my friend, too."

Goodnight stared at the cowhand. "You're serious?"

"Never been more so. But time's wasting."

Goodnight clapped him on the shoulder and, almost smiling, said, "Then let's get you some coffee and a fresh mount."

"I want something, Charles."

Goodnight hadn't realized his partner was awake. He dragged his chair close to Loving's bedside. "What can I get you, Oliver. You thirsty?"

"No, no. Later. Right now I want to make sure you'll do something for me."

"Of course."

The man in bed chuckled, a dry soft, coughing sound. "Just like you to volunteer before the facts are laid out."

Goodnight shifted in his chair, said nothing. Loving continued, "I don't want to be buried in this forsaken place. I want to spend eternity in Texas, dear sweet Texas."

Goodnight sat upright as if insulted. "Don't talk nonsense, Oliver. You're addled. Scot Moore will be here soon with the doctor and you'll be right as rain in no time."

Loving closed his eyes and shook his head. "No, no, Charles. I'm all done in. . . ."

Goodnight rose, knocking over the chair. "Enough of that talk, Loving. And I mean it."

The man in the bed laughed softly again and said, "You'll do it. I know you will."

For a few seconds the room was quiet, then Goodnight said, "Don't be so sure, Oliver."

"I'm sure. I'm the one who doesn't listen to friend's requests, not you. You're steadfast and true, pard."

"You ought not to have ridden in the daylight."

"I know, Charles. I know."

On his breakneck ride through inhospitable Navajo country to retrieve a doctor, Scot Moore dodged numerous bullets, and on the return trip, via wagon, he and the doctor were nearly waylaid several times by hostile warriors. Despite the hardships, they made it through. Unfortunately, Oliver Loving was by then too weak, and died during the surgery.

In the spring of 1868, Charles Goodnight had his best friend's body exhumed in Fort Sumner, New Mexico, where he'd been temporarily buried for the winter, allowing Goodnight to continue with the herd to Colorado. True to his word, Goodnight honored his friend's deathbed wish and brought Oliver Loving's body back to Weatherford, Texas, for burial. Loving, New Mexico, and Loving County, Texas, are named after him.

It is said that Charles Goodnight, famed cattle baron and rancher's rancher, carried a photograph of Oliver Loving with him for years after the event.

The abiding friendship between Oliver Loving and Charles Goodnight served as the inspiration for the Pulitzer Prize-winning novel, Lonesome Dove, *by Larry McMurtry.*

27

NATURAL BORN KILLER

From a near-fatal stabbing of a classmate when he was fourteen, John Wesley Hardin developed a lifelong taste for violent altercation. By his own admittance he would go on to kill forty-four men before his brutal ways caught up with him. In the fall of 1868, as a fifteen-year-old boy, he killed his first man. . . .

The powerful ex-slave's solid arm squeezed tighter around the thin young man's neck. "You had enough, white boy?"

John Wesley Hardin bucked and kicked, flailed like a man afire. He couldn't breathe to respond but if he could he would have told Mage, his uncle's ex-slave, to go to hell. He would never give up, even if it was just a wrestling match for fun. With a last lash out, he grabbed what he could with his free hand.

It was the big black man's face, and he dug in with his fingers, raking the man's nose and broad, smiling cheeks. It worked. Mage released him and jumped to his feet, holding his scratched face and bellowing like an enraged bull. "I'll kill you for that, white boy!"

Hardin felt rough hands on his shirt collar. His uncle, Clabe Holshousen, dragged him and his cousin, Barnett, away from Mage. "You ought to know better than to wrassle with youngsters, anyway." Hardin's uncle pointed off over the sugarcane field and said, "Now get on home, Mage, and cool yourself off."

Early the next morning, with the sun glinting through the trees and the mockingbirds calling far above, Hardin bounced along on his father's horse on the dirt road a few miles from his uncle's place. The scuffle of the previous afternoon was lost in his mind. He was a fifteen-year-old alone on a horse, on a fine promising morning with a Colt .44 rapping lightly against his thigh in its homemade holster. As the road curved, out stepped the big man Mage, a scowl drawing his scratched, menacing features into a frown. He swung hard with a stout stick and said, "Get down off that horse. I'll kill you." And then he snatched the startled horse's bridle.

Hardin said, "Get back, Mage. Leave me be." He drew the pistol. "Or I'll shoot."

The sight of the gun didn't seem to have an effect on Mage, unless it was to enrage him further. He lunged at the youth, the club whistling in close to Hardin's torso. Hardin cocked the pistol and fired at the man's chest. The shot knocked Mage to the ground, but he jerked back upright as if unharmed. Growling, he swung the club again. And again Hardin fired directly at the man's chest. Mage pitched to the ground, only to rise again, angrier than ever, his breath filling his cheeks in great bursts, his teeth gritted. He lunged at the horse, and Hardin fired a third shot into the bloodied chest. This time the man stayed down, writhing and moaning, his bare feet kicking and furrowing the gravel of the road.

On his return home later that day, Hardin's father predicted harsh retaliation for the shooting of a former slave by a member of a fiercely Rebel family. And he was correct. Within days three Union soldiers were sent to arrest young Hardin for the killing of Mage, who died the day after the scuffle. Hardin would shoot and kill those three soldiers, making a total of four men dead by his hand. And so at fifteen, John Wesley Hardin was already a fugitive, a title he grew familiar with at times throughout his life.

"Wes, you look like hell. I'm not so sure lawyerin' agrees with you."

Hardin looked up, red-eyed and squinting, at his friend, local merchant Henry Brown, with whom he was rolling dice at the bar of the Acme Saloon in El Paso. "I've killed men for less than that, Henry."

The men within earshot stopped their own conversations and stood still, not daring to lift their glasses or shift their gazes. To a man they knew who Hardin was, how many men he was alleged to have killed, and what he was capable of. They'd all seen him at various times perform his amazing "border rolls," quick draws, and gun twirling tricks—and the dead shots he'd made drunk or sober through playing cards that he'd later trade for stacks of poker chips or drinks. Men would stand him free drinks just to get one of those signed cards, ragged with bullet holes.

"Aw, I was just funnin' you, Wes."

"I've killed for less than that, too, Henry." Hardin looked up from the dice in his hand and winked quick at his friend, then leaned back to the counter and rolled. The surrounding conversation picked up as his dice tumbled to a stop showing pure luck. Hardin smiled and said, "You've got four sixes to beat, Henry."

Constable John Selman Sr. stepped up behind the gambling lawyer, raised a Colt revolver, and fired. Hardin dropped to the floor, dead. Selman, frenzied by the thought of what he'd done, continued to fire, squeezing off three more rounds, hitting Hardin with two—one in the arm, one in the chest, adding to the other bullet and knife wounds on his body, evidence of a lifetime of violence now drawn to a close.

John Wesley Hardin's legacy of death by smoking gun remains a point of fascination to this day for anyone interested in the history of the Old West. The killer's fierce reputation was well earned. It is true that he shot and killed a man for snoring. It is also true that Wild Bill Hickok, while a lawman in Abilene, Kansas, ignored his own law and allowed Hardin to keep his guns in town. He even caroused with the young killer, probably because Hardin was visibly enamored of Hickok's reputation.

Hardin was dogged for years by the Texas Rangers, several members of which he had killed in various altercations, and in 1877, while traveling on a train under an alias, he was captured by the Rangers. Hardin drew his pistol but it tangled in his braces. The arresting Ranger knocked the killer unconscious without firing a shot. In prison Hardin finished a law degree, and when he was released sixteen years later, he set up a practice, but it was not to last. Drinking and gambling became his preoccupations.

On August 19, 1895, in El Paso, Texas, while gambling with friends, Hardin was shot by corrupt local constable John Selman Sr., following a verbal altercation earlier in the day. The legendary killer was well and truly dead, killed by a man Hardin himself had hired to kill someone else—the jealous husband of a woman with whom Hardin had an affair. Despite this abrupt end, Hardin is remembered as one of the worst of the West's bad men.

28

GRAND CANYON HELL RIDE

On May 24, 1869, one-armed adventurer John Wesley Powell and nine companions launched four oak boats on the Green River in Wyoming. They hoped to be the first to travel, map, and collect geologic specimens from the length of the Green and Colorado Rivers through the Grand Canyon. But as the months wore on, each vicious rapid ride brought the men closer to hopelessness, starvation, and death.

John Wesley Powell stood on the graveled beach downstream from his men, water pooling about his boots. Before him the Green and Grand Rivers converged to form the Colorado, flowing swift but calm. The sun would be gone from view in another quarter hour, but right now, despite the day's travails, the world seemed a serene place. The canyon walls glowed honey-gold. He thought of his dear wife, Emma, and pushed down his emotions.

A slight breeze waved his empty right sleeve, reminding him of Shiloh seven years before. He closed his eyes and was again on the battlefield, the smoke filling his nostrils, the whistle and whine of bullets overhead, the screams of men all about him . . . He'd raised his arm to signal the order to fire, and agonizing pain coursed through his body. He staggered backward through the mud.

Powell inhaled deeply and opened his eyes. A laugh from the men reached him. It had taken them two months to travel 375 miles, and they'd only just arrived at the Colorado River. The party of ten he'd started with, himself included, had dwindled to nine—a man hiked out after one of the oak boats Powell designed had swamped one too many times, scaring the man into leaving the expedition early. Since then they'd permanently lost to the river's whims one boat, along with the crucial supplies—including cooking gear, guns, instruments, and food. Unexpected rapids and falls confounded them at every turn, and they were often forced to portage.

And now they had arrived at the Colorado, Powell's ultimate goal. This main braid of the famous river was unmapped territory and he was anxious to get to it. He walked back to the rock on which he'd rested his sextant and, pushing away thoughts of the past, of his wife, flipped open his tablet and scratched notes of the day's events.

He had predicted that the rapids would gradually ease and their travel would become safer the deeper they floated into the canyon. Instead, the river became a more turbulent, roiling snake with each passing day. They continued to suffer rollovers and, as a result, their foodstores became molded and spoiled. All this meant little to him when compared with the geologic treasure trove through which they traveled.

Powell collected fossils, explaining their significance to the men. Their own budding fascination with the landscape grew accordingly. They paused so that he might sketch a massive, beehive-like nesting mound populated with swallows, and he taught the men the intricacies of the various pieces of scientific equipment. This had the benefit of both engaging them even more in the expedition and of relieving him of duties he would have had to attend to himself. They were good companions, forever working to compensate for his lessened abilities due to his lost arm.

This paid off weeks before when Powell had scrambled and slipped down a rock face to retrieve what looked to be a promising fossil. But he'd found himself hopelessly stranded and in danger of slipping off the sheer face hundreds of feet above the wide, turbulent river. George Bradley, ever reliable, acted swiftly by lowering a set of long johns. Powell grabbed hold with his good arm, his precious fossil wedged deep in his trouser pocket.

By the time they reached the Grand Canyon on July 16, nearly two months after they began, morale was at its lowest ebb, although the level of danger was higher than ever. The river was lined with unbroken rock walls rising skyward hundreds of feet on either side. They often drifted for hours through stretches

Photograph of Powell's boat and chair by John K. Hillers. One-armed adventurer John Wesley Powell and his crew bucked the Colorado's rapids for months. Powell's seat was little more than a common wooden chair lashed to the deck. *Courtesy Library of Congress*

where sunlight didn't reach them. As they fought to maintain stability in the increasingly violent water, their exhaustion was more evident with every dip of the oars. Each day they struggled to bail out the three battered, leaking vessels. Their clothes were sodden and ripped, their boots slopping and tattered, and their food stores were mostly molded. Each day some unseen force seemed to undermine the trip, and while Powell didn't believe in such things, he resented the hardships.

In mid-August the men entered the most strenuous and demanding stretch yet of the canyon. Sheer walls rose straight up, lost in the mist, and at their base offered no sandy pull-outs where they might rest. When they finally found a place to spend a night, three of the men, after supping on near-raw dough balls and dried apples, announced they were leaving in the morning. Powell felt certain that, according to his maps and calculations, this hardship could not last much longer.

"Men, I beg of you to reconsider," he told them. "By my calculations we're nearly there." But he secretly doubted himself. He had also predicted that once they entered the canyon stretch of the Colorado, the river would gradually become smoother, the rowing easier, and the once-numerous rapids would disappear altogether. But the opposite had happened, and the seemingly impassable stretches of violent rapids reared their heads with increasing frequency.

That last meal together was a silent affair, and he knew his words fell on deaf ears. Powell spent a sleepless night, recalculating and taking stock of their meager stores of food—meat hadn't passed their lips in weeks. But come morning he still could not persuade the three men to remain with the group. They felt sure that a possible slow death by starvation was more preferable than a guaranteed quick death by drowning in the vicious whitewater they were convinced lay ahead.

Powell gave one man copies of some of his notes and a letter for his wife, for he knew there was the whisper of truth in the men's argument for abandoning the venture. Another remaining man entrusted a silver pocket watch to them to be given to his brother back east. The men took dough balls with them, shook hands all around, and scrambled up the steep but passable trail. As they climbed out of the canyon, the six remaining souls bid the three good luck, then readied themselves and their boats for the coming labors.

Later that day the men on the river once again nearly died. They lost sight of one man whose boat had been pulled into a roiling stretch of rapids. He popped up downstream, waving to them, but the relief was short-lived: In seconds his situation turned dire as the boat was nearly sucked from beneath him. Three men launched a second boat and drifted down the deadly stretch after him. But they, too, swamped in the boiling, crashing rapids. It was only by luck that they avoided serious injury on the hidden boulders. That night the six remaining adventurers slept as though dead, though they did dream of their cohorts and wished them well in their overland journey.

The following day, barely twenty-four hours after their three friends departed from them, the six adventurers drifted unexpectedly out of the canyon on a fine, clear stretch of river. Just downstream they came upon three men and a boy fishing. They had made it down the Colorado and through the Grand Canyon—the first men to do so. They had traveled one thousand miles in ninety-eight days.

Within days after emerging from the Grand Canyon, Powell headed back east and into the history books. Before leaving the Colorado Plateau country, he found out that his three companions who had hiked up out of the canyon mere days before had been murdered by angry Shivwit Indians who mistook them for a pair of whites who had killed a woman from their tribe. The Indians refused to believe that anyone could have come from out of the canyon because, they said, no one ever had.

John Wesley Powell, who had been reported as dead by all the eastern newspapers, was received with amazement and celebrated as a national hero. He embarked on a lecture circuit, recounting the trek and displaying elaborate sketches of the natural wonders they'd witnessed. Much of what he related to crowds was met with astonishment, if not skepticism. He published a book about his adventure, and in 1871 outfitted a second expedition to repeat the journey. This time he brought along a photographer.

Powell went on to write more books about the distinctive features of his beloved Colorado Plateau. In 1875 he relocated to Washington, D.C. as an administrator and founder of the U.S. Geologic Survey, an organization he later headed for thirteen years.

29

COLORADO CANNIBAL

In early April of 1874, thirty-one-year-old Alferd Packer emerged from Colorado's San Juan Mountains. He'd last been seen in the company of five ill-equipped prospectors in February, leaving the Ute camp of Chief Ouray. The five were later found murdered and partially consumed.

If I can just convince these gold hunters that I'm half the guide I'd like to be, I'll have a job for the winter and maybe a place in the diggings come spring, thought Alferd Packer. He fingered the few coins in his trouser pocket and stood a little straighter while a rugged fellow named Shannon Bell looked him up and down.

"We're looking to get through the mountains right away, it being November, and this being Utah. No sense sitting here waiting for spring. By that time every two-bit rock hound will already be there."

From what Packer could see, the group of twenty-one men facing him were just what Bell had described, but he kept his tongue in his mouth. No sense blowing another job before it even started. It had been a rum run of things, no mistake. Twice booted from the Union Army for epilepsy, he thought. And here he'd been a scout for Custer.

"I understand that sentiment and I agree with you," he told Bell. "Happens that I know my way through the San Juans. I figure we can make it to the Indian Agency in Saguache by mid-winter, if we get a head of steam on sooner than later."

Bell stared at him for a moment, then said, "I like the way you think, Packer. You're hired. Now let's set down and figure out this expedition."

"No, no, we did the right thing. That Ute Chief Ouray meant well but he doesn't realize that it's first-come, first-serve at the diggings. And I can smell the gold from here." Packer laughed and adjusted his bulky load. He wished the Utes could have spared more food, but with the weather as severe as it had gotten, they were lucky to have gotten anything at all. He had to admit the chief had something about waiting. As this was only January, this snow wasn't going away any time soon. But waiting there with the rest of the original group meant months with no pay. If these six were willing to chance a crossing, he was, too. For good or ill.

"I thought you said you were a guide," said Bell, eyeing Packer.

"I am. But that doesn't mean I won't try my hand at a little prospecting, now, does it?" He laughed again, but the leader just stared him down.

"Not sure I trust you, Packer. Not so sure that listening to you has been one of the wisest decisions we've made." Bell looked at the other four men, but they weren't paying attention. They were busy struggling through the waist-high snow, their gaunt faces straining with each half-step gained.

"Now let me see if I understand you, Packer. You mean to tell me that four of the men died of exposure, so you and the other two ate off them?" The eyes of General Charles Adams, supervisor of the Los Pinos Indian Agency at Saguache, bored into Alferd, but he only nodded.

"And then two of the remaining men, let's see," the General slid papers around in front of him on the desk, then looked up again over his half-glasses. "Shannon Bell, he shot a fellow named California something-or-other and then you shot Bell in self defense? And then you ate him?"

"It was a long winter. I tried to leave, but the snow turned me back every day for weeks." Packer shifted in his chair and looked down at his legs.

"How do you account for the fact that you initially told us that you became separated from them and were surprised to find they hadn't yet arrived in town? Despite the fact that you strolled down out of the San Juans looking fit, packing cash, wallets other than your own, and valuables belonging to your companions? And then you had the nerve to ask for whiskey . . . before you asked for food!"

Packer opened his mouth to speak, but the general beat him to it. "And how do you explain the strips of human flesh that Indian guide found along the trail?"

"I didn't think folks'd believe me."

"Which part?"

Packer opened his mouth again, but the General held up a big hand. "So you just lingered in our saloons and drank and lied, and lied some more." The General lowered his glasses to the end of his nose and regarded Packer. "Sheriff, take him back to his cell. I'll withhold sentencing until I hear what news the search party returns with."

Minutes later, Packer sat on the thin bunk in his cell and knew he couldn't be here when the search party returned from the mountains. What they most likely would find would contradict his statement. No sir, he'd wait until night, then make a move. He drew from an inner pocket of his trousers a small pen knife and set to work on the cell's flimsy lock.

If it hadn't been for that damned Frenchy Carbazon recognizing my laugh in that saloon, I'd still be a free man like I was for nine years, ever since I escaped from that joke of a jail at the Indian Agency, thought Alferd Packer as he sat listening to the judge. Curse me for a laugher. Joke wasn't even that good. Couldn't have been—I don't remember it. And I could surely use a joke, now that they've saddled me with a second jury trial.

"Mr. Packer," said the judge. "You have heard the testimony of various people, among them Mr. Nutter who found the bodies of five men clustered in a group, their skulls bashed in and meat carved from them. He was ready to testify as to his discovery of this grisly scene. But that was nine years ago and you had vanished from the prison at Saguache, picked the lock, I'm told with a pen knife, and fled, living for the following years under the name John Schwartze."

Alferd Packer nodded, regarded the twelve-man jury, and said nothing. But he felt their doubt. This time I'm in it for sure, he thought. Should have stayed in my cell and kept quiet.

"Mr. Packer, it is my opinion, and that of the jury, that you killed those five men while they slept, then robbed them and ate of their flesh . . . to save your own skin. And because your first trial two years ago was found unsuitable, owing to the fact that Colorado was a territory at the time of your crimes, we have acted on your request for a new trial. And while we were at it we also

Alferd Packer, prisoner #1389, in his first penitentiary photograph, 1883. In 1874, Alferd Packer wandered out of Colorado's San Juan Mountains well fed and with cash in his pockets. His five companions were later found partially consumed.

Courtesy Colorado State Archives

decided to try you for all five murders, this time on the charges of voluntary manslaughter. And it is my duty to report that you have been found guilty of all five murders."

The judge continued talking but Packer was interested in only one thing: How long would he serve? And before long he heard the judge give him eight years per man, for a total of forty years. Considering I'm now forty-four in this year of 1886, I'll be long dead before those forty years are up, he thought as he shuffled past the rows of spectators and out of the courthouse, his leg irons clanking on the hardwood floor.

"You hungry now, you son of a bitch?"

He wasn't sure who said it, but he thought it might be the jailer walking beside him. The man had been crabby all day, looking at Alferd as if he were a tin of milk gone off in the heat.

"Not much now," said Packer, one corner of his mouth raised in a slight smile. "But maybe later."

Though he contradicted himself in various confessions and testimonies over the years, it's now largely accepted that Alferd "Alfred" Packer, who used various spellings of his given name throughout his life, did indeed partake in the consumption of his fellows' flesh and probably murdered them in their sleep—whether in self defense, to rob them, or out of hunger, the world may never know.

Packer received various sentences at his subsequent trials, from death to forty years, but he only spent fifteen years in prison, though he was never pardoned for the crimes of murder for which he was convicted. Released in 1901, he was a physically weakened man suffering from various illnesses including Bright's Disease. He died on April 23, 1907. His last words reportedly were, "I'm not guilty of the charge."

Packer is today memorialized in various ways, from museum displays and roadside attractions to songs, films, books, a musical, and through the University of Colorado at Boulder's Alferd Packer Memorial Grill, where the motto is, "Have a friend for lunch."

30

ACES AND EIGHTS

On August 2, 1876, James Butler "Wild Bill" Hickok was playing poker in Nuttall & Mann's No. 10 Saloon, in Deadwood, Dakota Territory. He sat uncharacteristically with his back to the door. . . .

James Butler Hickok blinked hard to focus on his cards. He thought he'd quit the game after this hand. He'd been up all night riding bareback on a nag of a losing streak and he wanted some shuteye. Red Dill dealt him a second card and Hickok felt that creeping feeling come over him like a shade being drawn over a bright window. That's how it happened, more and more these past few years. Especially since Coe. That cursed Phil Coe in Abilene. If only Hickok had not made the mistake of shooting his own deputy marshal Mike Williams, too, he might not have lost that job.

It had been an accident, pure accident. And yet, no matter how many times he was told that, it still didn't change anything. Coe might have been a bad man and he himself might have been the marshal of the town, but Coe was a Texan, and a well-liked one at that, lawbreaker or no. Hickok had been a marked man since that day. He knew it was just a matter of time before his own death crept up on him and pulled him under.

He'd even written to his wife, Agnes Thatcher Lake, a retired circus proprietor, of his prescient feeling of impending death: "Agnes Darling, if such should be we never meet again, while firing my last shot, I will gently breathe the name of my wife—Agnes—and with wishes even for my enemies I will make the plunge and try to swim to the other shore."

"Bill . . . Wild Bill?"

He focused on the face saying his name. Tinhorn Toby.

"You still with us or what?"

Hickok took in a deep breath, let it out slowly, and said, "Course. Deal 'em up." He downed the last of the whiskey in the glass in front of him and poured again. Drive away death one way or another.

The dealer passed a third card. Wild Bill slid it toward himself and worked it around with the rest, not really looking at them, thinking instead of how much easier all this living had been when he was a green lad. Sure, that bear hadn't been an easy thing to deal with, but he'd killed it. He smiled and grunted at the memory.

They'd found him badly mauled, with that great, shaggy grizzly sprawled atop him. But he'd by God killed it with his knife and gun. He'd been a bit tender and off his feed for a time afterward, working at the Rock Creek freight station in Nebraska while he recovered.

Then that McCanles had taken to calling him "Duck Bill," on account of his protruding lip. He'd vowed to grow moustaches to avoid such names in the future, though he had to say that his looks didn't seem to stop the girls from showing their affections. But that McCanles had goaded him too far. So later that day, he'd waited inside the station for McCanles, then got the drop on him, and shot him dead. Shot his two friends, too, though they had to be finished off. The station master's wife had done for one of them with her garden hoe. Another feisty woman. Not unlike Calamity—a bit rough, but gold-hearted.

Hickok sighed. Seemed like life was nothing but a long line of drunks in saloons who needed locking up. And women. And gambling debt. Always that. Unbidden, he recalled July 21, 1865. The quick-draw showdown on the main street of Springfield, Missouri. Over a gold pocket watch. And a woman. At seventy-five yards, Tutt missed Hickok. Wild Bill took careful aim, steadied his right hand with his left, and shot Tutt in the heart. Now that had been good shooting.

"Look, Hickok, I don't want anyone saying I took advantage of you while you were glassy-eyed and dreaming."

Wild Bill focused on the dealer, Red Dill, and smiled. "Don't you worry 'bout old Wild Bill. If you fellas weep too hard I believe I have a kerchief here to help swab your tears." His smile faded. "Now deal out the cards and let's have at it."

The batwings swung in and boots sounded on the floor. They all turned their heads, mostly out of habit, to see who'd entered. Just like cattle, Hickok thought, as he resisted the urge to look. He'd sat with his back to the room and vowed that before the next hand he'd switch seats. He was not feeling much like himself lately, and that galled him, too. He never sat with his back to the door. He was losing his edge, losing his sight, losing his money, hell, he'd probably lose his life if he wasn't careful.

"Let's have that last card, Dill. I am here to play poker, not gawp at strangers."

Behind them the bartender said, "Well, look what the cat dragged in. What's the news, McCall?"

While Hickok waited for his fifth and final card to be dealt him, no one paid much attention to the man who walked up to the table. Poker was a spectator sport, after all. Even on a quiet day such as this, there was always someone to watch others win, lose, or draw.

Hickok snaked a hand out on the baize surface of the playing table, waiting for his last card. He heard the boots stop just behind him and heard the throaty clicking of a hammer ratcheting back into the deadliest position of all. He had just enough time to close his eyes.

Despite the mythology surrounding the man known as James Butler "Wild Bill" Hickok—from his dime-novel name of "Prince of the Pistoleers" to his own claims of having killed "upwards of one hundred men,"—Wild Bill was the genuine frontier article, a gunfighter almost without peer. He was respected by the many famous individuals he worked and rode with in his life, among them General George A. Custer and Buffalo Bill Cody.

As a scout and a guide, it was said that Hickok was effective, well-liked, and supremely competent. Cody said that each morning in camp, Hickok would practice his shooting with his Colt Model 1851s. Wild Bill was ambidextrous and could shoot as well with either hand (frequently with both at the same time), attested to by the way he wore his guns—in a dashing red sash with the pistols butt-forward in cross draw fashion. He was also famed for his coolness under fire and his ability to defuse tense situations, all attributes that served him well in his roles as a lawman in various rough towns throughout the West.

Ignoring increasing feelings of doom during a card game on August 2, 1876, James B. "Wild Bill" Hickok broke one of his personal rules and sat with his back to a saloon door. *Courtesy National Archives*

When he was shot in the back of the head by Jack McCall, he'd not yet been dealt his fifth card, and was left holding what forever after will be known as the "Dead Man's Hand," or two aces and two eights.

McCall, allegedly angry with Hickok over a gambling debt, was initially acquitted of the crime of murder. But then he bragged about the killing and was retried. The second time he was found guilty, hanged on March 1, 1877, and buried with the noose still about his neck.

31

CUSTER'S COMEUPPANCE

On June 25, 1876, Lieutenant Colonel George Armstrong Custer's Seventh Cavalry, a model of poor timing, poor decision making, poorly conveyed instructions, and severe underestimation of its enemy, met with an angry gathering of Plains Indians. Organized and powerful, Sitting Bull's Lakota Sioux and their allies helped set the stage for a savage battle of historic proportions.

It was a good day, beginning cool but with a clear sky and the promise of heat. Black Elk's father roused him from sleep to take the horses out to the pasture. But he was a weak-willed boy and the heat soon convinced him to swim in the river. He left the horses with a cousin and joined his older brother and friends for a swim. It was not long before they heard the warning shouts of the Hunkpapas. From high in the trees came a slapping sound like bugs being swatted. Even though it was but his thirteenth summer, the boy knew the sound of bullets tearing through bankside cottonwoods. They were under attack.

Black Elk's brother burst from the water and ran toward the sounds of battle. Shortly after, their father found Black Elk and gave him two pistols, instructing him to take one to his brother and then go back to camp. But when Black Elk found the fight, and saw the Sioux warriors led by Black Moon, he lost all thought of returning home.

Within minutes his cousin, Crazy Horse, thundered amidst them, drawing wild shrieks of praise from the gathered Sioux warriors. As a group they urged their horses forward. Black Elk was never happier in his young life than to be among them.

"Take that scalp!" It was Iron Tree speaking to the boy, pointing his long, bleeding arm at a blue soldier, twisting on the ground. The soldier moaned and kicked. His chest and side were ripped open and his innards glistened slick like those of a freshly killed deer.

Black Elk slid down from the horse and, with warriors all about him, felt as though he had swallowed meadow mice. The warriors looked at him as they rode by. Still he smiled. He could not help it. He pulled loose his knife and snatched the blue soldier's hair. It was the color of the horse, brown like mud. The man looked at him, his eyes forced open by the young man's grip, and his mouth worked like that of a fish. No sound, only bloody bubbles, came out.

Black Elk set to the task, pride swelling his chest. But it was more difficult than he had always dreamed it would be. The skin was tough, and the man made barking noises now and kicked more furiously. Black Elk put his knee to the man's chest, pushed it into his wound, but the scalp still would not come free and his knife, he knew now, was not sharp. He tossed it to the ground, stood up, and drew his pistol.

He pulled back on the mechanism as his father had taught him to do and aimed the weapon at the frantic bleeding man's forehead. He pulled the trigger. It was the most powerful medicine he had ever seen. The man was now gone to his own spirit world.

Black Elk dropped to his knees, his excitement causing his hands to shake. He did not dare look around him for fear of Black Moon or even Crazy Horse catching sight of him, a young warrior, taking so long at such a task. But his renewed vigor made the rest of the task quick. Within seconds he had swung himself onto the horse's back and whooped in triumph as he held aloft his first scalp, blood of the white man running down his arm. It felt like bugs on his skin or rain on a hot day. It felt good. The best feeling ever, perhaps.

He wheeled the horse back toward the village. With twenty paces still to go he jumped from the horse and ran to his mother, who was standing at the door to the lodge. She did not look happy with him. He lowered his head slightly and offered the scalp to her. She grasped the knot of bloody hair and shrieked her pride to the world. This was a boy who had disobeyed his father's wishes. But this was also a warrior who had taken his first scalp—a cavalry scalp—at thirteen years of age.

They had traveled from Fort Ellis with Colonel Gibbon. They had pressed hard, but had only just drawn close to where the Sioux were supposed to be camped on the Little Big Horn River. It was June 27, a whole day later than they'd been told they were to meet there. An emissary from Colonel Benteen rode out to meet them. Some of the men guessed the news was not good, because after that no one told them to pick up the pace. Then word spread around that Custer had been a whole day early. But what that meant wasn't made known to them.

"Hope ol' Iron Butt left some for us."

An officer spun in his saddle. "Who said that?" No one answered.

They walked in silence for a few minutes, then the smell reached them. It was the most unpleasant odor most of them had ever encountered. "What is that godawful stink?"

The same officer spun again. His eyes were hard and he was ready to bark at the young man who spoke. Then he swallowed and said, "That's the smell of death, Corporal."

"Injun, sir?"

The officer stared at him a moment, then shook his head. Within minutes the men knew what he meant. Spread before them, as if they were lounging in the sun, lay hundreds of men and horses. Many were stripped bare, some were skinned, split open. Their bellies, arms, and legs were all swollen, arching the bodies in unnatural positions. Carrion birds circled low. There were soldiers walking among the bodies, faces covered with kerchiefs.

The newly arrived troops soon learned whose company the men belonged to. And none of them believed it, even when his body was pointed out to them, stretched flat and covered with a blanket.

"I can't believe it's him. I can't believe he didn't whup the damned Sioux." Corporal Schmidt shook his head and leaned on his shovel.

"Yeah well, keep on diggin' while you're flapping your gums." Corporal Ryerson glanced at his companion as he bent down for another shovelful. "Because if Lieutenant Nichols catches you leaning like that, he'll put you on wagon duty. And with my luck I'll get throwed in with you, and then we'll both be heftin' dead soldiers."

"That's a terrible thing to say."

"I know. That's why I don't want to do anything but dig these here graves. Stink ain't so bad down here in a hole."

For a few minutes they pitched dirt in silence, then Schmidt said, "They fouled a lot of the bodies." Ryerson said nothing, just kept digging.

Lieutenant Colonel George Armstrong Custer severely underestimated Sitting Bull's Lakota Sioux and their allies at Little Bighorn, and paid the ultimate price. *Courtesy Library of Congress*

Schmidt continued, "Cut off fingers, noses, ears—even their rigs and sacks! Scalped a pile of 'em, too." He stopped again and leaned on the shovel. "Why, Driscoll told me there's bodies there they still ain't found heads for."

"Uh huh. Keep diggin', Schmidt. You can work and talk, can't you?"

Schmidt bent to his task, then said, "I still can't believe they got him."

Ryerson stopped, mopped his forehead and neck with his kerchief. "Just a man, like the rest of us."

"Yeah, but he was Custer."

Ryerson resumed digging the grave. "Yeah, I know."

The Battle at Little Bighorn has gained epic status in the consciousness of America, largely because it could have been prevented. What we know of the actual battle, however, is spotty because no U.S. soldier was left alive on the battlefield—the sole surviving member of Custer's party was Comanche, a captain's horse. Countless historians have spent the intervening years rebuilding the battle, though it is widely agreed that Lieutenant Colonel George Armstrong Custer made a series of poor tactical choices that resulted, in less than two hours, in the deaths of 210 officers, enlisted men, scouts, and civilians. Among them were five members of Custer's family, including Custer himself, two of his brothers, a nephew, and a brother-in-law.

The testimonies of the many Sioux warriors who participated in the battle provide a unique insight into an otherwise silent chapter of history. Black Elk, a young Oglala Sioux warrior at the Battle of Greasy Grass River (the Sioux name for the fight at Little Bighorn), would endure many more battles and hardships in the decades to come. Fourteen years after Greasy Grass, he survived the Battle of Wounded Knee and, in his later years, came to be a respected sage of the Oglala.

32

NO MORE FOREVER

In the summer and fall of 1877, fewer than seven hundred Nez Percé, of which less than two hundred were warriors, traveled for 1,700 miles across five states—Oregon, Washington, Idaho, Wyoming, and Montana—battling, humiliating, and evading more than two thousand cavalrymen.

We are not there yet."

Chief Looking Glass turned to face the speaker. It was his fellow Nez Percé chief, Joseph. "I know," he said, prodding the little fire in the middle of the tepee with a stick. "You forget I am the one who suggested this route. I am the one who has traveled the Lolo in search of buffalo. Not you."

"I know this. But we are beyond the Lolo now. We are at the place the whites call Big Hole Valley."

Looking Glass stood fast and faced his visitor. "I know where we are. Is this not a good place? General Howard is days behind us. We must rest the horses."

"Yes, but you heard Pile of Clouds. He said—"

"I know, Joseph. He said, 'Death is on our trail.'" The two men were silent for a few moments, then Looking Glass said, "Perhaps he is too old to share such medicine." He faced Chief Joseph, his eyebrows raised. "It is a good night, is it not? Surely there cannot be death on such a night."

Joseph wanted to smile, but he could not. He nodded. "Yes. It is a good night." He left the tepee, nodded to Looking Glass's first wife, and went to his own tepee.

When he awoke before dawn, Joseph was surprised that he had slept so well. That had not happened in many moons. Not since before they fled their home in July. If they could stay ahead of the persistent General Howard and his men, they might yet make it to Canada.

Still, they had traveled too far south. Even White Bird agreed. If they could but make it to Canada, perhaps they might reach their old enemies, the

Sioux. Sitting Bull was a reasonable leader. He might come to their assistance. He drew in a deep breath and sat up. His wife nursed the little girl, born the day of the march's beginning. Some of the tribe whispered that this was a bad omen. He chose to believe the birth of new life at the very beginning of their journey meant goodness and promise for the trail ahead.

He stood and stretched, the urge to relieve himself great. He touched the top of his wife's head briefly and reached for the tepee flap. Soft splashes from the stream flowing beside the camp gave him pause. He traded looks with his wife and, crouching, poked his head through the flap. Within seconds shouts of the few early risers sounded throughout the silent camp. The sun had not yet crested the trees and yet people were running by, clattering and shouting. Cavalrymen.

All about him warriors ran from their tents. Rifle shots filled the air. Angry shouts, screams of pain, the barking orders of the aggressors mingled with the neighing of horses. In the dim light of early morning, even as he scrambled for his rifle, he saw the bluecoats slamming through the water, weapons held aloft, some of them shooting before they reached the camp. Others, it seemed hundreds, were already swarming through the camp, firing at unarmed Nez Percé, some of them warriors, some of them women dragging their children. He saw his own nephew and sister receiving a clubbing from a burly, bearded cavalryman. Joseph aimed and fired, slumping the fat brute as he was poised to deal a death blow to the staring child.

Joseph's people fled in all directions away from the camp. It seemed to him they were all shot or clubbed or run down by the devils in blue. Five Wounds, swaying in a daze and blood flowering across his skull from a clubbing, was shot three times that Joseph saw before crumpling.

Joseph dashed between tepees, crouching in the dwindling shadows, shooting when he was sure of the form at which he aimed. From behind him, he heard his wife cry out his name in pain. She had made it to the edge of the camp but was now, even as he raced to her side, prone and holding tight to their infant daughter. He touched his wife's face, saw the pleading in her eyes. He left her there and snatched the child up. Shots snapped in the trees behind him. He crouched low, the uneven ground causing him to stumble, his baby daughter screaming in his arms.

Even as he ran, cradling his child, he caught sight of cavalrymen stomping babies' heads, clubbing running children. Anger such as he had never known

In the summer and fall of 1877, Chief Joseph led his people on a 1,700-mile trek across five states in a last attempt at freedom. *Courtesy Library of Congress*

rose in Joseph. Here were the whites he had been trying so desperately for months, for years, to avoid, to protect even in debates with his fellow Nez Percé chiefs. After all that work and ridicule and suffering, for it all to come to this.

It did not take long for Joseph to find White Bird and Looking Glass. From the eastern end of the camp, they could tell, as the day dawned brighter, that the soldiers were not as organized nor as strong a force as they should have been. Looking Glass sent a party of warriors across the river while the rest of the men worked back toward the camp. They now trapped the soldiers in a volley of crossfire.

The soldiers slowed their attack, grew more wary, and scrambled for anything that might protect them from the double-edged assault. Before them, from the east, warriors advanced, while from behind, across the river, they were sniped at by more Nez Percé. Most of the remaining soldiers managed a ragged retreat.

In the confusion following the attack, Joseph sought his children and wives. He'd left his infant with the wife of a fellow warrior, knowing she would be safe, but he was desperate to find his wounded wife. She was near where he left her, injured but alive. She stared up at him, worry in her eyes.

"Our child is well," he said, forcing a smile for her. She closed her eyes and nodded. Joseph left her, trusting her to the Great Spirit, and went to help his people. The wailing sounds of their grief accompanied them on their way out of what seemed such a peaceful little valley. They left much of their camp, taking with them only what they felt they would need. They walked as hurriedly as their wounds and grief would allow.

It was painful to watch family members leave the bodies of their slain mothers, fathers, babies. There was nothing Joseph could do but share with them the grief, the pain.

His younger brother, Ollikut, rallied a small band of fellow warriors, all of whom were sharpshooters, to stay behind for the day and night following the attack, to stop the soldiers from pursuing and harassing the weakened people further. The number of dead staggered Chief Joseph as if he'd suffered each death himself. Eighty-nine Nez Percé were gone, among them only twelve warriors. The rest were children, women, and old men.

Worst of all was the news that Red Echo, Five Wounds, and Rainbow were killed in the attack. Three vital chiefs. Joseph knew he was no strategist, but now their council of decision-makers had been reduced to him, White Cloud, and Looking Glass.

On October 5, 1877, two months after the Battle of the Big Hole, Chief Joseph surrendered to General Howard. He stood in a valley in Montana's Bears Paw Mountains just forty miles from the Canadian border and, surrounded by his starving people, he closed his now-famous impassioned speech with the words: "Hear me, my chiefs! I am tired. My heart is sick and sad. From where the sun now stands I will fight no more forever."

Many remaining Nez Percé were brought to a reservation in Oklahoma, dying in squalid conditions of epidemic diseases. Never allowed to return to his homeland, Chief Joseph died on September 21, 1904, on a reservation in Washington Territory. The doctor attending him said the chief died of a broken heart.

33

FATHER AGAINST SON

Bass Reeves was born into slavery, ran away to live with the Seminole and Creek Indians, and in 1875 became a U.S. Deputy Marshal, the first Black American to hold such a commission west of the Mississippi. He would go on to become one of the most revered lawmen in the United States. Though he was never shot himself, he did kill fourteen men, was responsible for three thousand arrests, and was known as a dogged tracker and man hunter, even when he had to track and arrest his own son for murder.

We're having troubles, Daddy." The young man, a smaller, more youthful version of the graying man with him, set down his glass of Forty-Rod and looked across the table at his father.

The big man stared straight back at his son. "Go on, son." He was close to the boy like no other of his five sons and five daughters. They had no secrets, shared many of the same passions, and enjoyed each other's company.

The young man swallowed, licked his lips, and said, "You know I got that new job, right?"

His father nodded.

"Well, I did that so I could be closer to home. She said I been working too much."

They were quiet a moment, then his father said, "That all?"

The young man sipped again, set his glass down on the worn wood of the little table, and said, "I come home early one day from the old job, to talk with her, you know. . . ."

His father nodded, sipped.

"And I caught her with . . . with one of them Williams brothers. J. P. is his name." His voice shook and he pushed a thumb and forefinger into his eyes. "I forgave her." He pulled his hand away from his damp eyes and said, "What would you have done, Daddy?"

Bass Reeves set down his empty glass and sucked the last of the fiery liquid through his teeth. He smoothed his big moustaches, looked straight into his son's eyes, and said, "I'd have shot the hell out of the man and whipped the living God out of her."

"Bass, I know you've been away from Muskogee for a couple of weeks. . . ."

"Yes, Marshal."

Marshal Bennett looked like he'd bit into a knob of pure salt. "Bass, something's happened."

The tall man splayed his fingertips on his boss's desk and said, "What is it, Marshal?"

Bennett said, "Aw, hell," and tossed a writ across the desk toward Reeves.

Reeves stood up, holding the paper. "You know I can't read, Marshal," he said in a low voice.

Bennett stood up and said, "I forgot. It's a writ."

"I can see that. For who?"

"It's for your son, Bass. For Benny."

"Benny?" Bass just stared at Bennett.

"Bass, no one here wants to take this on. At least without you knowing first."

Bass straightened, stretched his back, rasped a massive hand over his stubbled jaw, and said, "I'll bring him in."

"No, Bass. That isn't right."

"He's my son. I'll bring him in. Now, tell me what happened."

The boy would go to the hills in Indian Nation. Bass knew this as sure as he knew his own name. But to kill the girl? How bad could it have been? Had he caught her at it again? And what about that advice he'd given him. Bass cursed himself. How dumb could he be—he as good as told him if it was his situation he would have killed the man and beat the wife. Not good, Bass, he thought. Not good at all.

He urged the sorrel on. This reminded him of the trail he'd followed on Bob Dozier a few years before. The most wanted outlaw in Indian Territory and no one could track him. But this trail was the only thing his son had in common with Bob Dozier.

That man had been pure evil. He'd eluded Judge Parker's deputies for years. But he hadn't reckoned on being dogged by Bass Reeves. Bass half-smiled as he rode through the low, rolling hills, recalling that fine and final confrontation. He'd had a one-man posse with him, and they'd been closer than any lawman had ever gotten to that thieving, torturing, murdering Dozier.

Closed in on him all day and then, when they were about an hour behind him and his unknown partner, the sky darkened and lightning shafted down, wedging the blue-black skies and bringing on rain that washed out the scant trail.

Before long, full dark came on, quicker than usual, and Reeves and his man had looked for a dry spot to bed down, pick up the trail in the morning. They'd ridden down a ravine and into a stand of trees when a gunshot between lightning strikes split the air. Bass felt it zip by his right ear. He and his man dove off their horses, scrambled low for the trees.

In the next lightning flash, Bass saw a man off to his left hurry from one tree to between two others nearby. Bass fired twice at the spot and saw a form drop. One down, but his position was now known to the second man. As if timed with that thought, two shots cracked close by while lightning lit the scene. Bass pitched forward and onto his side, splashing heavily in the mud, the rain pelting down.

He was facing the shooter. He heard a laugh, saw the man step out from behind a tree, and in another flash recognized him as Dozier. The outlaw laughed long and loud when he saw Reeves, the famous lawman, prone in the mud. Bass waited until the killer was a few yards from him, then rolled up onto an elbow and shouted. "Drop the gun!"

Dozier's laugh choked to a halt and for a moment he just stared at the dead man who'd drawn a gun on him. Then he growled and dropped to one knee, raising his pistol. But Reeves squeezed the Colt's trigger and Dozier stiffened, dead from the bullet that passed through his neck.

Born a slave, Bass Reeves went on to become the nation's first black U.S. Deputy Marshal, arresting three thousand individuals in his long career. *Courtesy Western History Collections, University of Oklahoma Libraries*

His horse perked its ears and stared ahead, the slight movement pulling Reeves from his daydream. Two-and-a-half days into Indian Territory, Bass got that twinge in his gut and knew something was bound to happen soon. The trail was dusty, the sun beating down hard, and the sorrel was poking along slower than he'd like, but there was no hurry now. They rounded a boulder and there ahead of him stood his son, Benny, looking thin but rested, on the leaning porch of an old shanty. "Daddy. I thought you might come." The boy's saddled horse was tied close by, nosing the sparse grass.

Bass nodded, said, "Benny."

The two regarded each other for a moment, almost as if they were sharing a drink on the back porch. "I have to bring you in, Benny."

"I know." Benny stepped down off the porch. His father dismounted and they shook hands, hugged.

"Got coffee?"

"Won't take a minute."

"Good." Bass led his horse toward the shack and tied it near the boy's mount.

A half-hour later, Benny packed his few possessions, then he stepped back and held out his hands, palms down.

"What's this?" said Bass.

"For the shackles."

"No, Benny. That's not necessary."

The young man shook his hands once and said, "Yes it is. I've done wrong and you have a job to do. And a reputation to uphold. I expect no special treatment."

Bass Reeves straightened and stared at this young man, his son, then turned away for a moment, coughed, fiddling in his saddle bag, and pulled out a pair of handcuffs. "Mount up, then we'll put them on. Easier that way."

Benny did go to the federal penitentiary at Leavenworth, Kansas, for killing his wife. He proved to be a model prisoner and as word got out in his hometown of Muskogee about the nature of his crime, citizens started a petition to have him pardoned. People signed on the basis that he was the son of Bass

Reeves. "He's got the blood," they'd say. In time, Benny Reeves was pardoned, returned to Muskogee, and became a barber.

Bass Reeves was one of the most successful Old West lawmen, respected by the citizenry and his fellow peace officers. He was regarded as a family man, affable, and a sure shot who never gave up the chase. He was fluent in a handful of Indian languages and often operated alone, donning disguises and feigning ignorance to trick his quarry.

In thirty-five years on the job, Reeves was shot at numerous times—his reins were shot in two, his hat was shot from his head, his belt buckle was hit, buttons were shot from his shirt—but he was never struck by a bullet. He also never fired until he was drawn on.

In his later years, Reeves said that bringing in his son to stand trial for murder was the hardest thing he'd ever done.

34

LIKE A FREIGHT TRAIN

In the fall of 1880, Yellowstone's second superintendent, Philetus W. Norris, pursued a large, troublesome grizzly in the park. He attracted the bruin with the entrails of two freshly killed elk and opened fire on the massive male. The first shot dropped the beast—then it rose and bore down on him, closing the gap to within yards. . . .

The horse was barely recognizable as a horse anymore. But the sign associated with it—the savaged carcass, ripped apart as if by knives and mostly devoured, the piles of dirt and leaves—showed it was but one thing: a griz. And not just any griz, but the very beast Philetus Norris had been tracking. From the tracks at the various kill sites he'd found in the vicinity, it appeared a massive foe. If he could run it down, it would be his sixth grizzly of the season.

Elk were one thing, but a lamed horse—and one of his crew's best animals, recovering from a scalding in fire holes—was entirely something else. He had to track and kill this bear, for it was becoming far too familiar for Norris's taste. It was also a personal task. This was the first horse lost on his watch since he took over as Yellowstone Park's second-ever superintendent two years before, in 1877.

A couple of weeks later, Norris found himself trudging through fall snow that at times reached his knees. Cresting a knoll just off the rim of Beaver Lake, he spied two well-racked bull elk within a hundred yards, close by one another, pawing the snow in search of sustenance.

Knowing the target of his hunt was in the vicinity, he concocted a quick plan to attract the bear. Shouldering his Winchester, he dropped the two elk in rapid succession, then made his way down toward them even as the echo of his last shot rolled through the valley. He busied himself with gutting the warm elk, suddenly aware of the coming night, cursing the short daylight hours of autumn even as he slid out the steaming entrails of each fresh carcass.

With his trap laid, Norris retreated one hundred yards to await his visitor. It was a mostly sleepless night for him, knowing a potential record-size grizzly haunted the vicinity, and he only a short distance from the scene of ample fresh kills. Unnerving, even for a man of his long experience.

Norris dozed fitfully and was snapped awake by a rustling and the unmistakable heavy chuffing of a bear busy eating. In the day's early light, Norris peered toward the elk carcasses. There was his bear—had to be. It seemed heavier than a horse and massive in every way possible. The great head itself was down, busy nosing at something, while the beast's haunches rippled with its rich fur. It pawed and dug, busily covering the elk with earth. Norris noted that the bear had dragged one carcass closer to the other so that they were nearly side-by-side.

He rose slowly to a knee and lifted the Winchester, which he had triple-checked to ensure it was fully loaded: fourteen rounds and a special explosive shell in the chute, ready to fly. If they didn't do the trick at this distance, nothing would. And my hunting days will be over, thought Norris.

He drew in crisp breath silently through his nostrils, then slowly let it out as he snugged the stock to his cheek. Dead-on shot, he thought, and touched off the trigger. It caught the mighty bruin high on the shoulder. From the jolting impact, Norris knew it had done the necessary damage, probably severed the beast's spine. The bear dropped and Norris's suspicions were confirmed.

Then the bear bolted up as if jabbed with a bayonet and roared out his shock and pain. Before the bear could swing around Norris pumped four .44-caliber bullets into the same spot on the wounded animal. With each impact the animal staggered and dropped, then rose again. In its bawling, swinging rage, the big boar griz finally fastened his eyes on Norris—and bolted straight at him.

The park superintendent felt his heart hammering at the walls of his chest and throat. He gritted his teeth and worked at thumbing in a second dynamite shell. The massive grizzly's charge was a flat-out run, its impossibly wide head held low, the maw bellowing, curved fangs glinting through bloody froth, front legs pawing the snowed earth, the great curving claws lashing and clicking with each stride.

At fifty yards and closing fast, Norris aimed at the bulk of the hurtling furred mass and pulled the trigger. The explosive bullet caught the bear in the throat and shattered the beast's lungs. The kingly creature's front legs crumpled and his maw drove forward, furrowing the snow, its back end piling in a heap. Still groaning and chuffing, the grizzly pushed himself upright yet again. And Norris fired once more, breaking the bear's neck with another shell. The bear collapsed and the shoulder hump wagged its last as the animal came to rest, yards from the man.

Taking no chances, Norris plied the still form with .44 shells without let-up until no more cracking reports came. The echo of his last shot eventually washed away over the surrounding hills, as jarring sounds will, and a shocked stillness clung to the lakeside scene.

Norris held his pose, rifle tight to his shoulder, and touched the trigger one last time. It clicked on nothing. Slowly he pulled his face from the stock and let out the breath he'd been holding since the bear rose and charged. He stood from his kneeling position and finally lowered the rifle, but kept a firm grip on it. He knew the bear was dead, of course. It had to be—he'd pumped in more than a dozen regular shells and two exploding dynamite shells. But any creature that could rise again and again after being shot—in the shoulder, the lungs, and the spine—deserved nothing but caution.

Later, Norris and one of his employees, Stephens, loaded up their pack animals with as much of the elk and bear as they could carry and trudged twenty miles back to their base at Mammoth Hot Springs, at the park's northern end.

The two men spread the bear's hide flat and found it to measure nearly nine feet from snout tip to tail base, and six feet, seven inches wide. "This has to be a record, Phil," said Stephens, measuring for a third time and shaking his head.

"Wait until you render his blubber down, Stephens," said Norris with a wink. "Bound to be a whole lot of it."

When Stephens did render the fat of the beast, he ended up with thirty-five gallons of bear grease. "What do you think of that?" he said to his boss with a hint of pride at a job well done.

Yellowstone Park Superintendent Philetus W. Norris nodded, eyebrows raised, and said, "I'd say I shot one big bear." And as he watched Stephens pretend to be perturbed, an unbidden vision of the massive, roaring maw and slashing teeth barreling straight for him flashed in his mind's eye, and his smile faded.

In his line of work as Yellowstone's superintendent (1877–1882), Philetus W. Norris routinely faced massive grizzlies. One unstoppable brute almost got the better of him.

Courtesy National Park Service

In addition to bison, mountain lions, and grey wolves, grizzly bears are some of the most well-known (and threatened) creatures to inhabit Yellowstone National Park. There are currently approximately six hundred representatives of Ursus arctos horribilus *in the Greater Yellowstone Ecosystem, with roughly half that number residing within the park itself. Two hundred years ago grizzlies could be found throughout a wide region of the lower forty-eight states, and numbered an estimated fifty thousand.*

35

TOMBSTONE GUNDOWN

At 3:00 p.m. on Wednesday, October 26, 1881, in Tombstone, Arizona, thirty shots were fired in thirty seconds. When the gun smoke parted and people dared peek through shattered windows, three men were dead and three men were injured. And that was only the beginning.

In the waning daylight cast in squares on the floor of the little chamber that he'd come to accept would be his dying room, as soon as the pneumonia got its leg up and over him, Virgil Earp looked at his useless left arm lying limp on the quilt and let out a slow, rattling breath. All those years ago—twenty-four, if he figured right—that town had marked the entire Earp family for life. And death. The only one who'd come out of it whole was Wyatt, though judging from the fire in his eyes years later, he was as marked as any of them.

So many gunfights, so much killing and anger, and all for what? Money, money, power, greed. Steal this, steal that, see who could be the top dog. It had been a big pissing contest and no one really had come out the winner. At least not among the Earps and Clantons and McLaurys. And Doc Holliday, too. Most of 'em dead and gone now. Virgil chuckled, and the chuckle turned into a wracking cough that sent Allie in to rub more of her damnable liniment on his chest. Oh, for a chance at those days again. He'd do things a little differently, to be sure.

As he closed his eyes and sank back in his bed—it felt as though he were drawing breath through a pinched length of straw—Virgil Earp drifted back to their days in Tombstone. Three sets of brothers, two sides of the story, and one gunfight. In the end, that's about what it amounted to. Still, that little ragged town had seemed so right when they first got there—everything was new and shiny and full of promise. Tombstone had the potential to be the place the Earps could really gain some ground, set down roots, and make a whole lot of money. And it was happening, too, almost without effort it had seemed at times. Wyatt was a natural hand at dealing faro, so much so that he owned interest in the Oriental.

For all the hubbub made over it since, it had been a short fight, over in a half-minute. He sighed again, and not for the first time replayed every one of the short seconds of the fight.

He and Morgan and Wyatt and Doc Holliday had braced the McLaurys and Clantons in that little empty house lot—hell, it couldn't have been more than twenty-feet wide—and before he could tell them to hand over their guns, Billy Clanton and Frank McLaury had cocked their pistols, still undrawn.

"Hold! I want those guns!" Virgil had shouted at them. There were words sneered back by one of them, but the cowboys opened that ball, make no mistake.

Virgil had seen Billy draw on Wyatt and he'd pulled his hog leg out to end that rascal's life, but Morgan beat him to it. A good shot, their young brother had been, for he downed Billy, though not for good. He'd shot Billy's hand, then sent another into the whimpering man's breadbox.

Whether Wyatt knew Billy had pulled on him or not, he didn't seem to care, as he drew, cool as you please—just like Wyatt—and plugged Frank McLaury square in the gut. Then Tom McLaury had flung wide his coat and shouted, "I have nothing!" And Virgil had been sorely tempted to plug him anyway, and he fully expected to do it, for Tom McLaury had at the same time angled himself, grabbing like a half-squashed spider for a rifle hanging from his brother Frank's horse. He missed the rifle and instead crouched down behind the beast.

Virgil gritted his teeth and shook his head in the silent, grey room, head back against that pillow, as he thought of the fight. He could smell the powder, the haze of steel-colored smoke piling up as if a locomotive had torn through the alleyway.

Still, it amused Virgil, even after all these years, to think that the worst of the bunch, that rascal Ike Clanton, had come to the ball unheeled—just like the coward he was. And yet, as he'd seen Wyatt drill Frank, Ike dove at Wyatt, grabbing. Virgil had heard later that Ike claimed he was trying to stop the fight, but Virgil knew better—the coward wanted an Earp's head for shooting his brother, Billy. Virgil gave his brother the credit due him, Wyatt knew his attacker was unarmed and pushed Ike away, barking, "Go to fighting or get away!" Clanton scampered toward the nearest hidey-hole—the side door of the photography gallery of Camillus Fly—same spot that simpering Behan was holed up, ducking for cover. Before he reached the door Doc peppered at him with a blast from the shotgun. Doc missed him, but threw a goodly scare into his worthless hide.

Virgil had to admit that for a sickly drunk, Doc had sand like no man he'd met in all his days. And a fierce loyalty to Wyatt. Virgil hadn't particularly liked having the rogue around so much—he was a known outlaw—as his presence cast a devil of a glow on Virgil's attempts to build up an air of lawfulness in Tombstone. But to give the man his due, Doc had ridden with Wyatt, tracking the duplicitous cowboys, until his sickness had laid him low. A man couldn't ask any more of a friend than to be true to the end.

And then the horse behind which Tom McLaury had been hiding left that rogue high and dry. Doc opened fire with a shotgun blast that ripped into Tom, who staggered off down the street before collapsing in a bleeding pile.

But Frank McLaury and Billy Clanton, though both mortally wounded, had mustered strength enough to continue their deadly fusillade. And that's when Virgil felt the hot pain of a bullet in his leg. He'd collapsed because of that damnable Billy Clanton, near dead and still squeezing out lead.

Bad as he felt, Virgil had seen Frank McLaury, already sorely wounded by Wyatt's first shot, draw and fire at Doc Holliday. Three shots blended—Doc's and Morgan's dropped Frank for good while Frank's shot clipped Doc in the hip. Somehow, Billy Clanton still had strength enough to shoot—even as Wyatt and Morgan sent two more rounds into the gasping wreck. As he lay slumped there against the house, with his last bullet he managed to shoot Morgan in the shoulder. And still Billy lived. As he moaned and bled in the dirt, Virgil clutching his wounded calf, saw the photographer, Fly, come out of his shop and gently pull away Billy's pistol. Clanton didn't have the strength God gave a baby . . . and yet he begged for more cartridges. And Billy'd been the one who didn't want any more gun play, who'd tried to send his hot-headed, cowardly brother, Ike, home.

One of the most infamous gunfights in the Old West was also one of the most complex. It sported all the pieces to guarantee infamy: Warring factions like modern-day rival gangs (most members of which were proficient with their weapons of choice); public sentiment divided roughly equally in opposing favors; and all set in the most aptly named town imaginable: Tombstone.

And yet, the very name of the fight itself—the Gunfight at the OK Corral—is a misnomer. The thirty-second clash actually took place in a vacant lot between a business and a private home up the street from the infamous corral, and was but the first in a series of bloody gun battles between the Earps and the Clanton-McLaury Gang.

After the shootout, tensions between the factions increased until Wyatt Earp, Doc Holliday, and a handful of supporters set the law aside and rode down some of their rivals. In the end, Wyatt Earp outlived them all, surviving nearly another half-century, dying in 1929, at the age of eighty.

36

STAMPEDE!

In the late spring of 1882, with the age of the great cattle drives in full swing, the popular Doan's Crossing on the Red River, Texas, was a point of increasing congestion as more herds than ever used the spot to cross. An average-size herd, from two to three thousand animals, was difficult enough to control, but when eleven sizable herds, plus several herds of horses, and a thunder, lightning, and rain storm straight from hell came together on one particular day. . . .

For as far as Harlan Sykes could see, tens of thousands of head, primarily longhorns, were stretched for miles in every direction. He and the rest of the hands had done what they could, hoping to keep the herds separated. Boss had told him there were eleven cattle herds, three or more horse herds, and Lord only knew how many hands all doing the same thing he was—trying to keep the herds from mixing and getting agitated. Crossing was its usual slow process, made even more difficult by all the recent spring rains—Sykes heard one old-timer say the river was as swollen as he'd ever seen it. As the day progressed, a dark storm front, sky-wide and full of foreboding, drifted in over the valley.

By mid-afternoon nothing for miles held even the memory of being dry.

"If ever there was a time I'd gladly trade places with a shopkeeper, it's now," Harlan Sykes shouted out from under his sagged Boss of the Plains hat to his compadre, Julian Copper.

"What'd you say? I can't hear a lick, I swear the sky's fixing to drop straight down on our heads."

"You boys," it was the trail boss, Red Tonidas. "Break up the hen party and keep them leaders in sight. Any sign of trouble and I want to see this herd millin' tight and hard, you hear me?" He wheeled away and disappeared in a curtain of battering rain.

Both men shouted "Yessir!" even as they reined away from each other. But it was too late. The last of the day's light fell away and vicious shafts of silver lightning rent the very air about them. And in the time it took for the lightning to strike and thunder to crack, thousands of longhorns, their horns clacking and smacking others, stampeded, driven by the most base and unreasoning fear a creature can know, spurred on by the elements, the unfamiliarity of their surroundings, the multiplied deafening sound of their own bellows, the pounding of their hooves, the deep dark of the storming night slashed wide and bright at random moments—these reasons and more sped the flight of the eleven herds and forced them into one roiling mass of thirty-three thousand head of berserk cattle.

Boss Belcher hollered at the men—his and any others within hearing range—until his throat throbbed with the effort. "Let 'em scatter! Good God in heaven, boys, let 'em scatter. If you don't, they'll stomp each other sure as we're soakin' wet!" He rode hard and fast, cutting close to the mass of confused beasts, the great hooking horns slashing every which way, to get within shouting distance of any cowboy he could reach. Saving their lives, and as many head of the owner's property as they could, was the point.

This night couldn't last forever, he knew, but it damn sure as hell could last all night. His greatest fear was finding a yellow slicker in the morning, stomped and trampled into the mud. He'd been on plenty of stampedes. They were always a matter of when, and not if, on the trail.

Mixed in with the raging herd, Belcher saw terrified horses rearing and screaming for their own kind, searching for a way out of the crowd. Their heightened frenzies only served to stir up the cattle to greater confusions.

In a slashing flash of lightning, Belcher watched a chuck wagon, not ten yards to his left, collapse under the thundering mass. The sounds of the pelting rain, of the shouting cowboys, the drumming hooves nearly drowned out the cracking and crunching of the wagon's wood. Whoever that Cooky was, Belcher prayed he made it out in time.

Already he rode around downed cattle and horses gored and trampled, flopping in the mud, their bodies glistening and flayed open. Belcher knew the morning would bring to light miles of devastation, death, mud, grief, and work. Lots of work.

Seemingly anything could set a quiet herd of cattle running, from a sudden storm to bad singing. *Courtesy Library of Congress*

As dawn broke, and for as far as Belcher could see, the only steady visible movement came from cowboys on horseback, some with heads bobbing against their chests, their horses' heads not much higher, trudging around the edges of the now-stalled cattle.

The last clouds shunted past the distant cliffs. The river, engorged with pulsing brown water, flowed thick and strong southward. Between the river and the cliffs, for miles up and down the plateau, scattered cattle slept, ambled, or grazed already-nubbed grass.

"Where in hell's that Mexican?"

Belcher turned in the saddle to see a thin man with a bloodied rag wrapped around his topknot, a battered and filthy hat hung over one shoulder by a neck thong. "He's the cause of this damnable mess." The man looked up to see Belcher staring at him. "Just who are you?"

"I aim to ask you the same question, mister," said Belcher.

"Well I am the ramrod of the Circle Q."

"I'm a boss, too. No need to get your craw in a twist."

"You seen a Mexican?"

"Are you kidding? We're in Texas. Who do you expect to see?"

"This one works for me. Or he did. If the cattle didn't kill him, I will."

"Why?"

"Well he caused this mess, didn't he?"

"I think it had a little something to do with that storm, the bunching up of too many herds in too slight a space—lots of things. But one Mexican? Not so sure about that."

"He tried to turn 'em with his six gun. Of all the fool things. . . ."

Belcher shook his head and urged his mount into a lope. That boss took a helluva knock to think one man could be responsible for this. No doubt he was right about the gun—a smart cowboy never used a gunshot to rout a herd. Just made it worse. But any shots fired last night were drowned by all the other sounds of devastation that spring up on a stampede. And it would be a long time before he could forget them.

As he loped slowly to where it all began, miles downriver, he passed steer after steer, most of them longhorns, plus the odd horse here and there, stomped beyond meaning into the grime, their hides peeled from their bodies and pinned back into the mud as if by a buffalo skinner. No sir, he wouldn't forget that night for a long time to come.

It took 120 cowboys ten days to sort the thirty-three thousand head scattered in the stampede. Thousands of head of cattle, dozens of horses, and several men all lost their lives in the confusion.

It has been said that there are many (and, at the same time, no) excuses for a stampede, or "stompede," as the cowboys called them. It has been observed that even something as slight as a cowboy hitting a wrong note while singing to the beasts could cause a herd to bolt in bellowing confusion, oftentimes running for miles.

Stampedes, Indian attacks, rustlers, severe weather, and drowning were just a few of the many hazards a cowboy could face on the trail. It usually took two to three months to drive an average herd north, for which a typical cowboy could expect forty dollars per month, payable on the successful completion of the drive. Crew on drives consisted of a trail boss—oftentimes the herd's owner—plus a dozen or so cow hands who each required an average of six horses. In addition there was a horse wrangler and the cook, who also drove the chuck wagon and acted as barber, dentist, and doctor for the crew.

The herd typically covered ten to fifteen miles per day. Any faster and the cattle would lose precious weight by the time the herd reached the railhead, and the hoped-for forty dollars per head would diminish. After the Civil War and up to the turn of the century, approximately ten million head of cattle were herded from Texas north to the Kansas railheads for shipment by train to massive stockyards in Chicago. From there the meat made its way all over the country, though its largest market was the east coast, where Texas beef was held in high regard.

37

MASS HANGING

On December 8, 1883, five men descended on the general store in the mining-rich town of Bisbee, Arizona, waving pistols and demanding the payroll of the Copper Queen Mine from the store's vault. Chaos ensued, and four innocent shoppers—including a pregnant woman—were laid low. The murdering thieves were tracked down and brought to Tombstone.

Open the vault, now, or you're going to die right here in your damn store!"

A woman moaned audibly. One of the five gunmen, busy yanking a man's watch free from his vest pocket, spun on her and said, "Shut your mouth, woman. You shut it. And give me that ring."

"There's nothing in the vault," said the merchant, skittering his eyes over the four customers and five gunmen.

The gunmen all exchanged quick glances, then the rapid-breathing man holding the gun on the merchant thumbed back the hammer and said, "I'll be the judge of that. Now open it."

The merchant nodded fast, his hands shaking as if palsied, and dropped to his knees before the waist-high safe.

Finally, after what seemed a lifetime, the heavy safe door slowly swung outward. The gunman wagged the pistol at the kneeling merchant, who scrambled backward. The gunman peered into the safe, pulled out a handful of folded documents, several held closed with sealing wax, and yelled, "He wasn't fooling, boys. This here vault's empty as Heith's promises—"

"No names, you fool!"

The man at the safe spun on his cohort and said, "What'd you say? You callin' me a fool?" He raised the gun at him and sneered, breathing hard through his nose.

"Okay now, okay, the situation's got everyone feeling nervous. It's okay, it's okay. Let the lady go. She's due to have a baby."

The gunman from the vault spun on the speaker, a deputy sheriff, and shouted, "Shut your mouth!" He thrust the weapon at the man as if to emphasize his words and the pistol barked flame. The deputy's head snapped backward and he fell flat on the floor, twitching and gurgling.

"Oh god no, god no. I didn't mean to do that. I just wanted him to stop shouting. I needed to think. Oh god, what's going to happen now? Oh god, Heith never said this would happen. Oh Heith, you son of a bitch."

The woman beside him screamed and put her hands to her face. Another captive, the man who had lost his gold pocket watch, stepped forward and shouted, "You will pay for this!" his fat, pink hand balled in a fist, one thick digit almost touching the gunman's chest. "You will pay for this with your life. This atrocity will not go unpunished by the good citizens of Bisbee."

"Like hell." The gunman raised his pistol, cocked it, and shot the fat man in the neck, then in the chest. The woman continued to scream. He turned and shot her as well, catching her in the face, the shoulder, and the gut.

His cohorts were screaming and trying to get close enough to make him stop. But they didn't dare. He was like a different person. Never had they seen him so brutal.

At 8:30 on the morning of February 22, 1884, Sheriff Ward heard a soft knocking on the door of the Tombstone courthouse that led to the jail corridor. "Now that'll be the Chinaman with breakfast. I expect it'll be the last meal you get that'll be worth anything, Heith. When I heard the judge yesterday pass sentence of life at Yuma Territorial for you, I thought to myself, 'That boy ain't going to be eating too good for a while.'"

John Heith didn't respond. He just stared at the stone floor of the cell.

The sheriff opened the corridor door with a smile and seven men stared at him with guns drawn. "Give us the keys to the cell," said one. Ward did as requested since he wasn't in a position to overpower so many men. Within minutes the group led the prisoner out of the jail. When the sheriff followed them outside, he was faced with what looked to be 150 men. He pleaded with them to stop for the sake of the law, but they shook their heads, moved the sheriff off to the side, and proceeded to lead Heith by a rope through the crowd and down the street. The mass moved at a lope, the condemned man keeping up with them.

As he was urged forward with threats and nudges, and as he saw the faces of the men who surrounded him (hemming him in, making sure he wasn't going to run for it but half hoping he might), he knew this was well and truly the end of the line. He noted the grimy necks and ears of the miners in front of him, the worn elbows of the threadbare suit coats, the trousers held up with twine, boots that had seen better days, and he knew this wasn't being done just for the killings the other five had done at the store. This was also for the attempt to steal their money, their paychecks, their livelihoods, and he felt a deeper shame than he had even in the court-room when it had all been spelled out for him. And yet, this wasn't right. The judge had given him to life in prison, but it at least had been life. What they were about to do was not right.

And before he could think more on the matter, the crowd stopped before a tall telegraph pole at the corner of First and Toughnut Streets. Already a thin young man was shinnying up the pole, tossing a rope over the cross piece.

Heith saw himself as if from a distance, and he bent, folding his white handkerchief on his knee, then wrapped it across his eyes. "Someone tie this for me, please." Gentle but firm hands snugged it tight. He kept his eyes closed beneath the kerchief, felt the rope against his neck. Hands secured his own behind his back. His feet were bound together at the ankle and someone steadied him upright.

"You'll find," he shouted, calmly but with force. "when you hang the oth-ers, that I am an innocent man. You are hanging an innocent man." He paused, heard the comments, the jeers, then he spoke again. "I have faced death too often to be afraid, but I ask you this one thing."

"What is it?"

"Please don't shoot into my body."

A voice close by assured him this last wish would be respected. Heith nodded, licked his dry lips, whispered, "I am ready."

It took but a matter of seconds for countless hands to grasp the long rope and make a run with it, raising John Heith high into the air. It felt to him like a lifetime.

For his part as mastermind of the robbery turned murder, John Heith was lynched from a Tombstone telegraph pole by angry citizens. One month later, his five cohorts made the long drop in Arizona's largest mass hanging. *Courtesy Library of Congress*

The coroner attributed John Heith's death to "emphysema, which might have been caused by strangulation, self-inflicted or otherwise." The citizens attached a placard to the telegraph pole that read: "John Heith was hanged to this pole by citizens of Cochise County for participation in the Bisbee massacre as a proved accessory at 8:20 a.m., Feb. 22, 1884 (Washington's Birthday) to advance Arizona."

One month after Arizona's only public lynching, John Heith's five cohorts, all convicted murderers, stood on the specially built gallows and looked out on the assembled mass of outraged citizens one thousand strong. One after the other, the condemned proclaimed their innocence, some tearfully.

Whether by design or by poor planning, the gallows on which the five were hanged failed to perform as expected. Only the neck of one man snapped. The other four strangled to death. One man kicked for ten minutes. The still-outraged public didn't seem to mind. This was the largest mass hanging in Arizona history . . . and it was a well-attended event.

38

STUART'S STRANGLERS

In the summer of 1884, a group of Montana ranchers, weary of the drastic increase in rustling in the Judith Basin of Montana's Bitterroot Valley, took matters into their own hands.

Granville Stuart donned his hat and walked down the path to the bunkhouse, a hot cup of coffee in his hand. Though it was mid-June, there was a bite in the morning air. The sun felt as though it didn't yet want to commit to the day.

"Ted, you want to see me?"

"Morning, Mr. Stuart. I thought you'd want to know they hit again, another dozen steers and seven horses. And not the crow bait, neither."

Stuart sighed and nodded, knowing that his foreman was feeling low about this. But Stuart also knew it was the rustlers and not his men who were to blame. He sipped his coffee. "Ted, I'll need you and a few of the boys to visit our fellow stockmen. We'll have a meeting here, as it's a central location. Come on up to the house, I'll make a list." He turned and started up the path, then stopped, looked at Ted, and said, "This has to stop."

"You can count on me and the boys, Mr. Stuart."

"I know."

William Thompson sat up straight in his saddle, his hand on the butt of his booted rifle. The two men below him were leading seven horses, and three were unmistakably the property of the Stuart-Kohrs operation. Neither of those men were punching for Granville, that much he knew. If he wasn't mistaken they were Narciss Lavardure and Joe Vardner, hard cases both, and neither capable of buying more than a beer let alone seven horses. This had the makings of a dicey situation. "You men there! Halt!"

The two rogues below spun their heads in tandem. Lavardure, in the lead, raised his rifle with speed born of practice, and snapped off a shot at Thompson. But the thief's horse rose in a buck at the same time and the shot fouled, whizzing by Thompson's head.

"You son of a bitch!" Thompson ducked low and put a heel to his bay. The rustlers did the same, and Thompson found himself riding hard downslope to their trail, shucking his rifle and leaning low over the pommel, gritting his teeth against the dust of the nine horses ahead.

Well into their sixth mile, the dust cleared enough that Thompson could close to a safe distance and squeeze a shot from his Winchester. The second man, Vardner, twitched in the saddle as if being shaken awake and pitched sideways with nary a yelp. His mount and the three horses he led continued on at their breakneck pace behind the leading five runners.

Lavardure looked back quickly, then ducked low and kicked harder at his gasping mount. Thompson saw the beast's straining tongue, the foam spittling—the horse and those behind it were losing their steam. Then he saw his opportunity. He dug hard at his bay's barrel and sped ahead, gaining on the coursing mass of horseflesh. Within seconds he closed the gap on Lavardure. Before the flagging rustler could draw on him, Thompson reined hard into him, and rammed the thief hard with his rifle butt.

Lavardure slowed, then stopped. For a moment the men and horses stood still, trembling, dumb with the grit and fatigue of six miles of hard chase. Lavardure inched his hand down toward his sidearm and Thompson raised the rifle a few inches and shook his head. "Get down. Now."

In twenty minutes Thompson had Lavardure trussed up and mounted, and Vardner slung over his own horse. He retraced their route and delivered the stolen horses to their relieved owner, then sequestered the still-tied Lavardure in a stable with a guard at the door.

"Keep your mouth shut until we can get the law out here." Thompson felt his blood rise just looking at the rogue.

In the dark hours of early morning that followed, Lavardure was jerked to wakefulness by the thundering of a dozen horses. Men's voices drew close outside, and lantern light fingered through the slats in the crude siding. The horse thief heard a voice speak to the guard at the stable door. "We're officially overpowering you, Bardoff."

Bardoff chuckled, then said, "Looks like I got no choice."

"Drag him out of there."

Within five minutes, Lavardure was swinging from a corral gate's crossbar, a sign pinned to his coat: "Horse Thief." Stuart's Stranglers were born.

Twenty-four hours later Granville Stuart, William Thompson, and ten other cowboys rode in on two local law-straddlers, Billy Downes and California Ed.

"What say you boys tell us why there's, let's see . . . twenty-six horses in your corral. And with brands from every ranch around but this one." Stuart dismounted and strolled over to a stack of green hides bearing similar brands as the horses. "Oh, and I guess you have an explanation for these, too?"

Downes shouted, veins rising on his neck and temples, "You ain't got no right to be here. No proof to what you say!"

Granville Stuart took in a deep breath, let it out slowly. His fellow riders, local ranchers and ranch hands, all stood quiet, grim-mouthed, watching the two fidgeting rustlers, a pair of lanterns casting wavering light on the tight scene.

"I'd say that's a corral full of proof, let alone that stack of cattle hides, the top one bearing the Stuart-Kohrs brand." He turned to his fellows and said, "Boys, it's time."

The two thieves, clad only in their longhandles, kicked and screamed until their screams were choked off by the taut ratcheting of the ropes about their necks.

"Now, boys, I don't like this any more than you do, but we've all lost too much and we've only dug halfway. It didn't stop with those two thieves the other night. I fear the den's still crawling with the rustling vermin. It's July 8, 1884. We've been at this for a few weeks and, if fortune's with us, here's where it will end." Stuart looked at each of his nine fellow vigilantes in turn. They were with him, he knew, but it didn't hurt to restate their case.

"We're with you, Stuart," said Thompson. They all nodded in assent. "Sun'll be up soon, we best get situated."

Without another word, the men dismounted and left their horses with the young son of a rancher. The remaining eight men crept forward, surrounding the old logging camp at Bates Point. With any luck, thought Stuart, Stringer Jack and the rest of his outlaws will be holed up here. He was looking for one fell swoop to end this madness.

Below them sat a tent and, bare yards away, a ramshackle cabin. As the sun peered above the low, easterly ridge, old man James, whose two sons and nephew were never far away, tottered out to the latrine.

"James! Open that corral and shoo out the horses." As Stuart expected, the old thief froze in his tracks, peering at the trees for the source of the voice.

"Do it now." A hammer clicked back. The old man complied. Then, quicker than they expected of him, he rabbited back to the cabin. Seconds later rifle barrels poked through holes in the cabin's walls. The sharp snap of gunfire echoed across the slow-moving waters of the Missouri.

The tent held more men than they expected, and the three vigilantes covering it soon had their sights full of half-clad torsos, pumping arms, and churning legs as seven rustlers poured out and made for the river and its protective brush line. The bandit leader, Stringer Jack, was shot dead in the attempt. An hour passed, then two vigilantes belly-crawled under protective fire to set aflame a haystack beside the cabin. The dry wood of the structure soon caught fire, succumbing in a roar of sparks and fire, as did the men inside.

Five rustlers remained unaccounted for until Stuart telegraphed to Fort Maginnis, downstream. The fugitives were found on a makeshift raft and arrested two-hundred miles east. The U.S. Marshal charged with their return was waylaid by armed vigilantes, who lynched the five rustlers on the trail.

Within days of the battle at Bates Point, numerous cattle and 284 rustled horses were recovered from around the range. Rustling came to a standstill in Montana for years to come. None of Stuart's Stranglers were ever tried for participation in the cleanup of cattle and horse thieves. Granville Stuart himself always maintained no one else had anything to do with the killings.

In 1879, after several failed attempts, and with the cash of wealthy investors, Granville made a success of large-scale ranching. The Stuart-Kohrs operation grew to be one of the largest and most influential in Montana. In the harsh winter of 1886-1887, however (also known as the Great Die-Up), he lost two-thirds of his stock.

Disheartened, Granville Stuart sold his interest in the ranch. He would go on to many other pursuits, and is today celebrated for his contributions to Montana's history. Among other notable acts, he fought hostile Indians and rustlers, started a school, helped found the Montana Historical Society, and wrote numerous books. In 1894 he became the U.S. Ambassador to Uruguay and Paraguay, and in 1898 returned to his beloved home state. He is often referred to as "Mr. Montana."

39

FRISCO FUSILLADE

From October 29 to October 31, 1884, wet-behind-the-ears lawman Elfego Baca was pitted against eighty perturbed cowboys in the little town of Lower San Francisco Plaza, New Mexico. The showdown lasted thirty-three hours.

addy, what are you doing?" The burly barkeep, Bill Milligan, glared at the lanky little Hispanic with the Colt .45.

"What do you mean?"

"I mean these cowboys will cut you to ribbons if you go waving that thing around in here. And that fool cowpuncher, Charlie McCarty, has done enough damage. Look at my bar!"

Elfego Baca sighed and said, "I thought you wanted help from the law."

"Yes, I do, but if that's you and you alone, then I can tell you now this ain't going to end pretty." Milligan watched Baca, then said, "Him and his pals are all from the John B. Slaughter outfit, and you don't want to tangle with them."

Finally, the young lawman said, "I don't understand you at all. First, you want help. Now you are telling me they will kill me and that I should stay away from them. What is it to be? And besides, I'm not alone. I have three able fellows with me."

Milligan looked past Baca's shoulder and saw three more Hispanic men standing in a cluster by the door. Before the barkeep could answer, another shot cracked the air and sharp fingers of wood splintered out near the ceiling.

"Have at it, lawdog!" said Milligan, slapping a palm on the bar.

Baca watched the drunken McCarty weave toward the back door, then he left by the front. Followed by his three friends, Baca strode quickly around the side of the building in time enough to see the sagging wood door clunk shut on the drunken cowboy's backside. He cocked his Colt and scooted low beside an adobe wall next to the reeking latrine. The stench watered his eyes.

As McCarty stepped out, buttoning his fly with some difficulty, Baca appeared beside him, slipped the man's pistol from his holster, and jammed it in his own trousers.

"You're under arrest. Now don't talk at all. Just walk."

"You can't do this to—"

Baca held up his Colt and wagged it in his hand as if to cool it off. "No talking."

They rounded the corner of the bar building. Two cowboys stood smoking cigarettes not five feet from them on the boardwalk. "Boys," said McCarty. "This runty greaser's done arrested me." He laughed and kept walking.

One of the cowboys, Young Parham, the outfit's foreman, said, "Hey you. Yeah, you, law man. Just what do you think you're doing?"

Elfego Baca continued forward, prodding the weaving man in the back with his pistol barrel. "I am arresting this man for disturbing our peace."

"You can't."

"Talk with the magistrate about it."

Under his breath, Baca motioned one of his friends closer and said, "Where can we keep him until we decide what to do? Those two won't wait much longer."

"There's a house in Middle Plaza belonging to Geronimo Armijo where we can hold him."

Within a half-minute of slamming the house's door behind them, a dozen men from the Slaughter outfit converged on the little adobe house. A tall, fat man with bad teeth kicked at the bottom of the door. "Get on out of there! Let McCarty free or there'll be hell to pay!"

Baca, on the other side of the door, shouted, "Get away from here by the time I count to three or I start shooting."

The laughter of the gathered cowboys brought a smile to Baca's face. He heard one say, "How's he going to count that high?"

Baca backed away from the door, nodded to his three cohorts, inhaled deeply, and shouted, "Onetwothree!" The four armed men inside opened fire, pumping bullets through the wooden door.

Almost immediately they heard a horse whinny and the shouts and screams of a man. Someone said, "Parham! The shots spooked his horse. By God, it fell on him . . . I think he's dead!"

Within hours, Baca was convinced to surrender McCarty, who paid a fine of five dollars. Baca's helpmates also were let go. But Baca remained pinned down in the little house. He'd thought that because they had their own back they might let him go, but then a fat man named Hearne slammed against the door. "I'll get you, you lousy whelp!"

Baca sent two shots through the door. One of them drilled into the big man's guts. The screams froze everyone for a moment, then the noise and dust and danger really began.

The flimsy walls, made of upright sticks slathered in and out with adobe, wobbled with each shot that passed through them. From the time the onslaught began, Baca hunkered flat on the dirt floor, which was a foot-and-a-half lower than the base of the outside walls of the house.

And Baca thanked God for the eighteen inches, for it was saving his life. He had two pistols with which to defend himself, his own Colt and the side-arm he'd taken from the drunken cowboy. Whenever he found an opening, he'd carefully line up a shot, then squeeze the trigger. He'd wounded a handful of men and he knew he had killed that loudmouth Hearne, because his friends had said as much.

The attacks kept up throughout that day and all the next. The little town was lined with shooters ducked behind every available wall and corner. They sniped from atop the church, they ran off the residents and used their homes, and all the while they shot from every direction at the little house. Kerosene-soaked torches were thrown on the brittle dirt-and-wood roof, and part of the building collapsed in a shower of sparks, smoke, and flame. Dark descended on the beleaguered little town. The cowboys figured they'd drag out the body of Elfego Baca from the rubble come morning.

Night passed slowly. As the sun rose the next morning, there didn't seem to be a square inch of the little house left untouched, inside or out. Then the crowd of eighty cowboys saw smoke rising from the battered chimney of the little hovel—and they smelled tortillas warming. Baca not only lived through the attack, he was making himself breakfast.

The shooting began again in earnest.

Later that day a sheriff from Socorro convinced the little man to come out. Baca agreed, but on condition that he be transported back to Socorro in a buckboard, his pistols trained on the mass of angry cowboys trailing thirty feet behind. Due to a misunderstanding, two groups planning ambushes on Baca's wagon failed to attack, each thinking the other had already done the deed.

Although the basic facts of the incident now known as the Frisco Shootout vary slightly with each telling, it is widely accepted that the figures are close to accurate. The little house Baca sought refuge in received up to four thousand rounds of ammunition from the eighty gathered cowboys. The attack lasted between thirty-three and thirty-six hours.

At Baca's trial he was accused of murder. One man died from a bullet to the gut, one received a shot to the knee, and Young Parham, the Slaughter Outfit's foreman, died of injuries sustained when his horse reared and fell on him. Baca claimed in later years that he killed four men and injured another eight during the shootout, though he was never harmed in the fracas.

During the trial Baca was acquitted, in part because the jury was shown a number of items from the incident, among them the house's front door, which received nearly four hundred rounds. Elfego Baca went on to enjoy a long career as a lawman, lawyer, politician, and raconteur. He died in 1945 at the age of eighty, the only man in U.S. history to survive such a one-sided fusillade.

40

WINTERKILL

The winter of 1886–1887 was hard on the West, especially Montana. Following a series of early November blizzards, a ten-day storm blew in on January 9, 1887. Sixteen inches of snow fell in as many hours, and temperatures dropped to forty-six below zero. Cattle froze to death while standing upright and ranch hands perished in vain attempts to rescue stock.

Arlene Barr couldn't see through the cabin's one window. The snow was too high. It had fallen steadily, more or less without let up, since a month before Christmas. And now it was well into the new year. By her count it was either January 18 or 19, 1887.

A soft sound pulled Arlene from the window. It was Ned, their pride and joy, now nearly a year old, born a year after they'd built the place. She stood holding the baby close, sharing its warmth. Her husband, Joseph, pulled on his coat behind her. "I have to go out. Check on the stock. I have to see if there's something I can do." The money for the land, the stock, had come from her father, who owned a woolen mill back home in Maine, but the vision, the dreams, the hopes, they were all Joseph's.

She tried to talk Joseph out of it, but he continued to don the last of his winter gear, including the red and green scarf she'd made him for Christmas. Before leaving he made a face at his baby boy and touched his wife's cheek with a gloved hand. Then he tugged open the door.

Snow. Packed so tight that Joseph had to carve his way through the solid wall of it with the cinder shovel. It took him the better part of an hour to breach the surface. He yelled back to her to shut the door, for the wind was increasing and the snow was steadily falling. "I won't be long. Must check the stock!"

And so she shut the door behind him, reluctantly. Little Ned was already crying from the cold, even bundled in what layers of their spare clothes she could wrap about him.

And as the long hours dragged by and her wood ran low and her baby cried and the storm whistled through the roof, she prayed that Joseph was holed up in the barn.

The next morning, she awoke to silence. The cold stillness of the cabin shocked, then alarmed her. Even her child was silent—but only sleeping the oblivious slumber of babes. The fire had gone out, for instead of tending it and dozing through the night she had lain down just for a moment on their narrow bed. And now it was morning. She knew because light beaconed in at random points at the roofline—the result of the previous night's wind.

"Joseph!" Her whisper was loud in the dark. And there was no answer.

Minutes later she was bundled in as many of his spare clothes as she could find. She covered her hands with socks, three pair, the last being those she had knitted him for Christmas. He'd not worn them yet, said he was "saving them for a special occasion." Silly man.

The digging was easier than she expected because of Joseph's tunnel of the previous day. She broke through, expecting to see him standing over the hole, smiling. When her eyes adjusted to the light, however, she was shocked by what she saw: Drifts of snow had been sculpted by the wind, chiseled into mammoth peaks that resembled artists' versions of the Bears Paw Mountains surrounding their little valley. The very roof of their cabin was topped with a huge, dense drift of glistening snow.

It was finally spring. Kippy McWhorter and Teddy "Blue" Abbot continued to head out each morning. Each day's thaw brought new, gruesome discoveries in every coulee on the range. Their employer, the Stuart-Kohrs operation, was hit hard. The only work they were going to get, if they were interested, was skinning the dead beeves then setting the carcasses alight.

"I don't know how much more of this I can take," said Teddy Blue. "These beasts have plugged the Missouri. Why, if I didn't know they were beeves I'd swear they were logjams."

"You talk too much, Abbott."

"Sure beats ridin' around with a sour look on your face all day."

But the old man didn't respond.

"Hey," said Abbott, shaking out his rope. "You hear me, old dad?" He looked up and followed Kip's gaze to something bright in the river. Red, by the looks of it.

"What is that, Kippy?"

The old man shifted in his saddle, then said, "I can't be sure." He nudged his roan into a walk. "But it could be a man."

"What . . . ?" Teddy followed. Within moments they were on the riverbank staring down at a tangle of bloated cattle still lodged in the ice. Gouts of brown-green water rose over them, and here and there a clean hoof wagged in the current as if waving to them. And there was a red and green . . . something.

"Gimme your rope."

"What's wrong with yours?" said Teddy.

Kip looked at the young man, who handed it over. Teddy's gaze locked on the thing just under the water. It was a man. Had to be.

Once they dislodged the cows, the body freed itself and drifted, rolling and spinning downstream a hundred yards before fetching, face up, on the legs of a shaggy black and white beast.

"Aw hell," said Kip.

"What. You know him?"

The older man nodded and scratched with vigor at his sparse beard. "Mmm. What I thought. That's Joe Barr."

"Oh Lord, I plumb forgot he went missing. Oh Lord, Lord."

"Stop sayin' that. Lord ain't got squat to do with it now."

"Well I guess I disagree."

"Figured you might." Kip slid down the bank and said, "Get down here and help me. This ain't going to be pleasant and I ain't doing it alone."

Within minutes they had dragged him up on shore. He looked to Teddy less like a man and more like a swollen, made-up dummy of a man. Chunks of his face were missing and his fingertips were raw, some to the bone. One foot was bare and part gone, the other still booted. His left leg bent at the knee, but in a way that nature never intended.

"That boy should have stayed back East. And his girl, too. This ain't no place to be for the young."

"What about me?"

Drifting Before the Storm by Frederic Remington, circa 1904. During the winter of 1886–1887, the Great Die-Up, hundreds of thousands of cattle froze to death, and scores of cowboys perished in futile attempts to save the animals. *Courtesy Library of Congress*

"You're different."

"Thanks."

"Take it as you want to. Didn't say it was a compliment. Now quit jawin' and wrap him in your slicker."

"Why mine?"

"Because you're younger and got more chance than me to earn money for a new one."

"Oh."

They laid it down beside the man. "I ain't dressing him."

"No need to. Just let's roll him in it."

After they were done, parts of him still poked out the ends. They tied him tight with lengths of hemp rope and regarded their handiwork.

"He's ripe, Kippy."

"You'd be, too."

"I reckon." They were quiet for a time, then the young man said, "His wife will be relieved. You think?"

"Won't make much difference to her now, boy. Since her baby died when their cabin caved in from that snow load, she's been a crazy woman. Won't let anyone help her."

"How'd you reckon he got all the way over here to the river?"

"Turned around in the blizzard."

"But their place must be a mile or more from here."

"Yep."

"Wasn't much of a way to make a livin'."

"There's a big difference between livin' and survivin', Teddy. Now let's go."

"Where we takin' him?"

"Home. To his wife."

The young man looked back to the river, at the silent dogies clogging the flow, at more of the same littering the banks for as far as he could see. All over the flats on both sides of the river, carcasses lay in piles, exposing gaping wounds chewed by wolves and other scavengers.

"It's going to take a heap of money to rebuild a herd this size."

"Won't happen."

"What do you mean?"

"I mean," said Kip with a sigh, as he leaned on his horse, arms against his saddle. "That Montana's a changed place. Hell, most of the Plains is. Nearly every ranch, from what I've heard, is like this. There ain't hardly no beeves no more. Except dead ones."

"I don't believe it, Kippy." The young man looked at the big vista toward the Bears Paws and shook his head.

"Believe what you like, Teddy. I'm just telling what I heard."

COWBOYS, MOUNTAIN MEN, AND GRIZZLY BEARS

The winter of 1886–1887 saw the loss of hundreds of thousands of animals, mostly cattle, from Montana south to Texas. Following a drought-filled summer, blizzards began in November and continued through February. By the time spring arrived, dead cattle were everywhere—piled against fence lines, stacked in the coulees, clogging rivers. In spring, severe financial hardship and bankruptcy befell even the most solvent ranchers, including a young Theodore Roosevelt. The only populations who prospered that winter were the wolves.

After that devastating year, the face of western cattle ranching changed forever. Smaller, more concentrated outfits sprang up, and the harvesting and storage of winter feed became an industry in itself. It effectively put an end to the free-range system of grazing.

41

HELPLESS

On March 7, 1888, in New Rockford, North Dakota, Mrs. Olson, holding her baby girl, watched from her kitchen window as two-dozen half-starved timber wolves surrounded her young son and husband while they cleared snow from a haystack.

We'll be out there as long as it takes," Franz Olson told his son, Peter, when the boy asked how long they had to work on the haystack. His mother, Callie, understood. He was well into his Christmas present of Cooper's Leatherstocking saga and did not want to put it down.

Franz laid a big, calloused hand on his son's shoulder and said, "We'll be quick about it—your mother's stew is smelling good to me." He winked at the boy and pulled on his mittens. Callie helped them wrap and tie their scarves, then kissed them each on the forehead.

The wind had picked up during the night and with it the snow. But she could still see the barn through the little window beside the door. Franz joked that it was the "stock window" from which he could keep an eye on his empire, which at present consisted of a half-dozen cows, several dozen chickens, a horse, a mule, and six rabbits.

She watched the shapes of her husband and son, each so similar to the other. They worked with the shovels, Franz with the old wooden scoop and Peter with the newer steel scoop, carving out the path that once again had plugged tight with drifted snow. Franz stuck the shotgun, butt first, into the snow. He'd laughed and told Peter it was for Mohicans.

The baby's wail pulled Callie back from the window. She held the crying baby against her shoulder with one arm and worked the wooden spoon through the thick stew with the other, then walked back to the window with Delia to see how her men were progressing.

She had to breathe hard on the frozen glass to see out, but it looked like someone was around the haystack with them. She scratched at the ice and finally could see out again. But what she saw couldn't be real.

For seconds she watched as dark forms, like large dogs, hurtled from out of the snow-filled air at the upright forms of her husband and son. They were surrounded by a pack of wolves! Callie screamed as the dark shapes wavered like ghostly forms through the iced glass. She set the screaming baby in the cradle and rushed back to the window.

She could hear the wolves—and something more, the screams of her son, his voice high-pitched, and her husband's, too, wordless shouts amidst the terrible barking and growling and howling. She saw Franz trying desperately to help their son up onto the low mound of snow that was the haystack, but a large black wolf flew through the air and seized the boy's leg just above the boot. It hung there while Peter screamed, his head thrown back. He lost his grip on the stack and was dragged to the snow, crumpling among the savage beasts.

Eight or ten wolves lunged at the boy. She saw his arms clawing upward, and his wool hat flew out beyond the circle of lunging beasts. Franz dove at them even while two silver and black wolves hung off his back. One of them dragged its way upward toward his head. There must have been a dozen close in, with that many more circling beyond.

Callie grabbed her big carving knife and whipped open the door. Her husband and son were in the midst of a roiling mass of hair and gnashing teeth. The wolves were gaunt looking and desperate in their attack, hurling themselves without care at the two men. Peter and Franz screamed and flailed their arms.

She rushed out beyond the sheltered entryway, screaming at the wolves. Some of the animals noticed her. And at the same time she saw Franz's shotgun, still upright as if at attention, in the drift by the edge of the haystack. She should rush for the gun. But it was hundreds of feet away and there were a dozen wolves between her and the gun. And the shells for the gun would be in her husband's coat pocket.

Franz and Peter had both stopped moving, and still the wolves attacked them. Their slashing and gnashing teeth now dripped blood. She whimpered, and a scream, unbidden, rushed from her throat. Half of the mangy creatures turned to stare at her even while several others fought among themselves, drawing their own blood and whimpering. At least one wolf lay near death.

Several padded toward her, slavering, tongues out, red blood stringing from their panting mouths. Callie backed toward the house. The wolves would be upon her soon—and then where would Delia be? She looked behind her—she had left the door open. My God, they could get in!

The brutal winter of 1887–1888 in the Northern Plains claimed the lives of hundreds of people and caused widespread deprivation in the wild. Predators such as wolves resorted to any food source available. *Courtesy National Park Service*

The closer Callie Olson drew to the house, the faster other wolves, some pulling away from the roiling mass, padded toward her. She glanced behind her once to see how close she was to the door. When she whipped her head back around it seemed the pack had doubled in size. It bore down on her faster than ever.

They were within twenty feet and moving fast, silently, their chests heaving with exertion, their snouts and chest-fur covered in gore. She threw herself backward toward the kitchen door, stumbling into the room just as one large male, his slashing mouth blowing spittle, slipped in the doorway with her. She kicked and pushed at the door and caught the beast's snout hard enough that one of its curved incisors snapped off and spun under the stove. As she pushed against the wooden door, hearing it crack, other heads poked in, and clawed feet scratched and dug at the wood, scrabbling for entry.

Callie Olson hacked with the carving knife, bringing her arm up and down as hard and as fast as she could, severing the twitching black nose of one hellhound and hacking great hunks out of at least two paws. Another snout she cleft deeply. The howls of rage and pain were small solace as she slammed shut the door and slid the wooden safety bar across. But what if Franz or Peter tried to get in? She dropped the bloody knife and ran to the window. Behind her the baby screamed in the cradle.

She scratched at the scrim of ice on the glass pane and saw that her husband and son never would make it to the door. In fact, they hadn't moved from where the wolves had torn them away from the haystack. What was left of them lay prone on the ground before it, their clothes torn away, the snow now a smear of bright red. Through the jumping, whining, and howling pack of dogs she saw raw flesh. The wolves snapped and snarled at each other, coming away with hunks of meat.

Closer to the house a large wolf twisted on the ground like a cut snake, pawing at its face, blood gushing from its snout. At the scent of their fellow's blood, wolves lunged and attacked the wounded brute. Within seconds they had it down, devouring it as they had her husband and son.

There must have been two dozen wolves. Within half an hour after the attack began, they slinked away, their fur stained red as if they wore masks of blood. They left behind nothing but slick, picked-clean bones poking up at odd angles from the reddened, trampled snow. Much of the bodies had been carried off, piece by piece, until what remained was a jutting tangle of fleshless bones.

Callie finally screamed full and long, feeling the madness of this gruesome scene. Her screams frightened little Delia into an even greater frenzy, and the woeful sounds attracted the wolves back to the house. She heard them scratching at the wall, snuffling around the door. Callie moved to the bed, knife in hand once again, and trembled, huddling and rocking her baby in the cradle. The night was long and cold and dark. She didn't dare move.

The winter of 1888 was particularly brutal on the Northern Plains. On Thursday, January 12, 1888, a cold front swept from the northwest across the Dakota and Nebraska prairie. By the next morning, more than five hundred people, caught unaware, lay dead, one hundred of them children. Another result of the harsh conditions was a widespread starvation among wild animals, including wolves.

Although many wildlife biologists maintain that there have been few documented cases of healthy wolves attacking humans in North America, the anecdotal history suggests otherwise. A brief article in the March 8, 1888, edition of the Saint Paul Daily Globe reported the Olsons' sad tale. Extreme hunger, the result of a series of hard winters in the Plains, is the most logical explanation for the Olson attack.

Neighbors found Mrs. Olson and her daughter alive the morning following the attack. Within days she and her daughter had moved away. They were never heard from again.

42

BAD END FOR THE BANDIT QUEEN

A life spent infatuated with banditry and outlaws finally caught up with Myra Maybelle Shirley, a.k.a. Belle Starr, the Bandit Queen, on February 3, 1889. She was ambushed while riding home after visiting a neighbor near her home in Indian Territory. A handful of people, including her husband, her daughter, her son, former lovers, an employee, and a man she had cheated in horse trading, all had reason to want her dead.

Everybody knows why you took up with me while my cousin Sam's corpse was still warm."

The stern-faced woman spun on her new husband. For a moment, her face trembled in pent rage before softening. "Why, Jim July Starr, I'm sure I don't know what you mean by that." She dragged a hand across the pearl dress buttons at her throat, unfastened them slowly.

"Belle, you just wanted to keep your land here in Indian Territory." He watched her face while he spoke. "You can't do that unless you're married to an Indian. And I happen to be an Indian."

She smirked, ran her tongue over her lips, and kept working at the buttons. She pushed against him and whispered, "For the record, it was you who took up with me."

He laughed, pushed her away. "I know you too well, Belle Starr. Keep that gun in its holster." He plucked his wool coat from its peg by the door and said, "Besides, you're almost old enough to be my mother." He laughed again, shaking his head as he stepped out the door. A half-full jam jar shattered against it. A second later Jim July leaned back in, unsmiling, and said, "You know, I think your son has the right idea."

Belle Starr, just shy of her forty-first birthday, stood half undressed in the middle of her front room, staring at the closed door. "What the hell did he mean by that?" she said aloud to the empty room. Then she remembered the day before when she'd thrashed her spineless son with a broken pitchfork handle for quirting her favorite horse, Venus, in the face. Before he'd run off, welted and bleeding, he'd shouted, "I'll kill you for this, you witch! So help me, I'll kill you!"

The knock at the door came just as she swept up the last of the jar's shards. The blackberry preserves made an awful stain on the door and floor, and it seemed no amount of scrubbing was going to lift it out.

"What now?" she said, pushing the hair from her face.

"It's me, Watson, Mrs. Starr. I got to talk with you."

"Lord," said Belle, "this ought to be interesting." She opened the door and there stood Edgar J. Watson, hat in hand, and a mean look on his face.

"Edgar, what do you want?"

"You know why I'm here, Mrs. Starr. I can't sleep at night knowing . . . what you might do. . . ."

Belle sighed and said, "Edgar J. Watson, on the day the Good Lord doled out brains, you must have fallen asleep in the privy. I told you that as long as you do the work you were hired to do then the law will be none the wiser about the fact that you are a wanted man in Florida with a price on your head." She leaned toward him and said, "But if you keep this up, by God I'll see to it that the sheriff pays us a visit before another sunrise comes."

Watson's face slumped and he swallowed. "You wouldn't."

"I damn sure would. Matter of fact, you're becoming a human saddle sore and I just may put an end to this headache you've caused me since you got here. Now get out of here and leave me be." She slammed the door in his face.

Watson licked his lips, pulled on his hat, and said to himself, "Alright then, Missy. Two of us can play that tune."

Belle let her mare, Venus, slow to a walk. Though the day had grown bitter, she was in no hurry for home. The house would be cold and dark and empty. It

Wood engraving of Belle Starr in *The National Police Gazette,* May 22, 1886. Belle Starr made many enemies through the years. On a dark road one night shortly before her forty-first birthday, one of them finally caught up with her. *Courtesy Library of Congress*

was days like this she missed her Sam most of all. Still, it had been nice visiting with her nearest neighbor, Greta. She'd given Belle cornbread. The warmth of it through the muslin towel felt comforting in her hand, and she untied the little knot at the top of the bundle to slip out a piece. So good.

As she chewed, the horse stepping slow, the daylight nearly gone, she wondered about her birthday in two days. Forty-one, she thought. Two children who hate me, a husband who hates me, a hired man who hates me, other men displeased with horse deals we struck . . . is this all there is to it?

The serene quiet collapsed as the boom of a shotgun blast filled the quiet lane with sound. Her horse screamed. Lead balls slammed Belle from behind, catching her in the back and neck, driving her to the ground. She lay with her cheek to the gritty, packed dirt of the road, her eyes still open, sound coming to her as if from far off, like a train whistle on a stormy day.

Belle could no longer taste cornbread, though her mouth was full of it. Instead, something hot and sticky clogged her throat. She drew in a breath, but it felt like she was taking in water. She tried to rise but didn't seem to have any strength. She saw the dim outline of boots a few feet from her face. Then a flash.

Though one of her farm workers, Edgar J. Watson, an escaped convict from Florida with a price on his head, was tried for the murder of Belle Starr, he was acquitted for lack of evidence. Her husband at the time, Jim July Starr, had allegedly offered someone two hundred dollars to kill her. The offer was refused and Jim July was quoted as saying, "Hell, I'll kill the old hag myself and spend the money for whiskey." Belle Starr's own son also had motive to kill her, as she'd beaten him days before for abusing her horse. The murder of Belle Starr remains unsolved to this day.

Raised in a well-to-do family, Myra Maybelle Shirley was a stylish dresser and a crack shot. She left home to travel her own road, using her wits and body to seduce all manner of unsavory characters. She was romantically acquainted with a variety of notorious outlaws and once told a reporter, "I am a friend to any brave and gallant outlaw. There are three or four jolly good fellows on the dodge now in my section, and when they come to my house they are welcome, for they are my friends."

She bore two children, a girl, possibly to outlaw Cole Younger (a cohort of the James Brothers), and a son two years later to her husband at the time, outlaw Jim Reed. The girl grew up to become the successful madam and businesswoman, Pearl Starr. Belle's son, Ed Reed, grew up to become a convicted horse thief who was later pardoned with help from his mother's attorneys.

43

CATTLE KATE LYNCHED

In Wyoming in 1889, James Averell and Ellen "Ella" Watson (dubbed "Cattle Kate" by local newspapers) were homesteading on two parcels in Wyoming's Sweetwater Valley. Determined to prove up on the land and carve out a life for themselves, they planned to marry as soon as the land was theirs. But they had the bad luck to be neighbor to Albert Bothwell, one of Wyoming's largest—and most ruthless—landowners and ranchers. He wanted their land. And on July 20 of that year, he made his play.

What are you saying, Bothwell?" The angry young woman looked at the sneering rancher and threw her leather gloves to the ground, advancing on the rancher's wagon with a pointing finger. "I've about had enough of you and your accusations! I will tell you one more time—I bought that brand less than a year ago when you and your organization refused to let me register my own brand. I've had those cattle for more than a year! Bought legally! And you know it, Bothwell."

"I know nothing of the sort, damn you," the jowly cattleman sneered at her. "All I know is you're a rustler and we have proof."

"That's a lie. Just because your hired gun, George Henderson, says something doesn't make it so."

"It does when we're the law."

One of the men, another local rancher by the name of Durgin, grabbed a spare fence post and swung it hard at corral boards, at fencing, anything nearby.

"See here!" shouted Frank Buchanan a neighboring rancher Ellen Watson employed part-time to help with branding, fencing, and other chores. "That's none of your affair. You leave that fence be!"

"Shut up, Buchanan. You're next if you're not careful." Durgin's face was set as if carved from stone.

Another rancher joined in and within minutes they had driven Ellen Watson's cattle from the corral. The beef animals trotted before the shouting men.

"I see it takes six of you big men to harass a woman and her hired help."

Bothwell looked down at the red-faced young woman and said, "I've known women in my time, and you're no woman. You're a cattle thief." A couple of the other men chuckled. Bothwell wagged his rifle at her and said, "Now get in the wagon. In the back."

"I will not!" Ellen backed up, then tried to run toward her house. Durgin grabbed her by the arm and forced her toward the wagon. "Get in that wagon before we do something you'll regret, dammit."

The other ranchers on horseback surrounded the wagon with sidearms and rifles held at the ready, a few aimed at Watson's hired help, two young boys and Buchanan. The three of them watched helplessly while the raiding ranchers, ignoring them, rode off with their boss.

The boys and Buchanan raced to warn Jim Averell, Watson's fiancé, at his spread nearby. But Bothwell and the other ranchers were headed there, too. Bothwell's gang met Averell at the gate to his place just as Jim was heading to town.

"Get in the wagon, Averell," said Bothwell, gesturing with the rifle. "Beside your sweetie."

Faced with a half-dozen guns, Averell, confused, nonetheless complied, and soon the wagon rumbled onward. "Are you hurt, Ella?"

"No," she whispered, "but I'm afraid." She wiped at her grimed face with the back off a hand. "They said I'm a rustler, Jim. Bothwell's hired gun, Henderson, said he had proof I stole cattle from Bothwell and rebranded them." She collapsed against him, and he held her close. "You know that's not the truth, Jim. But what are we going to do? They own everything here. They own the law, Jim!"

Averell's jaw muscles worked hard, and he stroked Ella's hair and hugged her tight. What to do, indeed? Ella was right. He had a bad feeling that they weren't just being hauled to town to appear before a corrupt magistrate.

"What's the story here, Bothwell? You have no proof of anything. You want our land and you don't like having us as a burr under your saddle, is that it?"

The big man said nothing for a moment, just bounced in the seat. Then he nodded and said, "Something like that."

"Where are you taking us? I demand to know."

"We're headed in to Rawlins. Keep your mouth shut."

The wagon slowed and pulled to a stop beside a gulch along the Sweet-water River. Averell rose to his feet and, still holding Ella, said, "Why have we stopped? What are you planning to do?"

None of the armed men said a thing, but between them they muscled Averell and Watson under a gnarled tree on a knob overlooking the river. Averell kicked and shouted, "My God, my God, men, what are you doing? This is murder! You know the truth! We are innocent! Don't do this thing. I beg of you, don't do this thing!"

"Now you're innocent, eh? Now you're begging. Too little, too late, you squatters! You should have thought about it before you sent all those lies to the newspapers! You're on my pasture land and no amount of blubbering will change the fact that I'll have it in the end." Bothwell turned away from them, red-faced and shaking. He waved his rifle and said, "Hang them for rustlers, boys."

Ellen screamed as rough hands bound her wrists, pulled at her hair. Her fiancé lunged at the attackers, his face a savage, spittle-flecked mask of rage. But his shouts fell on seemingly deadened faces of the local power lords who owned the lion's share of the land in the region. They ignored the shouts of the two victims.

But the cries reached the ears of a friend. Riding at breakneck pace and sensing the worst, Frank Buchanan hastened to catch up with the wagon. He heard the shouts and, looking down from atop the gulch, he saw Bothwell toss a common rope up over the tree's largest branch then loop the rope about Averell's neck. Several men held the struggling victim firm. The same procedure was repeated for Ellen, though the ranchers had a time of it, Buchanan saw, as she fought as fiercely as Averell.

Enraged, Frank Buchanan began pouring lead down on the cluster of corruption. He managed to wound one man but was soon forced to retreat as a half-dozen guns blazed back at him in a vicious volley.

This was no hanging, Buchanan knew, but a strangling. It would take the victims, his friends, a long time to die. They were not weighted properly and so their necks would not break swiftly and mercifully. And there was nothing he could do about it. He cut across country, riding hell-bent for help. But he knew it would be too late. Far too late.

Their drop was less than two feet. The pair of innocent lovers, side by side on the same branch, kicked and wagged, their faces discoloring, their eyes and tongues bulging. The branch above, barely sufficient for the cause, bounced with their last efforts . . . and then was still.

Though word got out to the surrounding countryside right away, the bodies were left to hang for two-and-a-half days. The six murderers were arrested, then allowed to post a five thousand dollar bond for each other, and were released. The grand jury was set to convene on August 25, 1889. But then the witnesses for the prosecution, the two boys who worked for Ellen Watson, Gene Crowder and John DeCorey, disappeared. And then Frank Buchanan disappeared as well. Rumor has it that he spent the following years on the run, fearful of the long arm of the wealthy cattlemen. Ralph Cole, Jim Averell's nephew and ranch hand, died, most likely of poisoning, on the first day of the trial.

All charges were dropped for lack of witnesses. No investigations were made into the death of Cole or the disappearances of the other witnesses. In later years small ranchers in the area would claim that their families' lives had been threatened should they step forward with any information that might incriminate the lynching ranchers. Within a year Albert Bothwell ended up as owner of Averell and Watson's spreads, and several of the killers ended up holding seats in state legislature.

Even after their unfortunate deaths, Jim Averell and Ellen Watson were vilified in the stockman-controlled press. The fabricated rumors that Ellen was a prostitute known as Cattle Kate and Averell her pimp began there and, though they are popular notions, have never been substantiated. The events did have a positive outcome, in a manner of speaking. The Johnson County War of 1892 took place shortly thereafter, which eventually resulted in smaller ranchers gaining more control over their own lives and holdings.

44

HIGH PLAINS SLAUGHTER

At the start of the nineteenth century, the Great Plains were filled with herds of American bison, or buffalo, numbering in the tens of millions. By 1890 it is estimated that fewer than 750 buffalo were alive in the United States. Never before or since have so many large wild animals of one species been slain in so short a span of time. In a typical day, a Plains buffalo hunter could easily kill 250 of the unwitting beasts.

Once the band of Sioux warriors had surrounded the herd of buffalo, it was but a short time until all the great beasts were dead. But Swift Rain's heart was heavy. Despite the good hunting, which would help his people in the coming cold season, his brother, Blue Dog, had been trampled to death in the hunt. It was a noble way to die, but Swift Rain knew it could have been avoided had his brother not been so anxious to prove he was the bravest warrior among them.

Blue Dog had ridden his horse well ahead of them all to be at the front of the group when they formed the point. He had yelled the loudest to frighten the big animals and turn them back in on each other, and then he had been one of the first to drive his prized buffalo horse into the roiling mass of animals. Swift Rain, who had been on many buffalo hunts (while his young brother had only been on two), had seen the angry, wounded bull rake viciously and bring down Blue Dog's horse with a slashing horn wound that opened up the gut of the fine animal.

Swift Rain had expected his brother to jump free, to stay above the crowd of buffalo as they leapt and, in their frenzy, even attacked each other. He had been so long with his brother, the nimble young man who could inspire such confidence in warriors twice his age, that he had not expected to see him pulled so quickly beneath the massive black bodies.

Swift Rain was not the only one to see it. Even as the last of the small band of buffalo lay gasping, tongues extended and eyes wide in shock, Blue

Dog's young wife ran down the long grassy slope. Swift Rain kicked his horse hard and intercepted her just as she reached the edge of the killing ground. He had to hold her arms tight so she would not become injured in her grief by the still-thrashing animals. They stayed like that for some time, until the other warriors pulled Blue Dog from beneath a massive bull that had breathed its last.

Already the other wives came down the hill and streamed by them on their way to skin and butcher the buffalo. Despite the loss of so fine a young warrior, the entire tribe would soon celebrate the successful hunt by feasting on the brains and intestines of the beasts they vanquished.

And when they packed off everything they would use in the coming harsh months, they left behind the hearts of the buffalo they killed. This would help future herds to grow healthy.

"I'm going to need at least $2.25 per hide, Slocum, or you can forget the deal."

The wiry little man behind the long, low counter shook his head, smiling, and said, "I don't think so, Shaggy Bob. I told you I'm paying two dollars a hide and that's it. And that goes for young females. The full-growed shaggies and calves I'll do for $1.50 each."

The bearded hunter scratched his hairy cheeks. "We ain't even settled on a price and already you're telling me what to do."

The shopkeep didn't bother turning around, but kept on counting the cans of fruit on the shelves behind him. "I told you, Bob, there ain't no settling on a price. It just is what it is. And you had better like it or move along so someone else can tell me what they want and don't want. But if you do decide to sell hides to me, you'd better understand that I need at least five hundred to make it worth my time."

The hunter stared at the scarred counter, and thought to himself that five hundred would hardly make the trip worth the effort. "How come you ain't even paying what you did last month? Hides are just as good."

The merchant sighed and turned around, a can of peaches in each hand. "That may be, Bob, but it took me longer than ever before to sell that last pile of hides. Close to twenty thousand of the stinking things. There's still a slim market for them—for the time being. They make belts out of 'em for the mills back east."

"I know, I know. And I don't really give a good rat's ass."

The merchant's head snapped back as if he were struck. "Why, Shaggy Bob, no need to get surly about it."

"I ain't surly. Just that it takes a mite longer now to get one hundred of the things in any one place, let alone five hundred. I expect the Army's plan's working."

The shopkeep turned again and regarded the hunter. "Don't tell me that you disagree now, do you?"

Shaggy Bob yawned and rubbed his eyes. He was coming off a weeklong toot and had been hoping to get an advance from Slocum on a new pile of skins. But the damned bald merchant was the surly one today. "I don't rightly know what to think, Slocum. Except that once the buffs are gone them Indians are going to starve."

"You make that sound like a bad thing, Bob." The shopkeep smiled.

The grizzled hunter stared at the bald man and wanted to lay into him then and there. But he was tired. Tired of himself, of talk of hides, of the stink of hides, of everything. He stretched his shoulders, hefted his Sharps, and went out the store's front door. He'd try the Army depot, see if they'd give him another few hundred rounds. All his ammunition had been free for a few years now. So long as he showed up with his skin wagon piled high, the army doled out more ammunition than he could use.

Within fifteen years, from 1868 to 1883, the great Plains buffalo herds, which at one time may have numbered as many as one hundred million, were almost entirely killed off. In 1873, in the midst of the buffalo boom years, railroads transported 754,329 hides, 4,852,800 pounds of meat, and 8,229,300 pounds of bones. The very next year, twenty million pounds of buffalo bones were transported east to refineries for the manufacture of sugar and fertilizer. More often than not, the hides were stripped and the carcasses left to rot, though sometimes the tongues were cut out, salted, smoked, and sold as delicacies.

Forty thousand buffalo hides await shipment at Rath & Wright's buffalo hide yard in 1878, in Dodge City, Kansas. Though decades before they numbered in the millions, by 1890 fewer than 750 buffalo were left alive. *Courtesy National Archives*

Oddly enough, between 1873 and 1889, eighty-eight bison calves were captured by a group of businessmen and ranchers who sought (some for financial gain, some out of an urge to save the vanishing breed) to build up private herds. When these herds became difficult to manage the private owners turned them over to the Canada and United States governments. These disparate handfuls of animals formed the basis for the genetically narrow herds that exist today, largely in protected areas such as Yellowstone and Banff National Parks.

45

CARNAGE AT WOUNDED KNEE

On the bitterly cold morning of December 29, 1890, a Lakota Sioux refused to give up his rifle to the Army until he was paid proper compensation for it. His action was mistaken for hostility. Less than an hour later, hundreds of Lakota Sioux—men, women, and children—lay wounded or dead.

There was shouting from without the tent. For a brief moment the old sick chief and his first wife exchanged a look—their eyes shared the same fear. "That was Black Coyote," said Big Foot. "He says he paid for his gun and will not give it to any white. He is wrongheaded. We must do as Wovoka bids and not fight the whites. The Ghost Dance is the only way now. If he argues, it will come to no good."

As if intended to interrupt his musing, more shouts sounded. A man's scream was followed by the sudden and unmistakable sound of a single gun shot. Big Foot lurched to the flap of his tent and, as he pushed out of it into the chill morning air, the vicious thunder of hundreds of guns firing mingled with the screams of his people.

The first thing he saw was young Shaking Tree spinning toward him, a bullet lashing its way through her back and out through her baby's front. The pair of them faced him with widening eyes, blood streaking the air. They dropped at his feet, face down, mother on top of her baby. Sounds erupted all about him then, blossoming into countless bursts from countless directions.

He staggered forward into the open, his people running in all directions, soldiers in blue lashing at them with rifles while Indian knives flashed red. Through it all smoke rose from the Hotchkiss guns that poured death on them. He reached for a crying young girl and something like a horse hoof to the chest kicked him from his feet.

He saw his people slumping to the ground all about him, angry men in blue fighting them, his youngest warriors doing their best to fend off the attacks of the whites. But even as his vision fogged and his breath slowed, he knew there was no hope that his people, the once mighty Lakota Sioux, would survive. Already his half-brother, Sitting Bull, had been killed. Now it seemed only right that he be next. Wovoka was wrong. There would be no more ghost dances, there would be no more Sioux.

A bullet struck Chief Big Foot in the head and he slumped back to the frozen ground. He struggled to rise, managing only to make it to his elbows. His breath was leaving him for the last time. And as he stared up at the cold, gray sky, he was filled with grief. This was not a noble end.

On the slight rise above the charred remains of the Sioux encampment on Wounded Knee Creek, the army captain sat astride his dapple gray gelding. For the first time in a long time, perhaps not since he began fighting Indians nearly twenty years before, he felt a sharp pain in his breast at this scene. It had been three days since . . . the slaughter. There was no other word he knew to use for it—and they were just now returning to the scene. The blizzard had prevented them from getting here any sooner. He had been chosen to direct and oversee clean-up and burial details.

He had ridden his horse down to survey the scene, but it had been a mistake. He feared he trod upon some of the dead, buried as they were in snow drifts. He had seen Chief Big Foot, bundled like an old woman against the cold. He'd been told the man had pneumonia and that his shirt had been spattered with blood long before bullets in the first volley of the attack had laid him low. And now there he was, looking as if in the midst of rising from a nap, the makings of a curious almost-smile on his face. The sick, unarmed old man had been cut down, as had an as-yet-undetermined number of his tribe. Most unarmed, many women, children, and old men.

He inhaled the crisp air of the new year and let out his breath slowly. He thought back to the fight and saw the stumbling forms of the children, the elderly, the men and women, all shambling over the frozen ground and out through a ravine, the only direct way out of the camp. The Hotchkiss guns followed them, lacerating the group. By the time a cease-fire was called, nearly half of the 350 members of Chief Big Foot's band lay dead. Children, some naked, stumbled among the corpses, crying and shaking. The Hotchkiss guns continued to rake the ravine.

Now here they were to clean up their mess. He couldn't even talk with the other offices near him, could barely watch the farmers, shopkeeps, and other volunteers who were being paid two dollars for each corpse they pried, stiff and brittle, from the crusted drifts of snow and carried to the trench. But they bore watching, just the same. Many of them held no reverence for Indians, alive or dead, and he feared they would just as soon mutilate the dead as bury them. And as reprehensible as this thought was to him, he knew there was little he could do to prevent it, especially considering that some of the Indians managed to make their escape attempts last for two miles and more before succumbing to their wounds. The other survivors, too weak to go any further, had been hunted down and shot like sickly coyotes.

A young farmer's shouts pulled his attention from his perusal of the skyline. The man was bent low in the snow and pawing at something, a hunched dark shape.

"If he thinks I'll stand for looting, by God. . . ." said the captain aloud, his anger rising as he galloped his horse toward the gruesome scene. He made it to the young man. "Mister, if you think I'll let you desecrate this Indian's remains, you are mistaken." The man, whose back was partially to the captain, stood and held aloft a little form. It was a baby wrapped in a blanket. Its skin was a mottle of pink and blue splotches, and its mouth opened and closed like a baby bird's, though no sound came out.

The man was nearly crying. "It's a baby, sir. It's alive."

The meaning of the words did not fully present itself to the captain. What was a baby doing out here? The fight had happened three days ago, before the blizzard. How? He looked again at the little face matted with frozen gore, nearly black eyes, crusted and barely open, the black hair of the child . . . and tried to speak. But no sound came out. He was a man used to giving orders and making decisions, but now he was at a loss.

All about him men were staring, some walking toward them. The poor

Chief Big Foot of the Lakota Sioux, already stricken with advanced pneumonia, was one of the first shot dead at Wounded Knee. Before the day was over, 146 Sioux lay dead and frozen. A blizzard struck and it would be days before their bodies were recovered and buried in mass graves. *Courtesy National Archives*

thing would no doubt die. The fact that it had lived for three days under its dead mother was nothing short of a miracle.

"Sir," said a soldier in a fur hat. "There's an Injun doctor here somewheres, sir. From the res at Pine Ridge. Says he come to help survivors. I told him he was wastin' his time, but now I reckon not."

The captain looked back to the crusty, blue baby and said, "Find him. And make haste, soldier. Make haste!"

The army's misunderstanding of the peaceful Ghost Dance religion that had brought hope to many tribes suffering from decades of degradation and despair resulted in tighter control exerted over already mistreated Indians. On December 29, 1890, these tensions snapped and the Lakota Sioux paid a high price for it.

Five hundred members of the U.S. Seventh Cavalry, equipped with four Hotchkiss guns, opened fire on the Indians, most of whom were unarmed. Women and children, attempting to flee the chaos, were tracked for miles by officers on horseback, then killed. Those that weren't run aground were later found dead of hypothermia.

By the time the final counts were taken, twenty-five whites, mostly soldiers, were dead, and another thirty-nine wounded, the majority by friendly fire due to the indiscriminate effects of the fifty-round-a-minute Hotchkiss guns. The army's casualties were gathered and brought to Pine Ridge where they were treated, or at least treated with reverence. Three days later, after the blizzard, the Sioux were attended to.

The Lakota Sioux lost 146 tribesmen that day, some of exposure to the unforgiving elements after they fled the battle. Three days later, ten survivors were found. A native doctor from the nearby encampment at Pine Ridge treated four babies found huddled under their mothers' dead bodies. The children were eventually adopted by soldiers and raised among whites, though their lives were difficult, filled with racism and other forms of abuse. They led confused lives and found peace neither with the whites, nor with the Sioux.

46

VETTER'S BITTER END

On a warm September evening in 1892, in the Greybull River country of northwestern Wyoming, small game trapper P. H. Vetter left his little cabin after supper for a smoke on his pipe and a stroll to the river. He'd forgotten that plums were in season along the riverbank and that grizzlies were out in number, gorging on the plentiful fruit.

The light from the lowering sun laid a warm glow over the evening. The little twisting path down to the river that P. H. Vetter used nearly every day was just beginning to fill with shadows. Even the air was warm and soothing, and as he walked he took in great draughts, filling his lungs and swinging his tin bucket he'd brought along to fill at the river.

Just before it came to the riverbank, the path curved around a grey boulder, orange-tinged in the softening light. Vetter skirted it, stepping down over the worn roots of Ponderosas lining the bank. And not four feet below him a honey-brown grizzly swung its wide, proud head upward at the intrusion. For two clicks of the hands on a pocket watch, man and beast faced each other. Their eyes met and held. Vetter dropped the bucket and it rolled, clunk, clunk, down the bank to a stop at the bear's front feet. The bear looked down at it, then up at the man. Vetter's breath left him in a whoosh and the spell broke.

The grizzly's mouth opened, the lips flapping and sagging as a roar the likes of which Vetter had never heard rushed up at him. And as the bear bellowed its surprised rage, it dug its way up the gravel bank at the stunned trapper. The beast was nearly on him when Vetter remembered his sidearm. He clawed at the pistol as he ran backward. He had the gun cocked and was bringing it down to fire at the advancing beast when he was rammed from the side . . . by another grizzly. The shot sang out, whistling through the branches above.

Vetter spun in the path trying to regain his feet. He must have walked by this second bear on his way down the path. It bawled at him, inches from his face. Its presence slowed the advance of the first bear. They appeared annoyed as much with each other as with this intruder in their midst. Then Vetter tripped over a raised root in the path and they were on him.

The two angry bears growled alternately at him and at each other. The larger bear ignored the second, smaller bear, and bit down on Vetter's arm, shaking it hard in its jaws. Vetter felt something snap in his sleeve, knew it was his arm bones. He had to get away from these brutes. He screamed his fear and rage at them. The big bear let go of his arm and matched the mad trapper's bellowing, note for note.

The younger bear kept rushing in, clawing and biting at him. Vetter realized he still held his pistol in his left hand and tried to thumb back the hammer, but the younger bear drove its face at him. He brought the butt down hard on the bear's snout and it recoiled, shaking its head as if stung by a bee. The first bear resumed its attack on his arm.

He drove the gun butt at it and thrust an elbow underneath himself. As soon as he half-rose, the largest bear swatted him hard in the chest and sent him backward into the dirt once again. Hot pain washed through him and his screams were less manful, more urgent and desperate.

The bears directed their anger at each other while Vetter rose to his feet, staggering backward a few paces. He felt terrible and saw that his right arm hung limp. Blood ran from it as if from an opened spigot. He had no more time to waste in getting away from these killers. He struggled up the trail toward a large pine. The bears noticed the movement and simultaneously charged up the hill.

As the bears closed in on him, he thumbed back the pistol's hammer and squeezed off one, two shots, and the closest bear howled. Something slammed his good arm hard against the tree—a bear's paw. Dirt-crusted claws pinned his arm to the rough red bark. Vetter looked into the face of a third bear. The pistol had been knocked from his grasp. His vision buzzed and blurred, sweat ran in his eyes and it was so hard to breathe. Something bad had happened to his chest. Then all three bears were fighting but a few feet from him.

Vetter fled up the trail, stumbling and wobbling, glancing backward every few feet. No sign of bears yet. Something slapped against his leg as he ran—his now-useless right arm. He reached with his left and lifted it, and as he did so his hand rubbed against his chest, now a crater of sagged

P. H. Vetter had the misfortune to interrupt three sizable grizzlies as they dined on autumn plums one evening. And as he found out, even grizzlies in a fruit-induced stupor will turn on a man. *Courtesy National Park Service*

skin and what felt like small stones in a burlap sack. The bear had crushed his chest with one swat.

Vetter rounded the last bend and far ahead his cabin came into sight. Never had the little hovel looked so good. He knew if he didn't tend to himself he was likely to bleed out. He risked another look over his shoulder and saw no bears. Thank God. He lurched and staggered like a drunken man the last twenty feet to his door and dragged his weakening body through the threshold.

The inside of the cabin spun before him, the floor worked its way up to become the ceiling. There was the table, his plate and spoon, his stewpot, crusting over with the last of the rabbit in the bottom.

Beneath him on the boards he saw blood, running as if it were water poured from a cup. It trailed right off his dangling fingertips. That damn hand. He couldn't lift it nor move the fingers. He crashed onto the bunk and grabbed for a rag, his old blue kerchief.

Ragged breathing filled the little room and he realized it was his own breath. I sound like something old and dying, he thought. He strangled a whimper in his throat and fought with his good hand to tie off the kerchief high above his elbow. The arm was so bloodied and mangled it looked more like shank meat off a fresh kill than an arm.

"So . . . thirsty. . . ." But no one brought him a dipper of water. Hell, he snorted, no water anyway. It's all back at the river. And I'll be damned if I'm going back down there tonight. Something bubbled up from his broken chest. He didn't dare probe that mess again.

Vetter felt the stub of lead pencil under his hand as he groped with weak fingers on the low shelf by the bed. He'd write a note so people would know what happened when they found him, how to treat him. No treatment can save you now, fool, he told himself. He whimpered again and scratched letters on the edge of a newspaper so old he'd grown tired of rereading it.

He slipped one of his suspenders off his shoulder and fumbled the length of it around his arm, using his heaving mouth to tie it off. Maybe it would help. More than anything he wanted to rest a while. When he awoke, maybe he'd fetch the bucket and bring back water from the river.

Two to three weeks after the attack, John Corbett, a friend of P. H. Vetter, dropped by for a visit. He found his chum's bloated body lying in a blood-blackened bunk. Under the man's left hand, a few crudely lettered words were scratched in the margin of a newspaper, among them, "Franks" and "Dying." Corbett ran to the nearby Pitchfork Ranch to tell Vetter's friend, rancher Otto Franc. They determined that the largest of the attacking bears was a notorious local brute called "Old Two Toes," a name earned after he lost several claws in a trap years earlier.

Before Europeans ventured west of the Mississippi, grizzly bears roamed in great numbers from Canada south to Mexico, numbering 50,000 and more in what is now the United States. That figure today is approximately 1,100, though there are currently approximately 60,000 grizzly bears in all of North America. Most are found in Canada and Alaska.

47

DEADLINE LAW

In March of 1897, Diamondfield Jack Davis, a hired gun for the Idaho-based Sparks-Harrell Cattle Company, was convicted of brutally murdering two sheepherders. He spent five years in prison, awaiting his execution, but as he finally mounted the gallows, even the judge knew he wasn't guilty.

It was a big ranch. One of many the Sparks-Harrell Cattle Company owned across southern Idaho and northern Nevada. It was certainly the biggest outfit Jackson Lee Davis ever saw. He'd spent most of the past few years working at the Black Jack Mine near Silver City, then hit the surrounding hills when a diamond strike was reported. That didn't pan out and he ended up here. "God, but I hate punching cattle," he said low to himself, watching a half-dozen riders in the distance maneuver a huge herd of beeves toward a series of corrals and chutes.

"Mr. Davis?"

The man's voice behind him made him jump and he spun, hands dropping to his waist.

The tall, thin cowboy behind him laughed and said, "Easy now, gunhand. I'm no threat!" He held his hands up as if drawn on, then winked. His eyes narrowed and he said, "I need a young cowboy who can ride the deadline and make sure the sheep stay on their side. What I don't need is someone who's going to kill a damn sheepherder for no reason. Nor their stock, as little as I think of them woolly buggers. But if you do have to kill, the company will stand behind you no matter the circumstances. For that I pay fifty dollars a month. Are you up for this?"

"Diamondfield" Jack Davis glanced back out the window at the beeves and their billowing, choking dust cloud, and said, "You bet I am."

"Bill Tolman, I warned you, damnit. Now look what you've done." Jack Davis flopped the bleeding man off his horse and dragged him the last few yards to the man's campsite. "You've been told time and again to keep you and your woollies on this side of the deadline and there won't be trouble. But you start pushing your luck and see what happens?"

Despite his gruff talk, Davis was worried, crazy with worry should the sheepherder die. Sparks said he'd back him up in court, but that wasn't really the point. If Tolman died, Jack knew he'd swing for sure. He groaned at the thought and surveyed the man's camp. "I'll make you a fire, get you set up. Your pards'll be back soon to take care of you. You remember this now. Old Diamondfield Jack isn't one to shirk his duties, but I don't aim to swing on your account. Sparks-Harrell has deep pockets and frowns on people who disobey the deadline law."

He'd shot up a couple of other sheep camps in the past few weeks, just to make his point, show them he was serious. But you put a killing on top of those camp dustups and he could be looking at jail time. And that didn't sit right, no sir. Time to light a shuck. He nodded to the still-conscious, moaning sheepherder, mounted his horse, and hit the trail hard and fast, riding south for Nevada.

"If there ever was a time to shut your mouth and listen, it's now. I ain't saying you did it and I ain't saying you didn't, but you have to understand that it don't look good for you."

Jack Davis opened his mouth, then closed it and gripped the bars of the cell tighter. "Okay," he said. "What's it I'm supposed to have done?"

The man who was sent to fetch him back to Idaho from Arizona Territorial Prison, where he'd been arrested under an alias for a shooting incident involving a lawman, smiled and said, "Why, you almost seem innocent, Jack."

"I am, I think. Depends on what you're trying to pin on me."

"I ain't trying to pin anything on you. Facts are facts and you'll have to stand trial."

"For what, dammit . . . . "

The big man sighed. "Jack, you know what a sheepherder two weeks dead smells like? No? How 'bout two of 'em, and two near-dead dogs starved and barely able to move, tied to the wagon wheels. Not pretty."

Jack straightened and dropped his hands to his sides. "Now wait a minute. I never killed any sheepherders. I was hired by Sparks-Harrell Cattle Company to protect the deadline, make sure those sheepherders kept their woollies on their side, cattle on ours. Simple."

"You denying you shot one in November?"

Jack squinted in the dark cell and finally said, "You mean that herder I winged? He's alright, I lugged him back to his camp."

"Yep, you did. But then as you moseyed on down here, you stopped at every piss-pot watering hole and told everybody and their brother how you had a run in with a camp of herders. That you were paid top wage to get rid of the sheep problem."

"Well, I did. But nobody got shot. A horse, maybe, but that doesn't count."

"Easy now, Davis. I happen to like horses. Anyhow, I've been hired to drag you back to Idaho to stand trial."

"You're serious."

"You best believe it, Diamondfield Jack Davis. And what's more," the big lawman leaned close to the bars, his graying moustaches inches from Jack's face, "them two sheepherders were Mormons. And I don't have to tell you about the depth of the Mormon church's pockets. Or the length of its arms."

The caged man let his fingers slip from the bars. For the first time in a long time, Jack Davis felt real trouble closing in.

"How much more of this can a body take?" he asked the stone walls of his cell in a whisper. He rolled another cigarette and sat up on his bunk to light it, thinking back on the events of the past few years. The trial had raised enough attention at first. He'd been tried in sheep country, in an Idaho Mormon farming community, and sentenced to hang on July 4, 1897.

Then Sparks-Harrell ranch manager James Bower and cowboy Jeff Gray confessed to the killings, pleading self defense. So they stayed his execution on July 3, the day before he was due to die. But they didn't set him free. And it had been that way since. He dragged deep on the cigarette and blew the smoke out into the dark cell.

Five years full of appeals and execution dates that kept getting changed (though one stay wasn't issued until three hours before he was due to swing), and it didn't seem to matter that the courts had signed confessions, that they'd gone on to acquit the confessors, that they had no real proof that he'd been anywhere near the damned sheepherders in the first place. At least not near the ones that got murdered.

He ground out the butt and stretched his arms high in the dark. If he'd been guilty of anything it was of boastful talk. He always regretted that, sometimes not until he'd sobered up the next day, but he figured that's just the way he was built. But five years for something he knew he didn't do. . . . And the last he'd heard they'd given him life behind bars. He laid back down on the bunk and covered his eyes with his hands. Thought, should have kept my mouth shut and stayed hid in Arizona.

Widely regarded as a hothead who was handy with a gun, Diamondfield Jack Davis nevertheless did not commit the murders of which he was convicted. Even after the true killers were tried and acquitted on grounds of self defense, the judge refused to grant Davis a pardon, citing suspected collusion on the part of the two confessors. But Davis's former boss-turned-Nevada-Governor John Sparks, spoke on his behalf. Finally, on December 17, 1902, the Board of Pardons gave Diamondfield Jack Davis his freedom.

He left the region promptly and, as if to make up for the five years he lost in prison, he struck it rich within two years in the gold fields of the Tonopoh mining district of Nevada. Davis prospered for many years and when union troubles afflicted his consortium's mining camps, Diamondfield Jack Davis could be counted on to quell troubles with his ever-present weaponry. Local papers referred to him as "a walking arsenal" and "the most dangerous man in camp."

Davis later lost his fortune and, in Las Vegas in 1949, he was struck by a car and killed.

48

STEADY, TEDDY!

In Meeker, Colorado, on January 11, 1901, then Vice President-Elect Theodore Roosevelt, while hunting with two companions, found himself in fist-to-jaw combat with an enraged she-lion.

The pack of mixed-breed dogs surged ahead as if one sleek, muscled beast, bawling and baying at the top of their range toward something that the four men following on horseback could not yet see.

The hunt's guide, local ranch owner and sport, John H. Goff, took in the surrounding cragged landscape, chipped and gullied, and reined up beside the keenest of this hunt's three clients. "Mr. Roosevelt, I wouldn't be surprised if that is the hole of a denned she cat."

The broad, bespectacled face turned to him, a smile pulling it impossibly wide. With moustaches bristling, his barking laugh split the cold morning air. "Then I'm for it!" And he jumped from his mount and slid his rifle from its scabbard.

Within seconds the dogs had dug into the hole. Their frenzied barks were greeted with, and soon matched in intensity by, the slashing growl of a mountain lion. In those close quarters, though the dogs were experienced cougar fighters, the cat's bared fangs and swiping claws provided it with ample defenses. The other men of the party had by then dismounted and pressed close to the den. It wasn't long before the four hunters heard yelps of pain as the dogs felt the full effect of the trapped beast's fury.

A bevy of canine backsides was all the men could see, though they heard plenty of commotion from within the plugged chamber. "There's always another entrance," said Goff, cradling his rifle and crouching down to see into the gloom between the frantic bodies of the dogs. At that moment one dog backed out and when it was free of its fellows it whipped its head side to side with vigor. "Turk!" yelled Goff, but the dog was in the grip of a bloodlust and would not relinquish the limp body of the kitten in its maw.

"That's a shame," said Teddy. "I would like to have had a cougar to raise up."

In short order two other dogs followed Turk's lead, and emerged from the den backside first, each with a limp prize of its own. The men succeeded in freeing them from the dogs and the dead things were thrust in a game pouch for later study.

Within seconds after having lost her young, the cougar retreated with haste and emerged some thirty yards distant on the far side of the knoll into which she had denned. Flinging gravel with her massive round paws, she mounted the steep bank, topped it, and dove hard into the trees above. The dogs, once again surging after her, wasted no time in lessening the gap.

The men mounted their horses and dug in hard with their heels. "After them, boys! This is no time for dawdlers!" And with that Teddy Roosevelt led the four of them, plunging on their steeds, into the woods. The cougar had treed within a few hundred yards, and was barely man height off the ground in the low branches of a piñon.

The hunters dismounted even as their horses slid to a halt on the needles of the forest floor. On seeing the men, the horses, and the dogs below, the seemingly unruffled mountain lion neither growled nor swatted, but leapt from her branches into the pack of yapping dogs. She coursed like a flash of late-day sunlight through the dark forest. The shouts and hot-blooded roars of the pursuing men matched the howling of the pack of dogs.

Within yards of her jump-and-dash, the she-cat clawed her way up a new tree, seeking refuge from the madness that trailed behind. But these dogs were swift things, too, and of their snapping jaws, one set found purchase.

"Good boy, Baldy!" shouted Goff, leaping down once again from his saddle. The other men were in the midst of the same action when the cat, now seized by firm teeth, lost her grip on the tree, scarring the bark with long, fresh grooves. She growled, spinning on the lunging, snapping beasts, and faced them, her ears flat back against her man-like head.

The pack descended on her. She disappeared beneath it for but a moment before a foreleg thrust free, grabbing and swatting. A grey dog felt the full effects of a face raking. He recoiled, yelping and whipping furiously his bleeding chops.

The men advanced on the roiling, yowling mass of bodies, Teddy leading the group. In cases such as this he knew it was but a sliver of a second's work for the cat to disarm the man and tear his face from topknot to chin with a swipe of its savage curved claws. As he planned his attack, he was aware that an ill-placed lunge could well mean his end, for nothing fights so well as a cornered, wounded creature with nothing to lose.

With lightning speed Teddy elbowed his way between the flailing, lunging bodies of the dogs, inching closer, his teeth bared and gritted tight, his glasses riding high on his bunched cheeks. The other three men stood by, breath held and rifles at the ready.

The cat sensed his approach. With renewed vigor she swatted one hound back a few paces and sunk her fangs into another, whipping him aside as well. There was a moment of pause when Teddy and the cat faced each other. A low, guttering growl burred forth from the bleeding cat's gore-smeared mouth. She faced her stalker full on, eyes glinting like gold flake.

It seemed to the stocky man standing before her at the ready that for a moment even the dogs' yammering abated, and there were just the two of them, the hunter and the hunted. For the time it takes to breathe in and out, he wasn't sure which role was his. Then a broad smile stretched across his face, his teeth glinted, and all the noises of the world rushed back in on them.

The cat slashed and battled with the renewed, relentless attacks of the dogs. Once her forelegs were again occupied, the hunter saw his opportunity and lunged forward, ramming his rifle's butt straight into her glinting maw. It lodged there, her fangs piercing the wood and holding fast. At the same moment, seeing his opportunity, with the force and unerring power of an experienced hunter, he plunged the ten-inch blade straight into the great cat's heart.

For the second time in less than twenty seconds, the cat and the man stared into each others' eyes until one yielded—and then the glittering gold of her eyes filmed over and her tensed body sagged to the ground.

Teddy Roosevelt had to pry apart her jaws to release his gun butt from between her teeth. And a piece of the stock came away, so powerful and deep was her bite.

An inveterate hunter, Theodore "Teddy" Roosevelt took great pride in dispatching his quarry in close quarters, often engaging in fist-to-claw combat with the cornered beasts. *Courtesy Library of Congress*

Theodore "Rough Rider" Roosevelt was a lifelong, inveterate outdoorsman who pursued game the world over. But his favorite hunting grounds were those of the West, where he had ranched in the Dakota Badlands for a time as a young man.

Teddy went on to hold a variety of high-profile positions in public service before eventually becoming twenty-sixth President of the United States in 1901, finishing the assassinated McKinley's term before being elected to another in 1904. As President he oversaw construction of the Panama Canal and was awarded the Nobel Peace Prize in 1906. After he left office he hunted big game in Africa and continued a lifelong interest in writing books about his experiences. Most of his works are still in print today.

49

BOTCHED HANGING

After years of thieving and alleged killing, on April 26, 1901, in Clayton, New Mexico Territory, Thomas "Black Jack" Ketchum mounted the scaffold. He spoke his last words, the hood and noose were fitted, the trap door was sprung, and . . . something went wrong.

I am in more pain than you will ever know, you bastards!" Thomas Edward Ketchum rattled the steel-bar door of his cell. It clunked on its hinges but held firm. He was, after all, only using one arm. The other had been amputated a year before as the result, along with his incarceration, of a botched train robbery.

"Hey, shut up back there!"

The noise stopped, then the prisoner spoke in a slow, even tone. "You talk to me that way, you pup? Don't you know who I am?"

Now it was the deputy's turn to be quiet. Ketchum heard him walk toward the outer door of the cells and smiled. The young deputy said, "I know. And I'm sorry I said it that way."

"Aw, it's alright. It's just this stump. It's paining me something awful." Now he could see the deputy's fawn hat through the barred window in the door, the side of the young man's face glowing in the scant light from the hallway.

"But they took that arm off you more than a year ago."

"Don't mean the nub don't torment me like hellfire."

"Well I can't do anything for you. You know that. I got orders to not open this door."

"How 'bout a cup of coffee. That's all I want."

The boy didn't respond. Finally Ketchum said, "It's just a tin cup of hot coffee. I haven't asked for the world. Or a key to the cell. It's cold in here and I'm going to be in a place a damn sight colder than this in a month, come April 26. Besides, it's the wee hours and there ain't nobody here but us chickens. Hell, there ain't even any drunks in here tonight."

He heard the kid sigh, then clump back down the hall. Presently he heard the coffee pot scrape on the little potbellied stove, tink against a cup's lip, and clunk back down again. Then the boy's boots clumping down the short hallway, the dull rattle of the keys, and the cell block door swinging in, squawking slow. The boy brought a small oil lamp and the cup of coffee balanced on the same tray they used for his dinner plate.

He set the tray down on the wood visitor's chair and returned to the door, shutting and locking it from this side. "Move to the back of the cell. If you please, Mr. Ketchum."

The jailed man sighed, stepped back three paces, and waited.

After he'd set the cup in the cell the deputy stood back himself, let Ketchum sip, then said, "Why'd you do what you did?"

Ketchum closed his eyes, savoring the bitter bite of the hot coffee. "Well, it wasn't so I could be here talking to you. No offense, but this part wasn't exactly planned."

"You know what I mean."

"What is it I did?"

"The train. You tried to rob the train."

"Oh, that."

"It was for the money, then."

"You say that like wantin' money is a disease."

The young man just stared at the man in the dark cell and shook his head. "You shot that fella Bartlett in the mouth."

Ketchum held the cup under his nose for a moment, inhaling the warm coffee smell. "No, no, now there you're wrong. I shot at him and a piece of metal got in the way. Bullet bounced and caught him in the chops."

The kid stood there a moment more, shaking his head. When he'd gone from the cell block, Ketchum closed his eyes and said, "Hell, all he lost was a few teeth." Ketchum stretched out on the bunk and laid awake for hours.

"So you're the boy for it on Friday, April 26, at, what is it . . . 1:15 in the afternoon?"

"What do you mean, Handy?"

Despite the fact that he was convicted of "molesting a train," Thomas "Black Jack" Ketchum was nonetheless hanged. Sort of. *Courtesy National Archives*

"I mean you're in charge of Ketchum's necktie party."

Salome Garcia, Sheriff of Union County, New Mexico Territory, sat down heavily on the edge of the table that served as his desk. "That's what they tell me."

"You ever hung anyone before?"

"Nope."

Clarence Handy, of Handy's Dry Goods & Emporium, two doors down from the jail, set his empty coffee cup on the window sill and said, "Better get that rope right. You know what happens if your figures are off. . . ." He winked and walked out.

Garcia sat there a moment more thinking how annoying a man Handy was, then grunted and wondered just what he'd meant might happen. He also wondered who in town knew how to figure such things.

The territorial governor's representative retrieved his watch, glanced at it, 1:12 p.m., and slipped it back into its pocket. He looked at the man who in mere minutes would no longer be alive. Ketchum's eyes met his and the other man looked away first, toward Garcia.

The big sheriff was nervous. Hell, who wasn't? Ketchum didn't seem that bothered, but he was. A little white around the gills, if he had to guess. And now it was all set. The two deputies strapped Ketchum's legs together. The younger, nervous-looking boy got flustered when he reached for Ketchum's right arm and found the sleeve empty.

The governor's representative saw that Garcia kept licking his lips and wiping his palm on his coat front. The taller, older deputy arranged the noose about Ketchum's neck, placing the cumbersome knot to the side of his head. Before he arranged the black hood, the parson asked the condemned man if he had last words he'd like to speak.

Ketchum swallowed, then said, "Let 'er rip, boys."

Within another quarter minute, all the attendant men stood back, the crowd quieted, and the sheriff wiped his hand on his coat front one last time before grasping the little wood handle of his hatchet. The burly man held his breath, his face tensed, and he struck at the primary rope that released the trap below Ketchum's feet. His first whack didn't sever the rope. He raised the hatchet again, brought it down twice as hard, and the trap dropped away.

Ketchum's body rocketed downward. Before the men on top of the scaffold could look through the drop hole, they heard the shrieks and shouts from the crowd. Sheriff Garcia looked down through the hole and felt his late breakfast burble up his throat. Directly below them, sprawled on the gravel and not swinging as he should have been, was Thomas E. "Black Jack" Ketchum. But he was headless.

Later, one man close by on the ground said that he'd been to a few other hangings in his day and that he'd never seen a body drop so fast, nor had he ever seen a man's head just pop from the body before. "Just like you'd tear off a chicken's head, really."

"That's enough, Quimby, you old soak," said Garcia. "Git gone before I hang you, too." Garcia glared at the scrawny little man who had attracted the attention of two out-of-town reporters.

Despite the fact that Sheriff Salome Garcia asked many people about the finer points of hangings, it seemed the advice he received was less than proven. He ended up using too slender a rope, he rubbed it with soap so that it slid efficiently, and worst of all he miscalculated the length of the rope by nearly two feet. This combination of errors resulted in excess downward speed and force. The too-thin rope cinched fast and tight, and Ketchum's head separated from his body.

Before the dead man's head was sewed back on his shoulders for public display, the body was propped up with the hooded head still in the dirt before it. Photographs were made and later distributed as postcards. The caption read, "Body of Black Jack after the hanging showing head snapped off."

Though it was largely agreed that Ketchum did indeed deserve to die for some of the many crimes he committed over a long and brutal career as an outlaw, hanging for attempting to rob a train wasn't one of them. For that he made history as the only person in American history to hang for the crime of "molesting a train." Execution for such a crime is now considered unlawful.

50

WRONGED DETECTIVE

Range detective Tom Horn was, by sheer body count, one of the West's deadliest gunhands. He killed close to four-dozen men during his lifetime. In 1901, in Cheyenne, Wyoming, he was charged with the murder of a fourteen-year-old boy. Even as he mounted the gallows, one day before his forty-third birthday in 1903, he proclaimed his innocence . . . of that killing.

The first bullet probably would have killed him, but then again there was the chance that since he was so young he might have lived—the young are tough that way. But it was the second shot that spun him around, his arms wide and windmilling, as his father's hat flew off. With the first shot, the horse he'd ridden up the lane from the ranch, his father's horse, spooked and ran off. Not that it mattered, for the two slugs had done the job. His fourteen-year-old body just didn't know it yet. He lurched a few hundred feet back up the lane toward the ranch house, then pitched forward and bled his last into the dust on that dry summer morning of July 18, in 1901."

"That's just fanciful writing," said Joe LeFors, swallowing another gulp of beer.

LeFors was fatter than the young newspaperman had expected, and though there was gray in the former lawman's hair, there was still something youthful about him. Probably because he didn't appear to have worked too hard in the twenty years since the hanging.

"But it's about right, though, and sounds something like what Horn told me."

"But Horn was drunk," said the journalist. "And it's said that you plied him with alcohol, extracted a confession, and had someone in hiding taking notes."

LeFors set down his mug of beer, wiped a hand across his handlebar moustaches, then smoothed them. "Now look. I don't believe I remember the name you gave me, but it's a damn sure thing it ain't Joe LeFors, because that's me." He poked a thick, pink digit at his cravat. "You weren't there. I was."

"I'm sorry to have upset you. I'm a newspaperman by trade and training, you see, Mr. LeFors, and I have to ask the hard questions in order to get the full story. The story of your life, the man who brought in Tom Horn, as I've been led to believe, will fascinate readers." The young man snugged the goldwire glasses higher up on the bridge of his nose. The effect, thought LeFors, made him look like a rodent squeezed too hard. "Unless I've been led to believe otherwise, Mr. LeFors?"

The two men caught and held each other's glances in the mirror behind the bar. The older man sighed and said, "No, no. You've heard right, by gum. I was a lawman for years and I never received my due. And it is time to set the record straight."

"Good, good. Glad to hear it, Mr. LeFors. Now," the young man sipped his beer, licked his thumb, and flicked to a clean page in his tablet, "back to Tom Horn. Earlier you mentioned that you were offered a job in Montana that was substantially better paying than the law enforcement job you had at the time of the Nickell boy's murder?"

The man nodded. "Yep, $125 a month. Still law work, of a sort, but as an employee of the Iron Mountain Ranch Company. They were having trouble with rustlers and I'd had experience with just that sort of thing." He leaned on the bar and turned to face the young writer. "You recall ever reading about the Brown's Hole Gang? Stopped 'em cold, single-handed."

"I'd heard you chased them for months, but that turning them up proved to be too difficult."

"Now look here. . . ."

The young man held up a hand. "Mr. LeFors. I'm only trying to cover all the directions leading to your life story. Let's take a different approach. You're acquainted with famed Pinkerton Detective Charlie Siringo?" The young man saw his subject's jaw tighten and flex. "Bartender, I think it's time we had some whiskey, don't you Mr. LeFors?"

When the liquid fire was placed in front of them, LeFors stared at it, encircled the glass with his fingers, and said, "You may as well know now that me and Siringo didn't really hit it off all that well. He was a good lawman, no doubt, but he was. . . ."

"He called you incompetent, Mr. LeFors."

The older man spun from the bar and poked a thick finger in the young man's face. "Now see here. I've taken all I will take from you, you snap of a thing, what with your writing and questions and all. What gives you the right to lure me in here and try to ply me with alcohol like you were trying to get me to confess to something?" He stood there for a moment, one eye squinting, his teeth set tight under his bristling waxed moustaches, then his hard features seemed to the young man to sag.

LeFors stepped away from the bar, his color gone, his eyes dull. "I guess we've reached the end of this road, mister." He walked a few steps away, the young man watching him. Then LeFors turned back. "You never did tell me your name."

The young man smiled and said, "Kimmel. The name's Kimmel. I believe you've met my aunt, Glendolene Kimmel. She and Tom Horn were romantically involved. Some say they were each other's true loves. She was convinced of his innocence."

LeFors's face resumed its hard mask and his dark eyes burned.

"Just think, LeFors. Mr. Tom Horn could have been my uncle, of a sort. That is, if he hadn't been wrongfully hung."

The young newspaperman's grim smile faded as he watched the husky older man stalk from the bar. He heard the front door slam as he turned back to his whiskey. "Here's to you, Tom Horn," he said. "Innocent or not, it's been an entertaining afternoon." And he downed his shot.

Tom Horn packed a lot of living—and killing—into his forty-three years. He worked for the Pinkerton Detective Agency for four years and by his own admittance killed seventeen men during his tenure as an agency operative. No official counts are known, but it is said with a fair amount of historical accuracy that Horn's lifetime body count was between forty and forty-seven. Or roughly one death for each year he lived. He was admired by famed fellow Pinkerton agent Charlie Siringo and other notable lawmen of the day.

Horn went on to hire out as a private range detective. He played vital roles in a number of incidents involving rustling, resulting in the deaths of two dozen men. He was given to bragging when inebriated and often claimed that years before, as an army scout, he was responsible for Geronimo's surrender. Horn also stated: "Killing men is my specialty. I look at it as a business proposition, and I think I have a corner on the market."

At the turn of the century in Wyoming, in a complex series of violent incidents known as the Johnson County War, Horn was hired by Laramie cattleman John Coble in hopes that the famed gunman's presence might stop the rampant rustling plaguing local ranchers.

Horn was effective for a time, but finally met his end when he was charged with the murder of fourteen-year-old Willie Nickell. The charges were largely based on a flimsy drunken "confession" he made when coerced by lawman Joe LeFors, who had been acting out of his jurisdiction.

Horn escaped once from jail but was recaptured, in part because he couldn't figure out how to disengage the safety on the newfangled gun he'd stolen on his way out of the jail. He was hung at noon on November 20, 1903, the day before his forty-third birthday. To the end he claimed his innocence, a claim that has since largely been substantiated.

ART AND PHOTO CREDITS

Page 6: *Hunting of the Grizzly Bear*, by Ch. Bodmer. Library of Congress, LC-USZ62-59691.

Page 25: Jim Bridger. Pioneer Museum of Bozeman.

Page 51: Pioneer Trail Family. Courtesy National Archives (69-N-13606C).

Page 55: The Donner Party. William Gilbert Gaul; American, 1855–1919; *On the Way to the Summit*, circa 1891; Collection of the Oakland Museum of California, Kahn Collection.

Page 65: John "Liver Eater" Johnston. National Archives (111-SC-82944).

Page 87: Chief Quanah Parker. National Photo Company Collection, from Smithsonian Bureau of Ethnology. Library of Congress, LC-USZ62-98166.

Page 97: Christopher "Kit" Carson. From Brady-Handy Photograph Collection. Library of Congress, LC-DIG-cwpbh-00514.

Page 101: Robert McGee. Photograph by E. E. Henry, 1890. Library of Congress, LC-USZ62-105942.

Page 107: *Protecting the Herd*. Reproduction of painting by Frederic Remington, circa 1907. Library of Congress, LC-USZ62-99358.

Page 111: Fetterman Massacre. *Frank Leslie's Illustrated Newspaper*, Jan. 19, 1867, pg. 281. Library of Congress, LC-USZ62-108153.

Page 123: John Wesley Powell's Boat. Photograph by John K. Hillers. Library of Congress, LC-DIG-stereo-1s00756.

Page 129: Alferd Packer. Courtesy Colorado State Archives.

Page 134: James Butler "Wild Bill" Hickok. National Archives (111-SC-94122-A).

Page 139: Lt. Col. G.A. Custer. Civil War glass negative collection (Library of Congress). Library of Congress, LC-DIG-cwpbh-03110.

Page 143: Chief Joseph. Photograph by De Lancey Gill. Library of Congress, LC-USZ62-132047.

Page 149: Bass Reeves. Western History Collections, University of Oklahoma Libraries.

Page 155: Philetus W. Norris. Yellowstone Superintendent (4/18/1877–3/31/1882). National Park Service photograph.

Page 163: Texas Cattle Herd. Photograph by Erwin E. Smith. Library of Congress, LC-DIG-ppmsca-08790.

Page 169: John Heith. Photograph by N. H. Rose, San Antonio, Texas. Library of Congress, LC-USZ62-109782.

Page 183: *Drifting Before the Storm*. Reproduction of painting by Frederic Remington, circa 1904. Library of Congress, LC-USZ62-107673.

Page 188: Gray Wolf. Yellowstone National Park. National Park Service photograph by Jim Peaco.

Page 193: Belle Starr. Wood engraving in *The National Police Gazette* (May 22, 1886), p. 16. Library of Congress, LC-USZ62-63912.

Page 203: Buffalo Hides. National Archives (79-M-1B-3).

Page 207: Chief Big Foot. National Archives (111-SC-82412).

Page 211: Grizzly Bear. Yellowstone National Park. National Park Service photograph by Jim Peaco.

Page 221: Theodore "Teddy" Roosevelt. Photograph by George Grantham Bain. Library of Congress, LC-USZ62-23232.

Page 225: Thomas "Black Jack" Ketchum. National Archives (111-SC-93358).

BIBLIOGRAPHY

Adams, Andy. *The Log of a Cowboy*. New York: MJF Books, 1996.

Allen, Paul L., and Peter M. Pegnam. *Arizona Territory: Baptism in Blood*. Tucson: Tucson Citizen Publishing Company, 1990.

Ambrose, Stephen E. *Undaunted Courage*. New York: Touchstone, 1996.

Bagley, Will. *Blood of the Prophets: Brigham Young and the Massacre at Mountain Meadows*. Norman, OK: University of Oklahoma Press, 2002.

Bolgiano, Chris. *Mountain Lion: An Unnatural History of Pumas and People*. Mechanicsburg, PA: Stackpole Books, 1995.

Brown, Dee. *The Gentle Tamers: Women of the Old Wild West*. Lincoln: University of Nebraska Press, 1981.

————. *The Fetterman Massacre*. Lincoln: University of Nebraska Press, 1971.

Bunker, Robert, and Raymond W. Thorp. *Crow Killer: The Saga of Liver-Eating Johnson*. Bloomington: Indiana University Press, 1983.

Burton, Art. *Black, Red, and Deadly: Black and Indian Gunfighters of the Indian Territories*. Austin: Eakin Press, 1991.

Calvert, Patricia. *Great Lives: The American Frontier*. New York: Atheneum, 1997.

Casey, Denise, and Tim W. Clark. *Tales of the Wolf*. Moose, WY: Homestead Publishing, 1996.

Catlin, George. *Letters and Notes on the Manners, Customs, and Conditions of the North American Indians: Volumes I and II*. Mineola, NY: Dover Publications, Inc., 1973.

————. *Episodes from Life Among the Indians and Last Rambles*. Mineola, New York.: Dover Publications, Inc., 1997.

Cheney, Truman McGiffin. *So Long, Cowboys of the Open Range*. Helena, MT: Falcon Press, 1990.

Clark, Tim W., and Denise Casey. *Tales of the Grizzly*. Moose, WY.: Homestead Publishing, 1992.

Conard, Howard L. *"Uncle Dick" Wootton*. Chicago: W. E. Dibble & Co., 1890.

Crutchfield, A. James. *It Happened in Montana*. Helena, MT: Falcon Press, 1992.

Dary, David. *Frontier Medicine: From the Atlantic to the Pacific: 1492– 1941*. New York: Alfred A. Knopf, 2008.

DeVoto, Bernard. *Across the Wide Missouri*. Boston: Houghton Mifflin, 1947.

———(Editor). *The Journals of Lewis and Clark*. Boston: Houghton Mifflin, 1953.

Dimsdale, J. Thomas. *The Vigilantes of Montana*. Norman, OK: The University of Oklahoma Press, 1968.

Dobie, J. Frank. *The Longhorns*. New York: Bramhall House, 1982.

Dolnick, Edward. *Down the Great Unknown: John Wesley Powell's 1869 Journey of Discovery and Tragedy Through the Grand Canyon*. New York: HarperCollins, 2001.

Donovan, Jim. *Custer and Little Bighorn: The Man, the Mystery, the Myth*. Stillwater, MN: Voyageur Press, Inc., 2001.

Drago, Harry Sinclair. *The Great Range Wars: Violence on the Grasslands*. New York: Dodd, Mead & Co., 1970.

Drimmer, Frederick. *Captured by the Indians: 15 Firsthand Accounts, 1750–1870*. New York: Dover Publications, 1961.

Engel, Lorenz. *Among the Plains Indians*. Minneapolis: Lerner Publications Co., 1972.

Etling, Kathy. *Cougar Attacks*. Guilford, CT: The Lyons Press, 2001.

Etulain, W. Richard, and Glenda Riley, eds. *With Badges & Bullets: Lawmen & Outlaws in the Old West*. Golden, CO: Fulcrum Publishing, 1999.

Everett, George. *Butte Trivia*. Helena, MT: Riverbend Publishing, 2007.

Fifer, Barbara. *Montana Battlefields: 1806–1877*. Helena, MT: Farcountry Press, 2005.

Gard, Wayne. *The Great Buffalo Hunt*. New York: Alfred A. Knopf, 1959.

Geist, Valerius. *Buffalo Nation: History and Legend of the North American Bison*. Stillwater, MN: Voyageur Press, 1996.

Gowans, Fred R. *Rocky Mountain Rendezvous: A History of the Fur Trade Rendezvous, 1825–1840*. Layton, UT: Gibbs M. Smith, Inc., 1985.

Graham, W. A. *The Story of the Little Big Horn*. Mechanicsburg, PA: Stackpole Books, 1994.

Hafen, LeRoy R. *Mountain Men and Fur Traders of the Far West: Eighteen Biographical Sketches*. Lincoln, NE: Bison Books, 1982.

Haines, Francis. *The Buffalo: The Story of American Bison and Their Hunters from Prehistoric Times to the Present*. Norman, OK: University of Oklahoma Press, 1995.

Harris, Burton. *John Colter, His Years in the Rockies*. Lincoln, NE: Bison Books, 1993.

Hillerman, Tony. *The Great Taos Bank Robbery and Other Indian Country Affairs*. Albuquerque: University of New Mexico Press, 1973.

Hoffman, Wilbur H. *Sagas of Old Western Travel & Transport*. San Diego: Howell-North Books, 1980.

Hoig, Stan. *The Sand Creek Massacre*. Norman, OK: University of Oklahoma Press, 1961.

Horan, James D. *The Gunfighters*, vol. 1 of *The Authentic Wild West*. New York: Crown Publishers, 1976-1980.

———. *The Outlaws*, vol 2 of *The Authentic Wild West*. New York: Crown Publishers, 1976–1980.

Horwitz, Tony. *The Devil May Care: Fifty Intrepid Americans and Their Quest for the Unknown*. New York: Oxford University Press, 2003.

Howard, Helen Addison. *Saga of Chief Joseph*. Lincoln: University of Nebraska Press, 1978.

Hufsmith, George W. *The Wyoming Lynching of Cattle Kate, 1889*. Glendo, WY: High Plains Press, 1993.

Iverson, Peter. *The Navajos*. New York: Chelsea House Publishers, 1990.

Jacobson, Jude, and Andrea Merrill. *Montana Almanac*. Helena, MT: Falcon Publishing, 1997.

Johnson, Dorothy M. *The Bloody Bozeman*. Missoula, MT: Mountain Press Publishing, 1983.

Knowles, Thomas W. *The West That Was*. Avenel, NJ: Wings Books, 1993.

Krohn, Katherine. *Women of the Wild West*. Minneapolis: Lerner Publications, 2000.

Lamar, Howard R., ed. *The New Encyclopedia of the American West*. New Haven: Yale University Press, 1998.

Laskin, David. *The Children's Blizzard*. New York: HarperCollins, 2004.

Lavender, David Sievert, *The Fist in the Wilderness*. Garden City, New York: Doubleday, 1946.

Laycock, George. *The Mountain Men: The Dramatic History and Lore of the First Frontiersmen*. New York: Lyons and Burford, Publishers, 1996.

Macpherson, Margaret A., and Eli MacLaren, eds. *Outlaws and Lawmen of the West*, vol. 1. Edmonton, Alberta: Lone Pine, 2000.

Malloy, Denise Glaser, and Pioneer Museum of Bozeman. *Images of America: Bozeman*. Charleston: Arcadia Publishing, 2008.

Marrin, Albert. *Plains Warrior: Chief Quanah Parker and the Comanches.* New York: Atheneum Books, 1996.

McCoy, Michael, ed. *Classic Cowboy Stories: Eighteen Extraordinary Tales of the Old West.* Guilford, CT: Lyons Press, 2004.

McGlashan, C. F. *History of the Donner Party: A Tragedy of the Sierra.* Stanford: Stanford University Press, 1947.

McLynn, Frank. *Wagons West: The Epic Story of America's Overland Trails.* New York: Grove Press, 2002.

McMurtry, Larry. *Oh What a Slaughter: Massacres in the American West, 1846–1890.* New York: Simon & Schuster, 2005.

Monnett, John H. *Where a Hundred Soldiers Were Killed.* Albuquerque: University of New Mexico Press, 2008.

Morgan, L. Dale. *Jedediah Smith and the Opening of the West.* Lincoln: The University of Nebraska Press, 1953.

Moring, John. *Men with Sand: Great Explorers of the North American West.* Helena, MT: Two Dot Press, 1998.

Moulton, Candy. *Chief Joseph: Guardian of the People.* New York: Forge, 2005.

Murphy, Bob. *Bears I Have Known.* Helena, MT: Riverbend Publishing, 2006.

Myers, John. *The Saga of Hugh Glass: Pirate, Pawnee, and Mountain Man.* Lincoln: University of Nebraska Press, 1976.

O'Brien, Barmeyer Mary. *Heart of the Trail: The Stories of Eight Wagon Train Women.* Helena, MT: Two Dot Press, 1997.

———. *Toward the Setting Sun: Pioneer Girls Traveling the Overland Trails.* Helena, MT: Two Dot Press, 1999.

Osborn, William M. *The Wild Frontier: Atrocities During the American-Indian War from Jamestown Colony to Wounded Knee.* New York: Random House, 2000.

Pace, Dick. *Golden Gulch: The Story of Montana's Fabulous Alder Gulch.* Dick Pace, 1962.

Parkman, Francis. *The Oregon Trail.* New York: Signet Classic, 1978.

Parry, Ellis Roberts. *Montana Dateline.* Guilford, CT: Globe Pequot Press, 2001.

Patterson, Richard. *Butch Cassidy: A Biography.* Lincoln: University of Nebraska Press, 1998.

Paulsen, Gary. *The Legend of Bass Reeves: Being the True and Fictional Account of the Most Valiant Marshal in the West.* New York: Random House, 2006.

Picton, Harold. *Buffalo: Natural History & Conservation.* Stillwater, MN: Voyageur Press, 2005.

Place, Marian T. *Marcus and Narcissa Whitman, Oregon Pioneers.* Champaign, IL: Garrard Publishing, 1967.

Prodgers, Jeannette, ed., *The Only Good Bear Is a Dead Bear: A Collection of the West's Best Bear Stories.* Helena, MT: Two Dot Press, 1986.

Reed, Robert C. *Train Wrecks: A Pictorial History of Accidents on the Main Line.* New York: Bonanza Books, 1968.

Robertson, R.G. *Rotting Face: Smallpox and the American Indian.* Caldwell, ID: Caxton Press, 2001.

Roosevelt, Theodore. *Hunting Trips of a Ranchman & The Wilderness Hunter.* New York: Modern Library, 1996.

Rosa, Joseph G. *Age of the Gunfighter: Men and Weapons on the Frontier, 1840–1900.* London: Salamander Books, 2002.

Russell, Osborne. *Journal of a Trapper, 1834–1843*. Lincoln: University of Nebraska Press, 1955.

Rutter, Michael. *Upstairs Girls: Prostitution in the American West*. Helena, MT: Farcountry Press, 2005.

Schofield, Brian. *Selling Your Father's Bones*. New York: Simon & Schuster, 2009.

Schullery, Paul. *Yellowstone Bear Tales*. Niwot, CO: Roberts Rhinehart, 1991.

Schultz, James Willard. *Bird Woman: Sacagawea's Own Story*. Kooskia, ID: Mountain Meadow Press, 1999.

Seagreaves, Anne. *Soiled Doves: Prostitution in the Early West*. Hayden, ID: Wesanne Publications, 1994.

Sides, Hampton. *Blood and Thunder: An Epic of the American West*. New York: Doubleday, 2006.

Skarsten, M. O. *George Drouillard: Hunter and Interpreter for Lewis and Clark and Fur Trader, 1807–1810*. Lincoln, NE: Bison Books, 2005.

Steele, Volney, M. D. *Bleed, Blister, and Purge: A History of Medicine on the American Frontier*. Missoula, MT: Mountain Press, 2005.

Stewart, R. George. *Ordeal by Hunger: The Story of the Donner Party*. Lincoln: The University of Nebraska Press, 1986.

Stone, Irving. *Men to Match My Mountains: The Opening of the Far West 1840–1900*. Garden City, New York: Doubleday & Co., Inc., 1956.

Time-Life, eds. *The Old West Series*. 26 vols. Alexandria, VA: Time-Life Books, 1973–80.

Underwood, Lamar (Editor). *Tales of the Mountain Men*. Guilford, CT: Lyons Press, 2004.

Utley, Robert M. *A Life Wild and Perilous: Mountain Men and the Paths to the Pacific*. New York: Henry Holt, 1997.

Vestal, Stanley. *The Old Santa Fe Trail*. Lincoln: University of Nebraska Press, 1996.

Waldman, Neil. *Wounded Knee*. New York: Atheneum Books, 2001.

Walker, Paul Robert. *True Tales of the Wild West*. Washington, D.C.: National Geographic, 2002.

Walter, Dave, ed. *Speaking Ill of the Dead: Jerks in Montana History*. Guilford, CT: Two Dot Press, 2000.

Wellman, I. Paul. *A Dynasty of Western Outlaws*. Lincoln: The University of Nebraska Press, 1961.

Wilson, Gary A. *Tiger of the Wild Bunch: The Life and Death of Harvey "Kid Curry" Logan*. Guilford, CT: Two Dot Press, 2007.

———. *Outlaw Tales of Montana: True Stories of Notorious Montana Bandits, Culprits, and Crooks*. Guilford, CT: Two Dot Press, 2003.

WPA Montana Writers' Project. *An Ornery Bunch: Tales and Anecdotes Collected by the WPA Montana Writers' Project, 1935–1942*. Helena, MT: Two Dot Press, 1999.

Wright, William H. *The Grizzly Bear: The Narrative of a Hunter-Naturalist*. Lincoln: University of Nebraska Press, 1977.

INDEX

ABOUT THE AUTHOR

Matthew P. Mayo's previous books include the Western novels *Winters' War*, *Wrong Town*, and *Hot Lead, Cold Heart*. In addition to writing novels and non-fiction, Matthew has had short stories and poetry published in a variety of anthologies. He also edited the anthology *Where Legends Ride: New Tales of the Old West*.

Matthew is managing editor of *Big Sky Journal*, a culture and lifestyle magazine of the Northern Rockies. He is an active member of Western Writers of America and Western History Association. Along with his wife, documentary photographer Jennifer Smith-Mayo, and two dogs, Guinness and Nessie, Matthew divides his time between the coast of Maine and the mountains of Montana.

Visit him on the Web at www.matthewmayo.com.